The Best of Ogden Nash

THE BEST OF
OGDEN
NASH

Edited by
Linell Nash Smith

IVAN R. DEE

CHICAGO

www.ivanrdee.com

Library of Congress Cataloging-in-Publication Data:
Nash, Ogden, 1902–1971.
    [Poems Selections.]
    The best of Ogden Nash / Ogden Nash ; edited by Linell Nash Smith.
        p. cm.
    Includes index.
    ISBN-13: 978-1-56663-703-9 (alk. paper)
    ISBN-10: 1-56663-703-1 (alk. paper)
    1. Humorous poetry, American.   I. Smith, Linell Nash. II. Title.
PS3527.A637A6 2007
    811'.52—dc22   2007029851

Contents

Foreword

BY LINELL NASH SMITH

WHEN IVAN DEE first suggested that my sister Isabel and I edit a new collection of the poems of my father, Ogden Nash, we were excited by the prospect. Almost thirty-five years ago, in 1973, we had worked on a similar anthology, *I Wouldn't Have Missed It*, but the proximity of our father's death (1971) made us lean heavily on his own selections for his *Verses from 1929 On*. We were loath to discard or to add to his choices, and did so sparingly. This time around we hoped to take a fresh look at the whole body of his work in order to offer a fuller picture of the man.

We were to begin this assignment two years ago, but my sister, whose health had been failing for some time, became increasingly ill and unable to contend with the time-consuming task of amassing her choices, reviewing mine, and our coming to mutual agreement— "in or out"—on each poem. My much-loved Isabel, who had lived on determination and iron will alone for a number of years, finally succumbed and died at the turn of the old year—at home, with her family by her side.

I have not, therefore, had the benefit of her insight in gathering the poems for this new collection, and it has been sorely missed. Isabel was incredibly intuitive, extremely close to our father, and very like him in so many ways. I have tried to compile this anthology in a way that would meet with her approval, but I do so wish that it could have been graced with her magic touch.

From the time I was a very small child I can remember the ubiquitous yellow legal pads and Blackwing pencils that seemed almost an extension of my father. Thoughts, crazily rhyming words, and, occasionally, poems he jotted down on those pads. When they were left on the coffee table instead of his desk, Isabel and I would read them to each other, giggling at the funny ones and puzzling over some of the others. Here is a transcript of one page from my father's foolscap musings.

Under his own title of :

RHYMES AND SOUNDS—
Anatomy—anathema
Flourished—I'm discouraged
Methusaleh—lollapaloozala
Ennui—Can we?
Caribou—calaboose; hoosegow—moosegow
Ganymede—Runnymede
Monologue—dialogue—Bandarlog
Fishwives, housewives, alewives, mousewives
Meyerbeer—Biedemeyer
Cryptic—triptych
Vercengetorix—obstetrics

And these comments and verses, none titled:

Bear looks kind
From behind

Age once was young
Youth was never old

Does God believe in me?

Ogden's career is a cycle pictorial
Twixt Pimlico, Bowie and Union Memorial.
That Hollywood gold never reaches his bride—
What the mutuals leave him, the doctors divide.

In the month of February
I am fond of summer, very.
I find summer less alluring
After June and sometimes during.

What will become of the steeplejack now that
Ecclesiastical architecture has practically
Eliminated the steeple?
Is he self-sustaining between spires
As the mosquito is between people?

Who to blame?
Leaders who are feeders
Or followers who are swallowers?

Sometimes the notes lay stillborn, never to be published, but at other times the words scribbled down offhandedly would become a part of my father's legacy—those wildly galloping lines that threatened to run off the printed page but then would suddenly come to a precipitous halt, leaving the reader quite breathless. Perhaps they would morph into a limerick or a "Reflection" that tickled the funny bone, or the biting social commentary that made him more than just a writer of humorous verse or clever trivia. Those words on the pads that lay around the house would one day cement our father's place in the annals of American letters. He wrote for Everyman, incisively exposing both the beast and the best in us, evincing all the while an amused yet bemused acceptance of the foibles of the human race.

In this new collection will be found not only the familiar poems that shout "Nash" but also verse not previously selected for anthologies, lyrics from musicals and symphonic stage performances, and some unpublished work that merited inclusion. In addition, it seemed to me an important consideration to take note of those particular favorites of Nash fans through the years since his death. By reviewing permission requests and internet communications, it was not difficult to amass and incorporate these poems too (if they were not already counted in). Some of them were quite surprising to me—such as "A Tale of the Thirteenth Floor," "The

Wendigo," and "The Birthday That Never Was, A February Fantasy," all of which fitted into a sort of Nashian "Twilight Zone," which I have compiled under the chapter heading "The Thirteenth Floor." (I realize that the lyrics for "Haunted Hotspot" would fall nicely into this category as well but have left it with the other lyrics in "The Curtain Rises.")

While I have tried to omit poems that are too impossibly dated for today's reader to enjoy, I have included some that not only spoke to the times in which they were written but, because some things never change, are still pertinent. For instance, "The Beggar" of 1933 continues hopelessly to haunt the streets of 2007.

This book has been broken into chapters of sorts that cover various categories because our father's titles are often totally divorced from the poems' subject matter. If one were to search for an imperfectly remembered poem about a dog, the title "Please Pass the Biscuit" might not ring a bell. That poem can be found in the chapter "Nashional Menagerie," a potpourri of his animal poems. Other "chapters" cover family life, romance and marriage, travel, reflections on our corporate, social and governmental structure, daily living, and so forth. Admittedly, Nash poems often can be hard to categorize, so I have exercised a daughter's license in assigning each poem its place. (Doubtless some readers will consider my assignments misplaced, for which I apologize.)

To further help the reader find a particular poem, the book contains an index of first lines, which I have found to be of great usefulness to the Nash reader. Within each chapter the poems are placed in roughly chronological order to help students of Nash better sense the evolution of his work.

People often ask what inspired the unique flavor of my father's verse. They strive to learn the nature of the man who built a reputation and legacy upon such lines as "Candy is dandy / But liquor is quicker." Scholars have advanced different theories about Nash and his work; now, as a daughter but no scholar, I proffer mine. The story that follows illustrates my understanding of the man behind the writer. . . .

In 1906, in a world farther removed from today's than by years alone, a small boy stood beside his father on a footbridge near Rye, New York. Below them ran a line of metal rails. Like most young boys of his generation, he had a passion for trains. The child tugged excitedly at his father's hand and said, "See the train tracks, Father!"

Edmund Nash smiled but said, "No, Ogden, those are trolley tracks. They are for the new trolley car that runs from Rye to Portchester." The little boy's high spirits evaporated, yet he held on to his vision of a train. "Excuse me, Father, but I think they *might* be train tracks," he offered tentatively.

In 1906 fathers did not fudge the truth in order to enhance their children's self-esteem. "Ogden," said Edmund firmly, "those tracks are for the trolley, and we will stand here until the trolley comes."

The afternoon shadows lengthened as man and boy stood looking down on the line of rails. At last a vehicle came into view. It was the new trolley. Ogden's eyes filled with tears as it passed beneath them. He looked up briefly at his father's face, then bit his lip as he turned to watch the retreating trolley. At last he said softly, almost to himself, "Naughty trolley, running on the train tracks."

I am told that this was Grandfather's favorite story about my father, and it illustrates to me a core truth about him. That child, with a determined vision that often contradicted fact, was always at work in the man, dictating his need to coax others into seeing the world as he saw it. He himself would humorously attribute his unique outlook on life to his poor eyesight—he said it so distorted his perception of things that he related to them differently.

But that doesn't explain his dogged pursuit of the ideas, ideals, and aspirations that characterized his personal life as well as his work. Both as a boy and as a man he pursued what sometimes seemed impossible goals. Even though he knew that life was mostly full of trolleys, he still believed in trains. And, once in a while, the sheer force of his faith diverted a magic streamliner onto the trolley tracks of his world. It happened enough times to justify his faith and to nourish the romantic idealist carefully hidden inside the familiar humorist. I think he himself expressed it best in this quatrain:

> Cry welladay, this world is workaday,
> Where are the miracles for which we pray?
> Well, miracles, so few and far between,
> Must be believed, my brethren, to be seen.

Acknowledgments

I WOULD LIKE to thank Ivan Dee for the amazing and unlimited patience he has displayed as he waited for the completion of this collection; Doug Parker for suggesting it to Mr. Dee in the first place and for his wonderful biography *Ogden Nash: The Life and Work of America's Laureate of Light Verse*; George Crandell for his *Ogden Nash, A Descriptive Bibliography*, without which any true Nash scholar would be at a total loss and which has aided this nonscholar tremendously; and my goddaughter, Dancy Bruce Mills, for fearlessly leaping into the breach when it was clear that the necessary typing would never meet deadline without her help.

But most of all I want to thank my daughter, Frances: computer whiz, world-class organizer, indefatigable typist, and most valued sounding board, without whose help and encouragement this book would still be a mass of papers and notes on my desk.

L. N. S.

Sparks, Maryland
July 2007

The Best of Ogden Nash

Nashional Reflections, Limericks, Limicks

PEDIATRIC REFLECTION

Many an infant that screams like a calliope
Could be soothed by a little attention to its diope.

REMINISCENT REFLECTION

When I consider how my life is spent,
I hardly ever repent.

REFLECTION ON THE PASSAGE OF TIME,
ITS INEVITABILITY AND ITS QUIRKS

In nineteen hunderd
Jeunes filles wondered.

GENEALOGICAL REFLECTION

No McTavish
Was ever lavish.

REFLECTION ON THE FALLIBILITY OF NEMESIS

He who is ridden by a conscience
Worries about a lot of nonscience;
He without benefit of scruples
His fun and income soon quadruples.

REFLECTION ON CAUTION

Affection is a noble quality;
It leads to generosity and jollity.
But it also leads to breach of promise
If you go around lavishing it on red-hot momise.

BIOLOGICAL REFLECTION

A girl whose cheeks are covered with paint
Has an advantage with me over one whose ain't.

THEATRICAL REFLECTION

In the Vanities
No one wears panities.

REFLECTION ON A WICKED WORLD

Purity
Is obscurity.

SPECULATIVE REFLECTION

I wonder if the citizens of New York will ever get sufficiently
  wroth
To remember that Tammany cooks spoil the broth.

REFLECTION ON NATURE'S BEING SOMETIMES
INSCRUTABLE BUT ALWAYS WISE

Alcohol is an intoxicant
So gin can often do what Moxie can't.

REFLECTION ON INGENUITY

Here's a good rule of thumb:
Too clever is dumb.

ARTHUR

There was an old man of Calcutta
Who coated his tonsils with butta,
Thus converting his snore
From a thunderous roar
To a soft, oleaginous mutta.

BENJAMIN

There was a brave girl of Connecticut
Who flagged the express with her pecticut,
Which her elders defined
As presence of mind,
But deplorable absence of ecticut.

CARLOTTA

There was an old man in a trunk
Who inquired of his wife, "Am I drunk?"
She replied with regret,
"I'm afraid so, my pet,"
And he answered, "It's just as I thunk."

DRUSILLA

There was an old man of Schoharie
Who settled himself in a quarry.
And those who asked why
Got the candid reply,
"Today is the day of the soirée."

ÉDOUARD

A bugler named Dougal MacDougal
Found ingenious ways to be frugal.
He learned how to sneeze
In various keys,
Thus saving the price of a bugle.

FRAGONARD

There was an old miser named Clarence
Who simonized both of his parents.
"The initial expense,"
He remarked, "is immense,
But I'll save it on wearance and tearance."

REQUIEM

There was a young belle of old Natchez
Whose garments were always in patchez.
When comment arose
On the state of her clothes,
She drawled, When Ah itchez, Ah scratchez!

LATHER AS YOU GO

Beneath this slab
John Brown is stowed.
He watched the ads,
And not the road.

THE ORNITHOLOGIST

A young flirt of Ceylon,
Who led the boys on
Playing Follow the Leda,
Succumbed to a swan.

FIRST LIMICK

An old person of Troy
Is so prudish and coy
That it doesn't know yet
If it's a girl or a boy.

SECOND LIMICK

A cook named McMurray
Got a raise in a hurry
From his Hindu employer
By favoring curry.

THIRD LIMICK

Two nudists of Dover,
Being purple all over,
Were munched by a cow
When mistaken for clover.

UNTITLED LIMERICK

Asked a patient before appendectomy,
"What kind of a fee d'you expectomy?"
Said the doc, "If your pulse
Indicates the results,
Anything but a post-dated checktomy."

HOW PLEASANT TO APE MR. LEAR

I

A crusader's wife slipped from the garrison
And had an affair with a Saracen.
    She was not oversexed,
    Or jealous or vexed,
She just wanted to make a comparison.

II

A novelist of the absurd
Has a voice that will shortly be heard.
    I learn from my spies
    He's about to devise
An unprintable three-letter word.

III

There was a young girl of Milwaukee
Whose voice was sc-r-reechy and squawky.
    Her friends were emphatic
    It sounded like static
And called her their Milwaukee-talkie.

IV

An exiled Iraqi went back
To his home with a ewe in his pack.
    He said people all knew
    Every Q needs a U
So he put the ewe back in Iraqu.

V

A knight of the Garter long hence
Was expelled from that order of gents.
    He was fairly adroit
    When he cried "Honi Soit,"
But he couldn't pronounce "Mal y Pense."

VI

A lama of Outer Mongolia
Was seized with acute melancholia.
    When the Chinese asked why
    He could only reply,
You'd chop off my head if I tolia.

VII

A male entomologist author
Waxed wrother and wrother and wrother—
    He socked his own brother
    Who called him a mother
Instead of an eminent mother.

Family Matters

THE PARENT

Children aren't happy with nothing to ignore,
And that's what parents were created for.

TO A SMALL BOY STANDING ON MY SHOES
WHILE I AM WEARING THEM

Let's straighten this out, my little man,
And reach an agreement if we can.
I entered your door as an honored guest,
My shoes are shined and my trousers are pressed,
And I won't stretch out and read you the funnies
And I won't pretend that we're Easter bunnies.
If you must get somebody down on the floor,
What in the hell are your parents for?
I do not like the things that you say
And I hate the games that you want to play.
No matter how frightfully hard you try,
We've little in common, you and I.
The interest I take in my neighbor's nursery

Would have to grow, to be even cursory,
And I would that performing sons and nephews
Were carted away with the daily refuse,
And I hold that frolicsome daughters and nieces
Are ample excuse for breaking leases.
You may take a sock at your daddy's tummy
Or climb all over your doting mummy,
But keep your attentions to me in check,
Or, sonny boy, I will wring your neck.
A happier man today I'd be
Had someone wrung it ahead of me.

THE BABY

A bit of talcum
Is always walcum.

FAMILY COURT

One would be in less danger
From the wiles of the stranger
If one's own kin and kith
Were more fun to be with.

MY DADDY

I have a funny daddy
Who goes in and out with me,
And everything that baby does
My daddy's sure to see,
And everything that baby says,
My daddy's sure to tell.
You *must* have read my daddy's verse.
I hope he fries in hell.

SONG TO BE SUNG BY THE FATHER OF INFANT FEMALE CHILDREN

My heart leaps up when I behold
A rainbow in the sky;
Contrariwise, my blood runs cold
When little boys go by.
For little boys as little boys,
No special hate I carry,
But now and then they grow to men,
And when they do, they marry.
No matter how they tarry,
Eventually they marry.
And, swine among the pearls,
They marry little girls.

Oh, somewhere, somewhere, an infant plays,
With parents who feed and clothe him.
Their lips are sticky with pride and praise,
But I have begun to loathe him.
Yes, I loathe with a loathing shameless
This child who to me is nameless.
This bachelor child in his carriage
Gives never a thought to marriage,
But a person can hardly say knife
Before he demands a wife.

I never see an infant (male),
A-sleeping in the sun,
Without I turn a trifle pale
And think, is *he* the one?
Oh, first he'll want to crop his curls,
And then he'll want a pony,
And then he'll think of pretty girls
And holy matrimony.
He'll put away his pony,
And sigh for matrimony.
A cat without a mouse
Is he without a spouse.

Oh somewhere he bubbles bubbles of milk,
And quietly sucks his thumbs.
His cheeks are roses painted on silk,
And his teeth are tucked in his gums.
But alas, the teeth will begin to grow,
And the bubbles will cease to bubble;
Given a score of years or so,
The roses will turn to stubble.
He'll sell a bond, or he'll write a book,
And his eyes will get that acquisitive look,
And raging and ravenous for the kill,
He'll boldly ask for the hand of Jill.
This infant whose middle
Is diapered still
Will want to marry
My daughter Jill.

Oh sweet be his slumber and moist his middle,
My dreams, I fear, are infanticiddle.
A fig for embryo Lohengrins!
I'll open all of his safety pins,
I'll pepper his powder, and salt his bottle,
And give him readings from Aristotle.
Sand for his spinach I'll gladly bring,
And Tabasco sauce for his teething ring.
Then perhaps he'll struggle through fire and water
To marry somebody else's daughter.

FATHER-IN-LAW OF THE GROOM

Our times will be in books interred
As the era of the eaten word,
So tell my why should I alone
Be unprepared to eat my own?
The longer I live the sooner I find
How priceless is an open mind.
I trust that I am wiser plenty
At forty-nine than at nine-and-twenty.

How odd to think that once I rose
To sass my daughter's future beaux;
A newborn father, with arms akimbo,
Consigning all young men to limbo.
Since then I've lived a fifth of a century
Incredibly charming and adventury
As you would have, were your vicinity
One of exclusive femininity.

For years I saw no male but me;
Even the Bedlington was a she.
I stood apart and watched agog
My wife, my daughters, and my dog.
They are a higher form of life,
My dog, my daughters, and my wife,
Inhabitants of a fourth dimension
Too mystic for my comprehension.

Life was a song in Ancient Greece,
No debutantes disturbed the peace,
No sirens moaning o'er their hair
Left Mr. Paul for Mr. Pierre,
And ladies conscious of their backs
Avoided blue jeans, shorts and slacks;
Yet, alone among women, even Achilles
Got heebie-jeebies and the willies.

Therefore I hail this happy anomaly,
A fellow male within the family,
And cause a daughter's wrath to bloom
By monopolizing of her groom.
Oh, let the girls get on with the trousseau,
Here's a Friday at last for Crusoe,
To chew the fat and exchange the dope with,
And a simple masculine mind to cope with.

A girl and her words are equally random,
No use to attempt to understand 'em.
You behold in me a crafty vet

Of Hoover's day, and I'm trying yet.
But Johnny's talk is a green oasis
Of presidential and pennant races;
His forthright speech my mind relaxes,
Even when discussing taxes.

Linell, though I can't read you clearly,
You know I love you long and dearly.
You know I wish you barrel on barrel
Of joy and health and fine apparel,
And clinking, corpulent piggy banks,
And please to accept my heartfelt thanks
For bringing me, my angel chile
A man to talk to once in a while.

OUR CHILD DOESN'T KNOW ANYTHING
OR
THANK GOD!

I am now about to make a remark that I suppose most parents will
    think me hateful for,
Though as a matter of fact I am only commenting on a condition
    that they should be more than grateful for.
What I want to say is, that of luckiness it seems to me to be the
    height
That babies aren't very bright.
Now listen to me for a minute, all you proud progenitors who
    boast that your bedridden infant offspring of two months or so
    are already bright enough to get into Harvard or Stanford or
    Notre Dame or Fordham;
Don't you realize that the only thing that makes life at all bearable
    to those selfsame offspring is being rather backward, and that
    if they had any sense at all they would lose no time in perish-
    ing of boredom?
Good heavens, I can think of no catastrophe more immense
Than a baby with sense,
Because one thing at least, willy-nilly, you must believe,

And that is, that a baby has twenty-four hours a day to get through
    with just the same as we've.
Some people choose to wonder about virtue and others about
    crime,
But I choose to wonder how babies manage to pass the time.
They can't pass it in tennis or badminton or golf,
Or in going around rescuing people from Indians and then marry-
    ing somebody else the way Pocahontas did with the Messrs.
    Smith and Rolfe;
They can't pass it in bridge or Parcheesi or backgammon,
Or in taking the subway to Wall Street and worshipping Mammon;
How then do they manage to enthuse themselves,
And amuse themselves?
Well, most of the time they pass their time by sleeping and then
    waking up at inconvenient intervals and making the kind of
    noise that is made by a lummox as is really a lummox,
And lifting their heads up in a very smart-alecky way while lying
    on their stummox,
And the rest of the time they relax
On their backs,
And eat, by regime specifically, but by nature omnivorously,
And vocalize vocivorously.
That, to make it short,
Is about all they can do in the way of sport;
So whatever may come,
I am glad that babies are dumb.
I shudder to think what for entertainment they'd do
Were they as bright as me or you.

DON'T CRY, DARLING, IT'S BLOOD ALL RIGHT

Whenever poets want to give you the idea that something is par-
    ticularly meek and mild,
They compare it to a child,
Thereby proving that though poets with poetry may be rife
They don't know the facts of life.
If of compassion you desire either a tittle or a jot,
Don't try to get it from a tot.

Hard-boiled, sophisticated adults like me and you
May enjoy ourselves thoroughly with *Little Women* and *Winnie-the-Pooh,*
But innocent infants these titles from their reading course eliminate
As soon as they discover that it was honey and nuts and mashed
potatoes instead of human flesh that Winnie-the-Pooh and Little Women ate.
Innocent infants have no use for fables about rabbits or donkeys
or tortoises or porpoises,
What they want is something with plenty of well-mutilated corpoises.
Not on legends of how the rose came to be a rose instead of a petunia is their fancy fed,
But on the inside story of how somebody's bones got ground up to
make somebody else's bread.
They'll go to sleep listening to the story of the little beggar maid
who got to be queen by being kind to the bees and the birds,
But they're all eyes and ears the minute they suspect a wolf or a
giant is going to tear some poor woodcutter into quarters or
thirds.
It really doesn't take much to fill their cup;
All they want is for somebody to be eaten up.
Therefore I say unto you, all you poets who are so crazy about
meek and mild little children and their angelic air,
If you are sincere and really want to please them, why just go out
and get yourselves devoured by a bear.

IN WHICH THE POET IS
ASHAMED BUT PLEASED

Of all the things that I would rather,
It is to be my daughter's father,
While she, with innocence divine,
Is quite contented to be mine.
I'm conscious that in praising her,
I'm speaking as a connoisseur.
While she, poor dear, has never known
A father other than her own.

Within her head no notion stirs
That some are better men than hers;
That some are cleverer, some are braver,
Than the one that fortune gave her.
What fortune set us side by side,
Her scope so narrow, mine so wide?
We owe to this sweet dispensation
Our mutual appreciation.

A CHILD'S GUIDE TO PARENTS

Children, I crave your kind forbearance;
Our topic for today is Parents.

Parents are generally found in couples,
Except when divorce their number quadruples.

Mostly they're married to each other.
The female one is called the mother.

Paternal pride being hard to edit,
The male, or father, claims the credit,

But children, hark! Your mother would rather,
When you arrived, have been your father.

At last on common ground they meet:
Their child is sweetest of the sweet.

But burst not, babe, with boastful glee;
It is themselves they praise, not thee.

The reason Father flatters thee, is—
Thou must be wonderful, aren't thou his?

And Mother admires *her* offspring double.
Especially after all that trouble.

The wise child handles father and mother
By playing one against the other.

Don't! cries this parent to the tot;
The opposite parent asks, Why not?

Let baby listen, nothing loth,
And work impartially on both.

In clash of wills, do not give in;
Good parents are made by discipline;

Remember the words of the wise old senator:
Spare the tantrum, and spoil the progenitor,

But joy in heaping measure comes
To children whose parents are under their thumbs.

MR. TICKLEFEATHER

Timothy Ticklefeather, L.L.D.,
Lives in the top of a very tall tree.
He catches the rain in his christening cup,
And he nibbles nuts that the squirrels bring up.
His shoes are brown and his beard is gray,
And he sits and talks to the birds all day.
His beard is gray, but his shoes are brown,
And he lives in a tree, and he won't come down.

Hi, Mr. Ticklefeather,
Silly Mr. Ticklefeather,
What are you doing in that very tall tree?
It's all very well
To be friends with birds,
But suppose you fell?
You mark my words!
Come down, Mr. Ticklefeather,
Silly Mr. Ticklefeather,
Down on the ground and play with me!

Timothy Ticklefeather kicked his heels,
And he said, I know how a skylark feels!
And I've got my nuts and I've got my cup,
And I won't fall down, and I can't fall up,
And he polished his shoes and he brushed his beard,
And he climbed a little higher and he disappeared,

And all the policemen came from town.
But Mr. Ticklefeather never came down.

Poor Mr. Ticklefeather,
Silly Mr. Ticklefeather,
Where did he go with his beard on his knee?
Well, he didn't tumble down
With his christening cup,
And his shoes of brown,
So he must have tumbled up!
But I did, Mr. Ticklefeather,
Say, Mr. Ticklefeather.
Better come down and play with me!

BIRDIES, DON'T MAKE ME LAUGH

Once there was a poem, and it was serious and not in jest,
And it said children ought to agree like little birdies in their nest.
O forsooth forsooth!
That poem was certainly more poetry than truth,
Because do you believe that little birdies in their nest agree?
It doesn't sound very probable to me.
Ah no, but I can tell you what does sound probable,
And that is that life in a nest is just one long quarrel and squab-
    bable.
Look at that young mother robin over in that elm, or is it a beech,
She has two little robins and she thinks she has solved her problem
    because she has learned not to bring home just one worm but
    a worm for each.
She is very pleased with her understanding of fledgling psychology,
    but in just about two minutes she is going to lose a year's
    growth,
Because she's going to find that one little robin gets no worms and
    the other little robin gets both,
And if one little robin gets out of the nest on the wrong side and
    nothing can please it,
Why the other little robin will choose that moment to tease it,
And if one little robin starts a game the other little robin will stop it,

And if one little robin builds a castle the other little robin will knock it down and if one little robin blows a bubble the other little robin will pop it.

Yes, I bet if you walked up to any nest and got a good revealing glimpse,

Why, you would find that our little feathered friendlets disagree just like human imps,

And I also bet that their distracted feathered parents quote feathered poetry to them by whoever the most popular feathered poet may be,

All about why don't they like little children in their nurseries agree.

Well, to put the truth about youth in a very few words,

Why the truth is that little birds do agree like children and children do agree like little birds,

Because you take offspring, and I don't care whether a house or a tree is their abode,

They may love each other but they aren't going to agree with each other anywhere except in an ode.

It doesn't seem to have occurred to the poet,

That nobody agrees with anybody else anyhow, but adults conceal it and infants show it.

THE TALE OF CUSTARD THE DRAGON

Belinda lived in a little white house,
With a little black kitten and a little gray mouse,
And a little yellow dog and a little red wagon,
And a realio, trulio, little pet dragon.

Now the name of the little black kitten was Ink,
And the little gray mouse, she called her Blink,
And the little yellow dog was sharp as Mustard,
But the dragon was a coward, and she called him Custard.

Custard the dragon had big sharp teeth,
And spikes on top of him and scales underneath,
Mouth like a fireplace, chimney for a nose,
And realio, trulio daggers on his toes.

Belinda was as brave as a barrel full of bears,
And Ink and Blink chased lions down the stairs,
Mustard was as brave as a tiger in a rage,
But Custard cried for a nice safe cage.

Belinda tickled him, she tickled him unmerciful,
Ink, Blink and Mustard, they rudely called him Percival,
They all sat laughing in the little red wagon
At the realio, trulio, cowardly dragon.

Belinda giggled till she shook the house,
And Blink said "Weeck!" which is giggling for a mouse,
Ink and Mustard rudely asked his age,
When Custard cried for a nice safe cage.

Suddenly, suddenly they heard a nasty sound,
And Mustard growled, and they all looked around.
"Meowch!" cried Ink, and "Ooh!" cried Belinda,
For there was a pirate, climbing in the winda.

Pistol in his left hand, pistol in his right,
And he held in his teeth a cutlass bright,
His beard was black, one leg was wood;
It was clear that the pirate meant no good.

Belinda paled, and she cried, "Help! Help!"
But Mustard fled with a terrified yelp,
Ink trickled down to the bottom of the household,
And the little mouse Blink strategically mouseholed.

But up jumped Custard, snorting like an engine,
Clashed his tail like irons in a dungeon,
With a clatter and a clank and a jangling squirm
He went at the pirate like a robin at a worm.

The pirate gaped at Belinda's dragon,
And gulped some grog from his pocket flagon,
He fired two bullets, but they didn't hit,
And Custard gobbled him, every bit.

Belinda embraced him, Mustard licked him,
No one mourned for his pirate victim.

Ink and Blink in glee did gyrate
Around the dragon that ate the pyrate.

But presently up spoke little dog Mustard,
"I'd have been twice as brave if I hadn't been flustered."
And up spoke Ink and up spoke Blink,
"We'd have been three times as brave, we think."
And Custard said, "I quite agree
That everybody is braver than me."

Belinda still lives in her little white house,
With her little black kitten and her little gray mouse,
And her little yellow dog and a little red wagon,
And her realio, trulio little pet dragon.

Belinda is as brave as a barrel full of bears,
And Ink and Blink chase lions down the stairs,
Mustard is as brave as a tiger in a rage,
But Custard keeps crying for a nice safe cage.

THUNDER OVER THE NURSERY

Listen to me, angel tot,
Whom I love an awful lot,
It will save a barrel of bother
If we understand each other.

Every time that I'm your herder
You think you get away with murder.
All right, infant, so you do,
But only because I want you to.

Baby's muscles are prodigious,
Baby's beautiful, not higious,
She can talk and walk and run
Like a daughter of a gun.

Well, you may be a genius child,
And I a parent dull and mild;
In spite of which, and nevertheless,
I could lick you yet, I guess.

Forgive me, pet, if I am frank,
But truth is money in the bank;
I wish you to admire and love yourself,
But not to get too far above yourself.

When we race, you always win;
Baby, think before you grin.
It may occur to you, perhaps,
That Daddy's running under wraps.

When you hide behind the chair
And Daddy seeks you everywhere,
Behind the door, beneath the bed—
That's Daddy's heart, not Baby's head.

When I praise your speech in glee
And claim you talk as well as me,
That's the spirit, not the letter.
I know more words, and say them better.

In future, then, when I'm your herder,
Continue getting away with murder;
But know from him who murder endures,
It's his idea much more than yours.

LITTLE FEET

Oh, who would live in a silent house,
As still as a waltz left unwritten by Strauss,
As undisturbed as a virgin dewdrop,
And quiet enough to hear a shoe drop?
Who would dwell
In a vacuum cell,
In a home as mute as a clapperless bell?
Oh, a home as mute as a bell that's clapperless
Is forlorn as an Indian in Indianapolis.

Then ho! for the patter of little feet,
And the childish chatter of voices sweet,
For the ringing laughter and prancing capers

That soothe your ear as your read the papers,
For the trumpets that blow and the balls that bounce
As you struggle to balance your old accounts,
For the chubby arms that encircle your neck,
And the chubby behinds that your lap bedeck,
And sirens who save their wiliest wooing
For the critical spot in whatever you're doing.

Shakespeare's, I'm sure, was a silent house,
And that of Good King Wenceslaus,
And Napoleon's dwelling, and Alexander's,
And whoever's that wrote *The Dog of Flanders.*
Yes, Shelley and Keats
And other elites,
They missed the patter of little feets,
For he who sits and listens to pattering
Will never accomplish more than a smattering.

Then ho! for the patter of little feet!
Some find these footfalls doubly sweet,
Subjecting them to the twofold use
Of paternal pride and a good excuse.
You say, for instance, my modest chanteys
Are not so fine as Pope's or Dante's?
My deeds do not compare with those
Of Nelson, or Michelangelo's?
Well, my life is perpetual Children's Hour,
Or boy! would immortal genius flower!

JUDGMENT DAY

This is the day, this is the day!
I knew as soon as the sun's first ray
Crept through the slats of the cot,
And opened the eyes of a tot,
And the tot would rather have slept,
And, therefore, wept.
This is the day that is wrong,
The day when the only song

Is a skirling lamentation
Of continuous indignation,
When the visage is ireful,
The voice, direful,
And the early, pearly teeth
Snick like a sword in the sheath,
When the fists are clenched,
And the cheeks are drenched
In full-fed freshets and tumbling, tumultuous torrents
Of virtuous abhorrence,
When loud as the challenging trumpets of John at Lepanto
Rings the clarion, "I don't want to."
This is the day, the season,
Of wrongs without reason,
The day when the prunes and the cereal
Taste like building material,
When the spinach tastes only like spinach, and honey and sugar
Raise howls like the yowls of a quarrelsome puma or cougar,
When the wail is not to be hushed
Nor the hair to be brushed,
When life is frustration, and either
A person must be all alone or have somebody with her, and toler-
    ates neither,
When outdoors is worse than in, and indoors than out, and both
    too dull to be borne,
And dolls are flung under the bed and books are torn,
When people humiliate a person
With their clumsily tactful attempts to conciliate a person,
When music no charm possesses,
Nor hats, nor mittens, nor dresses,
When the frowning fortress is woe
And the watchword is No.
You owners of children who pass this day with forbearance,
You indeed are parents!

CHILDREN'S PARTY

May I join you in the doghouse, Rover?
I wish to retire till the party's over.
Since three o'clock I've done my best
To entertain each tiny guest;
My conscience now I've left behind me,
And if they want me, let them find me.
I blew their bubbles, I sailed their boats,
I kept them from each other's throats.
I told them tales of magic lands,
I took them out to wash their hands.
I sorted their rubbers and tied their laces,
I wiped their noses and dried their faces.
Of similarity there's lots
Twixt tiny tots and Hottentots.
I've earned repose to heal the ravages
Of these angelic-looking savages.
Oh, progeny playing by itself
Is a lonely fascinating elf,
But progeny in roistering batches
Would drive St. Francis from here to Natchez.
Shunned are the games a parent proposes;
They prefer to squirt each other with hoses,
Their playmates are their natural foemen
And they like to poke each other's abdomen.
Their joy needs another's woe to cushion it,
Say a puddle, and somebody littler to push in it.
They observe with glee the ballistic results
Of ice cream with spoons for catapults,
And inform the assembly with tears and glares
That everyone's presents are better than theirs.
Oh, little women and little men,
Someday I hope to love you again,
But not till after the party's over,
So give me the key to the doghouse, Rover.

RAINY DAY

Linell is clad in a gown of green.
She walks in state like a fairy queen.
Her train is tucked in a winsome bunch
Directly behind her royal lunch.
With a dignified skip and a haughty hop
Her golden slippers go clippety-clop.
I think I am Ozma, says Linell.
I'm Ozma too, says Isabel.

Linell has discovered a filmy veil;
The very thing for a swishy tail.
The waves wash over the nursery floor
And break on the rug with a rumbling roar;
The swishy tail gives a swishy swish;
She's off and away like a frightened fish.
Now I'm a mermaid, says Linell.
I'm mermaid too, says Isabel.

Her trousers are blue, her hair is kinky,
Her jacket is red and her skin is inky.
She is hiding behind a green umbrella:
She couldn't be Alice, or Cinderella,
Or Puss in Boots, or the Fiddlers Three:
Gracious Gulliver, who can she be?
I'm Little Black Sambo, says Linell.
I'm Sambo, too, says Isabel.

Clack the shutters. The blinds are drawn.
Click the switch, and the lights are gone.
Linell is under the blankets deep,
Murmuring down the hill to sleep.
Oh, deep in the soft and gentle dark
She stirs and chirps like a drowsy lark.
I love you, Mummy, says Linell.
Love Mummy too, says Isabel.

THE FACTS OF LIFE

Daughter, dim those reverent eyes;
Daddy must apologize.
Daddy's not an engineer;
Never will be, now, I fear.
Daddy couldn't drive a train,
Not for all the sherry in Spain.

Daddy's not a fireman, too;
He couldn't do what firemen do.
Clanging bells and screaming sirens
Are no part of his environs.
In case of fire, no hero he;
Merely a humble rescuee.

Also, greatly to his grief,
Daddy's not an Indian chief.
Daddy cannot stealthy walk
Or wield a lethal tomahawk.
Hark to Daddy's secret grim:
Feathers only tickle him.

Better learn it now than later;
Daddy's not an aviator.
Daddy cannot soar and swoop,
Neither can he loop the loop.
Parachutes he never hung on to,
And what is worse, he doesn't want to.

As long as Daddy's being defiant,
Daddy, child, is not a giant.
You'll travel far if you would seek
A less remarkable physique.
That's why he feels a decade older
When you are riding on his shoulder.

Another thing that Daddy ain't,
I frankly tell you, is a saint.
Daddy, my faithful catechumen,
Is widely known as all too human.

Still, if you watch him, you will find
He does his best, when so inclined.

One final skeleton while I dare;
Daddy's not a millionaire.
Alas, his most amusing verse
Is not a Fortunatus purse.
What I should buy for you, my sweeting,
Did journals end in both ends meeting!

There, child, you have the dismal truth,
Now obvious as an absent tooth.
Your doom it is to be the daughter
Of one as flat as barley water.
Do you mind so much, since he was made so?
What's that, my own? — I was afraid so.

A WATCHED EXAMPLE NEVER BOILS

The weather is so very mild
That some would call it warm.
Good gracious, aren't we lucky, child?
Here comes a thunderstorm.

The sky is now indelible ink,
The branches reft asunder;
But you and I, we do not shrink;
We love the lovely thunder.

The garden is a raging sea,
The hurricane is snarling;
Oh happy you and happy me!
Isn't the lightning darling?

Fear not the thunder, little one.
It's weather, simply weather;
It's friendly giants full of fun
Clapping their hands together.

I hope of lightning our supply
Will never be exhausted;

You know it's lanterns in the sky
For angels who are losted.

We love the kindly wind and hail,
The jolly thunderbolt,
We watch in glee the fairy trail
Of ampere, watt, and volt.

Oh, than to enjoy a storm like this
There's nothing I would rather.
Don't dive beneath the blankets, Miss!
Or else leave room for Father.

ADVENTURES OF ISABEL

Isabel met an enormous bear,
Isabel, Isabel, didn't care;
The bear was hungry, the bear was ravenous,
The bear's big mouth was cruel and cavernous.
The bear said, Isabel, glad to meet you,
How do, Isabel, now I'll eat you!
Isabel, Isabel, didn't worry,
Isabel didn't scream or scurry.
She washed her hands and she straightened her hair up,
Then Isabel quietly ate the bear up.

Once in a night as black as pitch
Isabel met a wicked old witch.
The witch's face was cross and wrinkled,
The witch's gums with teeth were sprinkled.
Ho ho, Isabel! The old witch crowed,
I'll turn you into an ugly toad!
Isabel, Isabel, didn't worry,
Isabel didn't scream or scurry.
She showed no rage and she showed no rancor,
But she turned the witch into milk and drank her.

Isabel met a hideous giant,
Isabel continued self reliant.
The giant was hairy, the giant was horrid,

He had one eye in the middle of his forehead.
Good morning, Isabel, the giant said,
I'll grind your bones to make my bread.
Isabel, Isabel, didn't worry,
Isabel didn't scream or scurry.
She nibbled the zwieback that she always fed off,
And when it was gone, she cut the giant's head off.

Isabel met a troublesome doctor,
He punched and he poked till he really shocked her.
The doctor's talk was of coughs and chills
And the doctor's satchel bulged with pills.
The doctor said unto Isabel,
Swallow this, it will make you well.
Isabel, Isabel, didn't worry,
Isabel didn't scream or scurry.
She took those pills from the pill concocter,
And Isabel calmly cured the doctor.

IT IS INDEED SPINACH

People by whom I am riled
Are people who go around wishing O that Time would backward
    turn backward and again make them a child.
Either they have no sense, or else they go around repeating some-
    thing they have heard, like a parakeet,
Or else they deliberately prevarikete,
Because into being a marathon dancer or a chiropodist or a tea-
    taster or a certified public accountant I could not be beguiled,
But I could sooner than I could into being again a child,
Because being a child is not much of a pastime,
And I don't want any next time because I remember the last time.
I do not wish to play with my toes,
Nor do I wish to have codliver oil spooned down my throat or al-
    bolene pushed up my nose.
I don't want to be plopped at sundown into a crib or a cradle
And if I don't go to sleep right away be greeted with either a lul-
    laby or an upbraidal.

I can think of nothing worse
Than never being out of sight of a parent or nurse;
Yes, that is the part that I don't see how they survive it,
To have their private life so far from private.
Furthermore, I don't want to cry for the moon,
And I do want to hold my own spoon;
I have more ambitious ideas of a lark
Than to collect pebbles in my hat or be taken for a walk in the
   park;
I should hate to be held together with safety pins instead of but-
   tons and suspenders and belts,
And I should particularly hate being told every time I was doing
   something I liked that it was time to do something else.
So it's pooh for the people who want Time to make them a child
   again because I think they must already be a child again or else
   they would stand up and own up
That it's much more fun to be a grown-up.

THE SNIFFLE

In spite of her sniffle,
Isabel's chiffle.
Some girls with a sniffle
Would be weepy and tiffle;
They would look awful,
Like a rained-on waffle,
But Isabel's chiffle
In spite of her sniffle.
Her nose is more red
With a cold in her head,
But then, to be sure,
Her eyes are bluer.
Some girls with a snuffle,
Their tempers are uffle,
But when Isabel's snivelly
She's snivelly civilly,
And when she is snuffly
She's perfectly luffly.

I WANT A DRINK OF WATER,
BUT NOT FROM THE THERMOS

Have you ever lost your early start on a six-hundred-mile trip and
had to spend the night in an individual wayside slum instead of
the cozy inn at which you had foresightedly engaged rooms be-
cause child A couldn't find her absolutely favorite doll, and
when she did find it, child B hadn't finished plaiting her hair
yet?

Then you will agree with me that an accurate definition of a mil-
lionth of a second is the interval between the moment when
you press the starter as you begin a six-hundred-mile trip and
the moment when two little tired voices inquire from the back
seat, "Are we nearly there yet?"

Then again, consider the other millionth of a second which lasts a
year, when Time stands still, and Eternity in the lap of Infinity
lingers,

Which is while you sit in helpless paralysis while child B carefully
slams the door on child A's fingers.

Take the battle royal whose results no bachelor need ever have
computated,

Which is the struggle to sit nearest to the open window, a struggle
the prize for which is the privilege of sticking the head and
arms out in just the right position to be immediately ampu-
tated.

Yes, for the father of none to thank his stars I think it only be-
hooving,

If merely because he has not to contend with little ones who will
descend from the car only on the traffic side, and preferably
quite some time before the car but not the traffic has stopped
moving.

Yes, he can roll along as confident as brass;

No restlessly whirling little leg will knock his spectacles off as he
confronts a bus, no little hand groping the floor for a vanilla
ice cream cone with chocolate thingamajigs on it will suddenly
alight heavily upon the gas.

As the father of two there is a respectful question which I wish to
ask of fathers of five:

How do you happen to be still alive?

WATER FOR THE GANDER

You take a man who has ever possessed an infant son or daughter,
And he feels pretty superior about drinks of water.
His voice is full of paternal lenience
As he describes how their thirst is always adjusted to his utmost in-
convenience,
And you gather that there is no rest for the married,
If only because of the little ones who choose to be perpetually in-
opportunely arid.
I assume that these little ones have never seen their sire in session
At his business or profession,
So listen closely, infant son and infant daughter,
His business or profession is what he carries on between getting up
to get a drink of water.
It requires a dozen visits to the nearest water cooler or fount
Before he can face drawing up a report or balancing an account.
You may be interested to note
That the driest point in America is not Death Valley, but a man
with lots of important work on his desk's throat.
Therefore, children, when he next complains at midnight about
your everlasting thirst,
Simply ask him how many hours he spent that day at his desk and
how many at the water cooler, and he may answer you, but I
bet he has to go and get himself a drink of water first.

ASK DADDY, HE WON'T KNOW

Now that they've abolished chrome work
I'd like to call their attention to home work.
Here it is only three decades since my scholarship was famous,
And I'm an ignoramus.
I cannot think which goes sideways and which goes up and down,
a parallel or a meridian,
Nor do I know the name of him who first translated the Bible into
Indian, I see him only as an enterprising colonial Gideon.
I have difficulty with dates,
To say nothing of the annual rainfall of the Southern Central
States.

Naturally the correct answers are just back of the tip of my tongue,
But try to explain that to your young.
I am overwhelmed by their erudite banter,
I am in no condition to differentiate between Tamerlane and Tam
   o'Shanter.
I reel, I sway, I am utterly exhausted;
Should you ask me when Chicago was founded I could only reply
   I didn't even know it was losted.

FIRST CHILD . . . SECOND CHILD

FIRST

Be it a girl, or one of the boys,
It is scarlet all over its avoirdupois,
It is red, it is boiled; could the obstetrician
Have possibly been a lobstertrician?
His degrees and credentials were hunky-dory,
But how's for an infantile inventory?
Here's the prodigy, here's the miracle!
Whether its head is oval or spherical,
You rejoice to find it has only one,
Having dreaded a two-headed daughter or son;
Here's the phenomenon all complete,
It's got two hands, it's got two feet,
Only natural, but pleasing, because
For months you have dreamed of flippers or claws.
Furthermore, it is fully equipped:
Fingers and toes with nails are tipped;
It's even got eyes, and a mouth clear cut;
When the mouth comes open the eyes go shut,
When the eyes go shut, the breath is loosed
And the presence of lungs can be deduced.
Let the rockets flash and the cannon thunder,
This child is a marvel, a matchless wonder.
A staggering child, a child astounding,
Dazzling, diaperless, dumbfounding,
Stupendous, miraculous, unsurpassed,
A child to stagger and flabbergast,

Bright as a button, sharp as a thorn,
And the only perfect one ever born.

SECOND
Arrived this evening at half-past nine.
Everybody is doing fine.
Is it a boy, or quite the reverse?
You can call in the morning and ask the nurse.

TABLEAU AT TWILIGHT

I sit in the dusk, I am all alone,
Enter a child and an ice cream cone.

A parent is easily beguiled
By sight of this coniferous child.

The friendly embers warmer gleam,
The cone begins to drip ice cream.

Cones are composed of many a vitamin
My lap is not the place to bitamin.

Although my raiment is not chinchilla,
I flinch to see it become vanilla.

Coniferous child, when vanilla melts
I'd rather it melted somewhere else.

Exit child with remains of cone,
I sit in the dusk, I am all alone.

Muttering spells like an angry Druid,
Alone, in the dusk, with the cleaning fluid.

TARKINGTON, THOU SHOULD'ST BE
LIVING IN THIS HOUR

O Adolescence, O Adolescence,
I wince before thine incandescence.
Thy constitution young and hearty
Is too much for this aged party.

Thou standest with loafer-flattened feet
Where bras and funny papers meet.
When anxious elders swarm about
Crying "Where are you going?", thou answerest "Out."
Leaving thy parents swamped in debts
For bubble gum and cigarettes.

Thou spurnest in no uncertain tone
The sirloin for the ice-cream cone;
Not milk, but cola, is thy potion;
Thou wearest earrings in the ocean,
Blue jeans at dinner, or maybe shorts,
And lipstick on the tennis courts.

Forever thou whisperest, two by two,
Of who is madly in love with who.
The car thou needest every day,
Let hubcaps scatter where they may.
For it would start unfriendly talk
If friends should chance to see thee walk.

Friends! Heavens, how they come and go!
Best pal today, tomorrow foe,
Since to distinguish thou dost fail
Twixt confidante and tattletale,
And blanchest to find the beach at noon
With sacred midnight secrets strewn.

Strewn! All is lost and nothing found.
Lord, how thou leavest things around!
Sweaters and rackets in the stable,
And purse upon the drugstore table,
And cameras rusting in the rain,
And Daddy's patience down the drain.

Ah well, I must not carp and cavil,
I'll chew the spinach, spit out the gravel,
Remembering how my heart has leapt
At times when me thou didst accept.
Still, I'd like to be present, I must confess,
When thine own adolescents adolesce.

SOLILOQUY IN CIRCLES

Being a father
Is quite a bother.

You are free as air
With time to spare,

You're a fiscal rocket
With change in your pocket,

And then one morn
A child is born.

Your life has been runcible,
Irresponsible.

Like an arrow or javelin
You've been constantly travelin'.

But mostly, I daresay,
Without a *chaise percée,*

To which by comparison
Nothing's embarison.

But all children matures,
Maybe even yours.

You improve them mentally
And straighten them dentally,

They grow tall as a lancer
And ask questions you can't answer,

And supply you with data
About how everybody else wears lipstick sooner and stays up later,

And if they are popular,
The phone they monopular.

They scorn the dominion
Of their parent's opinion,

They're no longer corralable
Once they find that you're fallible

But after you've raised them and educated them and gowned them,
They just take their little fingers and wrap you around them.

Being a father
Is quite a bother,
But I like it, rather.

UNTITLED

. . . Few creatures others less admire
Than a lass of seventeen her sire.
What humiliation must you weather
When we are seen in public together!

PIANO TUNER, UNTUNE ME THAT TUNE

I regret that before people can be reformed they have to be sinners,
And that before you have pianists in the family, you have to have
    beginners.
When it comes to beginners' music
I am not enthusic.
When listening to something called "An Evening in My Doll
    House," or "Buzz, Buzz Said the Bee to the Clover,"
Why I'd like just once to hear it played all the way through, instead
    of that hard part near the end over and over.
Have you noticed about little fingers?
When they hit a sour note, they lingers.
And another thing about little fingers, they are always strawberry-
    jammed or cranberry-jellied-y,
And "Chopsticks" is their favorite melody,
And if there is one man who I hope his dentist was a sadist and all
    his teeth were brittle ones,
It is he who invented "Chopsticks" for the little ones.
My good wishes are less than frugal
For him who started the little ones going boogie-woogal,
But for him who started the little ones picking out "Chopsticks"
    on the ivories,

Well I wish him a thousand harems of a thousand wives apiece, and a thousand little ones by each wife, and each little one playing "Chopsticks" twenty-four hours a day in all the nurseries of all his harems, or wiveries.

THERE'S NOTHING LIKE INSTINCT, FORTUNATELY

I suppose that plumbers' children know more about plumbing than plumbers do, and welders' children more about welding than welders,

Because the only fact in an implausible world is that all young know better than their elders.

A young person is a person with nothing to learn,

One who already knows that ice does not chill and fire does not burn.

It knows that it can read indefinitely in the dark and do its eyes no harm,

It knows it can climb on the back of a thin chair to look for a sweater it left on the bus without falling and breaking an arm.

It knows it can spend six hours in the sun on its first day at the beach without ending up a skinless beet,

And it knows it can walk barefoot through the barn without running a nail in its feet.

It knows it doesn't need a raincoat if it's raining or galoshes if it's snowing,

And knows how to manage a boat without ever having done any sailing or rowing.

It knows after every sporting contest that it had really picked the winner,

And that its appetite is not affected by eating three chocolate bars covered with peanut butter and guava jelly, fifteen minutes before dinner.

Most of all it knows

That only other people catch colds through sitting around in drafts in wet clothes.

Meanwhile psychologists grow rich

Writing that the young are ones parents should not undermine the self-confidence of which.

LINES TO BE EMBROIDERED ON A BIB
OR
THE CHILD IS FATHER OF THE MAN, BUT NOT FOR QUITE A WHILE

So Thomas Edison
Never drank his medicine;
So Blackstone and Hoyle
Refused cod-liver oil;
So Sir Thomas Malory
Never heard of a calory;
So the Earl of Lennox
Murdered Rizzio without the aid of vitamins or calisthenox;
So Socrates and Plato
Ate dessert without finishing their potato;
So spinach was too spinachy
For Leonardo da Vinaci;
Well, it's all immaterial,
So eat your nice cereal,
And if you want to name your own ration,
First go get a reputation.

A BOY'S WILL IS THE WIND'S WILL?

Mr. Longfellow spoke only part of the truth,
Though a fatherly poet of pre-eminent rank;
A girl's will is the twister's will.
It can drive a parent through a two-inch plank.

FEE, FI, HO HUM, NO WONDER BABY
SUCKS HER THUMB

I don't know whether you know what's new in juvenile literature
or not,
But I'll tell you what's new in juvenile literature, there's a new plot.
I grew up on the old plot, which I considered highly satisfactory,
And the hope of having stories containing it read to me restrained
me occasionally from being mendacious or refractory.
There were always two older sons and a youngest son, or two
older daughters and a youngest daughter,
And the older pair were always arrogant, selfish rascals, and the
youngest was always a numskull of the first water,
And the older ones would never share their bread and cheese with
little old men and women, and wouldn't help them home with
their loads.
And ended up with their fingers caught in cleft logs, or their con-
versation issuing in the form of toads,
And the young numskulls never cared what happened to their sib-
lings, because they had no family loyalty,
They just turned over all their bread and cheese to elderly ec-
centrics and ended up married to royalty, which I suppose ex-
plains what eventually happened to royalty.
That was admittedly not a plot to strain the childish understand-
ing,
But it was veritably Proustian compared to the new plot that the
third generation is demanding.
Whence these haggard looks?
I am trapped between one lovable grandchild and her two de-
testable favorite books.
The first is about a little boy who lost his cap and looked every-
where for it, behind the armchair and inside the refrigerator
and under the bed,
And where do you think he found it? On his head!
The second is about a little girl who lost one shoe on the train, and
until she found it she would give the porter and the other pas-
sengers no peace,
And finally where do you think she found it? In her valise!

A forthcoming book utilizing this new plot will tell the story of a
child who lost her grandfather while he was reading to her, and
you'll never guess where she discovered *him*.
Spang in the middle of Hans Christian Andersen and the Brothers
Grimm.

DADDY'S HOME, SEE YOU TOMORROW

I always found my daughters' beaux
Invisible as the emperor's clothes,
And I could hear of them no more
Than the slamming of an auto door.
My chicks would then slip up to roost;
They were, I finally deduced,
Concealing tactfully, pro tem,
Not boys from me but me from them.

UNTITLED POEM
(For the Baptism of a Friend's Daughter)

No wonder little Mary grins;
She's been washed of all her sins.
When she leaves St. Andrew's door
Mary plans to sin some more.

GRANDPA IS ASHAMED

A child need not be very clever
To learn that "Later, dear" means "Never."

THE GENTLEMAN LADY'S MAID

A treat which I consider mild
Is dressing an impatient child.
It proves impossible to insert
The child in socks or drawers or shirt.

The process baffles brain and brawn,
The socks will just go halfway on,
The drawers cut the child in two
And the shirt won't let the head get through.
It's presently clear that one cannot
Force last month's clothes on this month's tot.

ONE TIMES ONE IS EIGHT

Either old magic or new math
Into our house has beat a path.
How else could Einstein or Diogenes
Explain an exploit of our progeny's?
While at the table with his ilk
A child upsets a glass of milk.
The glass held half a pint when filled,
And half a gallon when it spilled.

THE ROMANTIC AGE

This one is entering her teens,
Ripe for sentimental scenes,
Has picked a gangling unripe male,
Sees herself in bridal veil,
Presses lips and tosses head,
Declares she's not too young to wed.
Informs you pertly you forget
Romeo and Juliet.
Do not argue, do not shout;
Remind her how that one turned out.

He and She

WHAT ALMOST EVERY WOMAN KNOWS, SOONER OR LATER

Husbands are things that wives have to get used to putting up
with,
And with whom they breakfast with and sup with.
They interfere with the discipline of nurseries,
And forget anniversaries,
And when they have been particularly remiss
They think they can cure everything with a great big kiss,
And when you tell them about something awful they have done
they just look unbearably patient and smile a superior smile,
And think, Oh she'll get over it after a while.
And they always drink cocktails faster than they can assimilate
them,
And if you look in their direction they act as if they were martyrs
and you were trying to sacrifice, or immolate them.
And when it's a question of walking five miles to play golf they are
very energetic but if it's doing anything useful around the house
they are very lethargic,
And then they tell you that women are unreasonable and don't
know anything about logic,

And they never want to get up or go to bed at the same time as you
do,
And when you perform some simple common or garden rite like
putting cold cream on your face or applying a touch of lipstick
they seem to think you are up to some kind of black magic like
a priestess of Voodoo,
And they are brave and calm and cool and collected about the ail-
ments of the person they have promised to honor and cherish,
But the minute they get a sniffle or a stomachache of their own,
why you'd think they were about to perish,
And when you are alone with them they ignore all the minor cour-
tesies
And as for airs and graces, they utterly lack them,
But when there are a lot of people around they hand you so many
chairs and ashtrays and sandwiches and butter you with such
bowings and scrapings that you want to smack them.
Husbands are indeed an irritating form of life,
And yet through some quirk of Providence most of them are really
very deeply ensconced in the affection of their wife.

A LADY THINKS SHE IS THIRTY

Unwillingly Miranda wakes,
Feels the sun with terror,
One unwilling step she takes,
Shuddering to the mirror.

Miranda in Miranda's sight
Is old and gray and dirty;
Twenty-nine she was last night;
This morning she is thirty.

Shining like the morning star,
Like the twilight shining,
Haunted by a calendar,
Miranda sits a-pining.

Silly girl, silver girl,
Draw the mirror toward you;

Time who makes the years to whirl
Adorned as he adored you,

Time is timelessness for you;
Calendars for the human;
What's a year, or thirty, to
Loveliness made woman?

Oh, Night will not see thirty again,
Yet soft her wing, Miranda;
Pick up your glass and tell me, then—
How old is Spring, Miranda?

ASIDE TO HUSBANDS

What do you do when you've wedded a girl all legal and lawful,
And she goes around saying she looks awful?
When she makes deprecatory remarks about her format,
And claims that her hair looks like a doormat?
When she swears that the complexion of which you are so fond
Looks like the bottom of a dried-up pond?
When she for whom your affection is not the least like Plato's
Compares her waist to a badly tied sack of potatoes?
Oh, who wouldn't rather be on a flimsy bridge with a hungry lion
    at one end and a hungry tiger at the other end and hungry croc-
    odiles underneath
Than confronted by their dearest making remarks about her own
    appearance through clenched teeth?
Why won't they believe that the reason they find themselves the
    mother of your children is because you think of all the looks in
    the world, their looks are the nicest?
Why must we continue to be thus constantly ordealed and cri-
    sised?
I think it high time these hoity-toity ladies were made to realize
    that when they impugn their face and their ankles and their
    waist
They are thereby insultingly impugning their tasteful husbands'
    impeccable taste.

EVERYBODY EATS TOO MUCH ANYHOW

You gulp your breakfast and glance at the clock,
Through eleventh-hour packing you gallop amok,
You bundle your bags in the back of the car,
You enter, she enters, and there you are.
It's au revoir to your modest abode,
You're gypsies, away on the open road;
The conversation is sweet as clover,
With breakfast practically hardly over.
"Darling, light me a cigarette?"
"At once and with all my heart, my pet;
And by the way, we are off the track;
We should have turned left a half-mile back."
You swing around with a cheery smile,
Thus far, a mile is only a mile.
The road is romance, so let it wind,
With breakfast an hour or so behind.
Under the tires the pebbles crunch,
And through the dust creep thoughts of lunch.
The speedometer sits on a steady fifty
And more and more does lunch seem nifty.
Your eyes to the road ahead are glued,
She glances about in search of food.
She sees a place. She would like to try it.
She says so. Well, you're already by it.
Ignoring the road, you spot an eatery;
The look of it makes her interior teetery.
She sees a beauty. It's past and gone.
She's simmering now, like a tropical dawn.
She snubs the excuse as you begin it:
That there'll be another one any minute.
She says there won't. It must be a plot;
She's absolutely correct. There's not.
You finally find one. You stop and alight.
You're both too annoyed to eat a bite.
Oh, this is the gist of my gypsy song:
Next time carry your lunch along.

CURL UP AND DIET

Some ladies smoke too much and some ladies drink too much and
some ladies pray too much,
But all ladies think that they weigh too much.
They may be as slender as a sylph or a dryad,
But just let them get on the scales and they embark on a doleful
jeremiad;
No matter how low the figure the needle happens to touch,
They always claim it is at least five pounds too much;
To the world she may appear slinky and feline,
But she inspects herself in the mirror and cries, Oh, I look like a
sea lion.
Yes, she tells you she is growing into the shape of a sea cow or
manatee,
And if you say No, my dear, she says you are just lying to make
her feel better, and if you say Yes, my dear, you injure her van-
ity.
Once upon a time there was a girl more beautiful and witty and
charming than tongue can tell,
And she is now a dangerous raving maniac in a padded cell,
And the first indication her friends and relatives had that she was
mentally overwrought
Was one day when she said, I weigh a hundred and twenty-seven,
which is exactly what I ought.
Oh, often I am haunted
By the thought that somebody might someday discover a diet that
would let ladies reduce just as much as they wanted,
Because I wonder if there is a woman in the world strong-minded
enough to shed ten pounds or twenty,
And say, There now, that's plenty;
And I fear one ten-pound loss would only arouse the craving for
another,
So it wouldn't do any good for ladies to get their ambition and
look like somebody's fourteen-year-old brother,
Because, having accomplished this with ease,
They would next want to look like somebody's fourteen-year-old
brother in the final stages of some obscure disease,
And the more success you have the more you want to get of it,

So then their goal would be to look like somebody's fourteen-year-
old brother's ghost, or rather not the ghost itself, which is fairly
solid, but a silhouette of it,
So I think it is very nice for ladies to be lithe and lissome,
But not so much so that you cut yourself if you happen to embrace
or kissome.

THE EVENING OUT

You have your hat and coat on and she says she will be right down,
And you hope so because it is getting late and you are dining on
the other side of town,
And you are pretty sure she can't take long,
Because when you left her she already looked as neat and snappy
as a Cole Porter song,
And so goes ten minutes, and then fifteen minutes, and then half
an hour,
And you listen for the sound of water running because you suspect
she may have gone back for a bath or a shower,
Or maybe she is taking a nap,
Or possibly getting up a subscription for the benefit of the children
of the mouse that she said mean things about last night but she
is now sorry got caught in a trap,
Or maybe she decided her hair was a mess and is now shampoo-
ing it,
But whatever she is up to, she is a long time doing it,
And finally she comes down and says she is sorry she couldn't find
the right lipstick, that's why she was so slow,
And you look at her and she looks marvelous but not a bit more
marvelous than she did when you left her forty-five minutes
ago,
And you tell her she looks ravishing and she says No, she is a sight,
And you reflect that you are now an hour late, but at any rate she
is now groomed for the rest of the night,
So you get to your destination and there's the ladies' dressing room
and before you know it she's in it,
But she says she'll be back in a minute,
And so she is, but not to tarry,

No, only to ask you for her bag, which she has forgotten she had
  asked you to carry,
So you linger in the lobby
And wish you had a nice portable hobby,
And you try to pass the time seeing how much you can remember
  of the poetry you learned in school, both good verse and bad
  verse,
And eventually she reappears just about as you have decided she
  was in the middle of *Anthony Adverse,*
And she doesn't apologize, but glances at you as if you were Blue-
  beard or Scrooge,
And says why didn't you tell her she had on too much rouge?
And you look to see what new tint she has acquired,
And she looks just the same as she did before she retired,
So you dine, and reach the theater in time for the third act, and
  then go somewhere to dance and sup,
And she says she looks like a scarecrow, she has to go straighten
  up,
So then you don't see her for quite a long time,
But at last you see her for a moment when she comes out to ask if
  you will lend her a dime,
The moral of all which is that you will have just as much of her
  company and still save considerable on cover charges and bev-
  erages and grub
If instead of taking her out on the town, you settle her in a nice
  comfortable dressing room and then go off and spend the
  evening at the Club.

I NEVER EVEN SUGGESTED IT

I know lots of men who are in love and lots of men who are mar-
  ried and lots of men who are both,
And to fall out with their loved ones is what all of them are most
  loth.
They are conciliatory at every opportunity,
Because all they want is serenity and a certain amount of impunity.
Yes, many the swain who has finally admitted that the earth is flat
Simply to sidestep a spat,

Many the masculine Positively or Absolutely which has been di-
luted to an If
Simply to avert a tiff,
Many the two-fisted executive whose domestic conversation is lim-
ited to a tactfully interpolated Yes,
And then he is amazed to find that he is being raked backwards
over a bed of coals nevertheless.
These misguided fellows are under the impression that it takes two
to make a quarrel, that you can sidestep a crisis by nonaggres-
sion and nonresistance,
Instead of removing yourself to a discreet distance.
Passivity can be a provoking *modus operandi;*
Consider the Empire and Gandhi.
Silence is golden, but sometimes invisibility is golder.
Because loved ones may not be able to make bricks without straw,
but often they don't need any straw to manufacture a bone to
pick or a chip for their soft white shoulder.
It is my duty, gentlemen, to inform you that women are dictators
all, and
I recommend to you this moral:
In real life it takes only one to make a quarrel.

THAT REMINDS ME

Just imagine yourself seated on a shadowy terrace,
And beside you is a girl who stirs you more strangely than an
heiress,
It is a summer evening at its most superb,
And the moonlight reminds you that To Love is an active verb.
And your hand clasps hers, which rests there without shrinking,
And after a silence fraught with romance you ask her what she is
thinking,
And she starts and returns from the moon-washed distances to the
shadowy veranda,
And says, Oh I was wondering how many bamboo shoots a day it
takes to feed a baby Giant Panda.
Or you stand with her on a hilltop and gaze on a winter sunset,
And everything is as starkly beautiful as a page from Sigrid Undset,

And your arm goes round her waist and you make an avowal
   which for masterfully marshaled emotional content might have
   been a page of Ouida's or Thackeray's,
And after a silence fraught with romance she says, I forgot to or-
   der the limes for the Daiquiris.
Or in a twilight drawing room you have just asked the most mo-
   mentous of questions,
And after a silence fraught with romance she says, I think this
   little table would look better where that little table is, but
   then where would that little table go, have you any sugges-
   tions?
And that's the way they go around hitting below our belts;
It isn't that nothing is sacred to them, it's just that at the Sacred
   Moment they are always thinking of something else.

TO MY VALENTINE

More than a catbird hates a cat,
Or a criminal hates a clue,
Or the Axis hates the United States,
That's how much I love you.

I love you more than a duck can swim,
And more than a grapefruit squirts,
I love you more than gin rummy is a bore,
And more than a toothache hurts.

As a shipwrecked sailor hates the sea,
Or a juggler hates a shove,
As a hostess detests unexpected guests,
That's how much you I love.

I love you more than a wasp can sting,
And more than the subway jerks,
I love you as much as a beggar needs a crutch,
And more than a hangnail irks.

I swear to you by the stars above,
And below, if such there be,

As the High Court loathes perjurious oaths,
That's how you're loved by me.

THOUGHTS THOUGHT ON AN AVENUE

There would be far less masculine gaming and boozing
But for the feminine approach to feminine fashions, which is dis-
tinctly confusing.
Please correct me, if, although I don't think I do, I err;
But it is a fact that a lady wants to be dressed exactly like every-
body else but she gets pretty upset if she sees anybody else
dressed exactly like her.
Nothing so infuriates her as a similar hat or dress,
Especially if bought for less,
Which brings up another point which I will attempt to discuss in
my guttural masculine jargon;
Her ideal raiment is costlier than her or her dearest friend's purse
can buy, and at the same time her own exclusive and amazing
bargain.
Psychologists claim that men are the dreamers and women are the
realists,
But to my mind women are the starriest-eyed of idealists,
Though I am willing to withdraw this charge and gladly eat it un-
complaineously
If anyone can explain to me how a person can wear a costume that
is different from other people's and the same as other people's,
and more expensive than other people's and cheaper than other
people's, simultaneously.

SUMMER SERENADE

When the thunder stalks the sky,
When tickle-footed walks the fly,
When shirt is wet and throat is dry,
Look, my darling, that's July.

Though the grassy lawn be leather,
And prickly temper tug the tether,

Shall we postpone our love for weather?
If we must melt, let's melt together!

I'M SURE SHE SAID SIX-THIRTY

One of the hardest explanations to be found
Is an explanation for just standing around.
Anyone just standing around looks pretty sinister,
Even a minister;
Consider then the plight of the criminal,
Who lacks even the protective coloration of a hyminal,
And as just standing around is any good criminal's practically daily
    stint,
I wish to proffer a hint.
Are you, sir, a masher who blushes as he loiters,
Do you stammer to passers-by that you are merely expecting a
    streetcar, or a dispatch from Reuter's?
Or perhaps you are a safeblower engaged in casing a joint;
Can you look the patrolman in the eye or do you forget all the
    savoir faire you ever loint?
Suppose you are a shoplifter awaiting an opportunity to lift a
    shop,
Or simply a novice with a length of lead pipe killing time in a dark
    alley pending the arrival of a wealthy fop,
Well, should any official ask you why you are just standing
    around,
Do you wish you could simply sink into the ground?
My dear sir, do not be embarrassed, do not reach for your gun or
    your knife,
Remember the password, which, uttered in a tone of quiet despair,
    is the explanation of anyone's standing around anywhere at
    any hour for any length of time: "I'm waiting for my wife."

DON'T EVEN TELL YOUR WIFE, PARTICULARLY

All good men believe that women would rather get rid of a piece
    of gossip than a bulge,

And all good women believe that gossip is a feminine weakness in
which men never indulge.
Rather than give ear to scandalous rumors,
Why, men would rather play golf in bloomers,
And rather than talk behind each other's backs,
They would go shopping in a mink coat and slacks.
It is one of each sex's uniquenesses
That men's talk is all of humanity's aspirations, and women's all of
their friends' weaknesses.
Yes, this is a universal credo that no amount of evidence can alter,
Including that of Petronius, Suetonius, Pepys, Boswell, the locker
room of the country club, and Mrs. Winchell's little boy, Wal-
ter.
Allow me to ask and answer one question before departing for
Mount
Everest or Lake Ossipee:
Who says men aren't gossipy? — Men say men aren't gossipy.

THE TROUBLE WITH WOMEN IS MEN

A husband is a man who two minutes after his head touches the
pillow is snoring like an overloaded omnibus,
Particularly on those occasions when between the humidity and
the mosquitoes your own bed is no longer a bed, but an in-
somnibus,
And if you turn on the light for a little reading he is sensitive to the
faintest gleam,
But if by any chance you are asleep and he wakeful, he is not slow
to rouse you with the complaint that he can't close his eyes,
what about slipping downstairs and freezing him a cooling dish
of pistachio ice cream.
His touch with a bottle opener is sure,
But he cannot help you get a tight dress over your head without
catching three hooks and a button in your coiffure.
Nor can he so much as wash his ears without leaving an inch of
water on the bathroom linoleum,
But if you mention it you evoke not a promise to splash no more
but a mood of deep melancholium.

Indeed, each time he transgresses your chance of correcting his faults grows lesser,
Because he produces either a maddeningly logical explanation or a look of martyrdom which leaves you instead of him feeling the remorse of the transgressor.
Such are husbandly foibles, but there are moments when a foible ceases to be a foible.
Next time you ask for a glass of water and when he brings it you have a needle almost threaded and instead of setting it down he stands there holding it out to you, just kick him fairly hard in the stomach, you will find it thoroughly enjoible.

WE DON'T NEED TO LEAVE YET, DO WE?
OR
YES WE DO

One kind of person when catching a train always wants to allow an hour to cover the ten-block trip to the terminus,
And the other kind looks at them as if they were verminous,
And the second kind says that five minutes is plenty and will even leave one minute over for buying the tickets,
And the first kind looks at them as if they had cerebral rickets.
One kind when theater-bound sups lightly at six and hastens off to the play,
And indeed I know one such person who is so such that it frequently arrives in time for the last act of the matinee,
And the other kind sits down at eight to a meal that is positively sumptuous,
Observing cynically that an eight-thirty curtain never rises till eight-forty, an observation which is less cynical then bumptuous.
And what the first kind, sitting uncomfortably in the waiting room while the train is made up in the yards, can never understand,
Is the injustice of the second kind's reaching their seat just as the train moves out, just as they had planned,
And what the second kind cannot understand as they stumble over the first kind's feet just as the footlights flash on at last
Is that the first kind doesn't feel the least bit foolish at having entered the theater before the cast.

Oh, the first kind always wants to start now and the second kind
   always wants to tarry,
Which wouldn't make any difference, except that each other is
   what they always marry.

TIN WEDDING WHISTLE

Though you know it anyhow
Listen to me, darling, now,

Proving what I need not prove
How I know I love you, love.

Near and far, near and far,
I am happy where you are;

Likewise I have never learnt
How to be it where you aren't.

Far and wide, far and wide,
I can walk with you beside;

Furthermore, I tell you what,
I sit and sulk where you are not.

Visitors remark my frown
When you're upstairs and I am down,

Yes, and I'm afraid I pout
When I'm indoors and you are out;

But how contentedly I view
Any room containing you.

In fact I care not where you be,
just as long as it's with me.

In all your absences I glimpse
Fire and flood and trolls and imps.

Is your train a minute slothful?
I goad the stationmaster wrothful.

When with friends to bridge you drive
I never know if you're alive,

And when you linger late in shops
I long to telephone the cops.

Yet how worth the waiting for,
To see you coming through the door.

Somehow, I can be complacent
Never but with you adjacent.

Near and far, near and far,
I am happy where you are;

Likewise I have never learnt
How to be it where your aren't.

Then grudge me not my fond endeavor,
To hold you in my sight forever;

Let none, not even you, disparage
Such valid reason for a marriage.

FOR FRANCES

Geniuses of countless nations
Have told their love for generations
Till all their memorable phrases
Are common as goldenrod or daisies.
Their girls have glimmered like the moon,
Or shimmered like a summer noon,
Stood like lily, fled like fawn,
Now like sunset, now like dawn,
Here the princess in the tower,
There the sweet forbidden flower.
Darling, when I think of you
Every aged phrase is new,
And there are moments when it seems
I've married one of Shakespeare's dreams.

I DO, I WILL, I HAVE

How wise I am to have instructed the butler to instruct the first
    footman to instruct the second footman to instruct the door-
    man to order my carriage;
I am about to volunteer a definition of marriage.
Just as I know that there are two Hagens, Walter and Copen,
I know that marriage is a legal and religious alliance entered into
    by a man who can't sleep with the window shut and a woman
    who can't sleep with the window open.
Moreover, just as I am unsure of the difference between flora and
    fauna and flotsam and jetsam,
I am quite sure that marriage is the alliance of two people, one of
    whom never remembers birthdays and the other never forget-
    sam,
And he refuses to believe there is a leak in the water pipe or the gas
    pipe and she is convinced she is about to asphyxiate or drown,
And she says, Quick get up and get my hairbrushes off the window-
    sill, it's raining in, and he replies, Oh they're all right, it's only
    raining straight down.
That is why marriage is so much more interesting than divorce,
Because it's the only known example of the happy meeting of the
    immovable object and the irresistible force.
So I hope husbands and wives will continue to debate and combat
    over everything debatable and combatable,
Because I believe a little incompatibility is the spice of life, partic-
    ularly if he has income and she is pattable.

THE PERFECT HUSBAND

He tells you when you've got on too much lipstick,
And helps you with your girdle when your hips stick.

ALWAYS MARRY AN APRIL GIRL

Praise the spells and bless the charms,
I found April in my arms.
April golden, April cloudy,
Gracious, cruel, tender, rowdy;
April soft in flowered languor,
April cold with sudden anger,
Ever changing, ever true—
I love April, I love you.

CONFESSION TO BE TRACED
ON A BIRTHDAY CAKE

Lots of people are richer than me,
Yet pay a slenderer tax;
Their annual levy seems to wane
While their income seems to wax.
Lots of people have stocks and bonds
To further their romances;
I've cashed my ultimate Savings Stamp—
But nobody else has Frances.

Lots of people are stronger than me,
And great athletic menaces;
They poise like gods on diving boards
And win their golfs and tennises.
Lots of people have lots more grace
And cut fine figures at dances,
While I was born with galoshes on—
But nobody else has Frances.

Lots of people are wiser than me,
And carry within their cranium
The implications of Stein and Joyce
And the properties of uranium.
They know the mileage to every star
In the heaven's vast expanses;
I'm inclined to believe that the world is flat—
But nobody else has Frances.

Speaking of wisdom and wealth and grace—
As recently I have dared to—
There are lots of people compared to whom
I'd rather not be compared to.
There are people I ought to wish I was;
But under the circumstances,
I prefer to continue my life as me—
For nobody else has Frances.

THEY WON'T BELIEVE, ON NEW YEAR'S EVE, THAT NEW YEAR'S DAY WILL COME WHAT MAY

How do I feel today? I feel as unfit as an unfiddle,
And it is the result of a certain turbulence in the mind and an un-
    certain burbulence in the middle.
What was it anyway, that angry thing that flew at me?
I am unused to banshees crying Boo at me.
Your wife can't be a banshee,
Or can she?
Of course, some wives become less fond
When you're bottled in bond.
My Uncle George, in lavender-scented Aunt Edna's day,
If he had a glass of beer on Saturday night, he didn't dare come
    home till the following Wednesday.
I see now that he had hit upon the ideal idea,
The passage of time, and plenty of it, is the only marital panacea.
Ah, if the passage of time were backward, and last night I'd been
    a child again, this morning I'd be fragrant with orange juice,
Instead of reeking of pinch-bottle foreign juice;
But if I should turn out to be a child again, what would life hold
    for me?
The woman I love would be too old for me.
There's only one solution to my problem, a hair of the dog, or
    maybe a couple of hairs;
Then if she doesn't get mad at me life will be peaceful, and if she
    does, it will show she really cares.

THE ANNIVERSARY

A marriage aged one
Is hardly begun;
A fling in the sun,
But it's hardly begun;
A green horse,
A stiff course,
And leagues to be run.

A marriage aged five
Is coming alive.
Watch it wither and thrive;
Though it's coming alive,
You must guess,
No or yes,
If it's going to survive.

A marriage aged ten
Is a hopeful Amen;
It's pray for it then,
And mutter Amen,
As the names
Of old flames
Sound again and again.

At twenty a marriage
Discovers its courage.
This year do not disparage,
It is comely in courage;
Past the teens
And blue jeans,
It's a promising marriage.

Yet before twenty-one
It has hardly begun.
How tall in the sun,
Yet hardly begun!
But once come of age,
Pragmatically sage,

Oh, blithe to engage
Is sweet marri-age.

Tilt a twenty-first cup
To a marriage grown-up,
Now sure and mature,
And securely grown up.
Raise twenty-one cheers
To the silly young years,
While I sit out the dance
With my dearest of dears.

UNTITLED

No Petrarch I, but you're my Laura;
I'm Tithonus to your Aurora.
With every passing year I wither,
While you develop more come-hither.
If I reach ninety still alive
You'll still be looking thirty-five,
But don't despise him who adored you—
Whistle, and I will hobble toward you.

THE NYMPH AND THE SHEPHERD
OR
SHE WENT THAT-A-WAY

Few things are less endearing than a personal comparison,
But I know a lady who is very like the elusive mother of Mr. Milne's
James James Morrison Morrison.
She would be a perfect wife could she but be restrained by a leash
    or a fetter,
Because she has the roving tendencies of an Irish setter.
Her husband assists her from the cab and stops to pay the fare,
And when he turns around she isn't there,
She is a hundred yards off, blithe as a flock of linnets,
And in a fair way to do the mile under four minutes.

He assists her from the train and by the time he has caught a porter
    she is at the top of the moving stairway,
And again to do the mile under four minutes she is in a fair way.
She shoots ahead of him in London crowds and leaves him behind
    fumbling with lire in Pisa,
Despite the fact that he is in sole possession of all the travelers'
    checks and their joint passport and visa.
If in the Louvre she exclaims, "Oh, look at the Mona Lisa!" and
    he pauses to look at the Mona Lisa,
By the time he has looked she is three corners and forty master-
    pieces away, and himself alone with the same old money and
    passport and visa.
Sometimes he is touched and flattered by her faith in him, but
    mostly he feels like Queen Victoria's chair,
Which Queen Victoria never looked behind at before she sat down,
    because she just knew it would be there.

MY DREAM

Here is a dream.
It is my dream—
My own dream—
I dreamt it.
I dreamt that my hair was kempt,
Then I dreamt that my true love
unkempt it.

HOW TO HARRY A HUSBAND
OR
IS THAT ACCESSORY REALLY NECESSARY?

Husband stands at door of flat,
Coat in elbow, hand on hat,
In his pocket, from broker shady
Two good seats for *My Fair Lady*.
Patiently he stands there humming,
Coming, darling? Darling, coming?

But she's a freak and she's a hag,
She's got the wrong, she murmurs, bag,
She's got, she adds in wild distress,
To change the bag or change the dress.
She'd as soon appear with stockings ragged,
As be seen incongruously debaggèd.

Husband rings the bell for lift,
Hears it chunk and upward drift,
Well knows taxis in the rain
Rarer than the whooping crane.
Impatiently he stands there snarling,
Darling, coming? Coming, darling?

Another bag at last she chooses
And everything in the first bag loses.
She fumbles with many a dainty curse
For lipstick, glasses, keys and purse.*
He grunts, as dies preprandial liquor,
To change from the skin out would have been quicker.

They disrupt the middle of the show,
Their seats are middle of the row,
They crawl and climb like tandem tractors
Between the audience and the actors,
Whose delicious rapport might have lagged
Had she been incongruously bebagged.

*Then—
She turns it inside out and scratches
For handkerchief, cigarettes, and matches,
Tweezers, compact, and aspirin,
And Band-Aids redolent of My Sin,
Driver's license and Charga-Plate,
A sweepstake ticket one year late,
A colored chart of a five-day diet,
A Penguin commended by Gilbert Highet,
A tearful appeal from a charitymonger,
And a catalogue from Lewis & Conger.
This is she whose eyes start from their sockets
At the content of her small son's pockets.

THERE'LL ALWAYS BE A WAR BETWEEN THE SEXES
OR
A WOMAN CAN BE SOMETIMES PLEASED, BUT NEVER SATISFIED

I used to know a breadwinner named Mr. Purefoy who was far
    from the top of the heap,
Indeed he could only be called a breadwinner because he had once
    won half a loaf of whole wheat in the Irish Sweep.
His ambition was feverish,
His industry was eager-beaverish,
His wife was a thrifty helpmeet who got full value for every dis-
    bursement,
Yet their financial status showed no betterment, just perpetual
    worsement.
The trouble with these two was that they dissipated their energies,
They didn't play the percenages.
If he got angry at a slovenly, insolent waiter when they were din-
    ing in town
She would either bury her face in the menu or try to calm him
    down.
If she got angry at the woman in front of her at the movies and
    loudly suggested that she push her hat a little lower,
He pretended he didn't know her.
He defended his unappreciative employer against her loyal wifely
    ire,
And when he got burned up about the bills from the friendly ex-
    orbitant little grocer around the corner she tried to put out the
    fire.
One day they had a thought sublime,
They thought, Let's both get mad at the same person or situation
    at the same time.
I don't know about Mars, but Earth has not a denizen,
Who can withstand the wrath of a husband and a wife being
    wrathful in unison.
To be said, little remains;
Only that after they merged their irascibility, it required the full
    time of three Certified Public Accountants and one Certified
    Private Accountant to keep track of their capital gains.

EXCUSE ME DEAR, BUT IT DOESN'T
GO THISAWAY, IT GOES THATAWAY

I address this appeal to a lady named Mrs. Waldemar Reiland
Who lives with her husband in Amityville, Long Island.
They not only live in Amityville, they live in amity,
Except when he embarks on an anecdote and she turns his antici-
pated social triumph into a calamity.
She loves him dearly, she caters to his every comfort, she has sewed
buttons on his shirt, she has with her own hands breakfasted
and supped him,
But when he attempts to tell a story she cannot help but interrupt
him.
If he says something happened on a Thursday she says, No, love,
it was on a Friday;
If he says his bathrobe caught fire while he was watching the late
late movie which was "Bambi" she laughs and says she remem-
bers very clear that it wasn't "Bambi," it was "Heidi."
If he displays a gold doubloon that he says came from a sunken
Spanish galley she says, Not galley, dear, galleon,
And if he tells of the kind Irish cop who gave him a warning in-
stead of a ticket she says, He wasn't Irish, he was Italian.
She is a stickler
For the irrelevant particular.

Dear Mrs. Reiland, does it really matter, do his spellbound listen-
ers really care exactly where or when the episode he is strug-
gling to describe occurred?
Does it affect the point if he places it at noon on Forty-second
Street when it actually happened at 12:15 on Forty-third?
Suppose the man does get the minor details wrong, after all it is his
story, it is his alone,
Just let him finish it on his own.
Promise me this, Mrs. Reiland, and in return I, prince of inaccu-
rate raconteurs,
Promise never again to interrupt my wife, whose stories are as ac-
curate as they are entertaining, while she is telling one of hers.

THE SPOON RAN AWAY WITH THE DISH?

The ideal TV commercial pins the attention of the viewer,
And I am suffering from one that has pinned my wandering
thoughts like shish kebab on a skewer.
Did I ever prick up my ears
When the other night a smiling announcer presented what he
called the most revolutionary dishwashing discovery in twelve
years!
I readily agree that the new discovery is great;
What pinned my attention was trying to remember what revolu-
tionized dishwashing in 1948.
I was in the most frustrating of the countless predicaments I have
been among,
Because the answer wasn't even on the tip of my tongue.
I could remember that in 1948 the Cleveland Indians took the
World Series, four games to two, from the Boston Braves, and
Citation won the Derby;
Also that 1948 marked the publication of *The Golden Hawk,* by
Frank Yerby.
Frank Yerby did not win the Nobel award for literature that year,
but T. S. Eliot did—may he long on life have lease—
And there was no Nobel award for peace.
I recalled clearly that the Pulitzer Prize went to *Tales of the South
Pacific,* by James Michener,
But that was literary stuff—I was groping for something pantrier,
something kitchener.
For that twelve-year-old dishwashing discovery my mind continues
sleeplessly to grope.
Could it have been the discovery of dish towels? Of paper plates?
Of hot water? Of soap?
Of course, there was my wife's welcome discovery that without my
assistance it took her only half the time to get the dishes spot-
less and arid,
But that was in 1931, shortly after we were married.
Anyhow, that's the way my brain has been eroded,
Worrying about a once-revolutionary method of dishwashing that
has now been outmoded.

HOW CAN ECHO ANSWER
WHAT ECHO CANNOT HEAR?

Why shouldn't I laud my love?
My love is highly laudable;
Indeed, she would be perfection
Were she only always audible.

Why shouldn't I laud her voice,
The welcomest sound I know,
Her voice, which is ever soft?
It is likewise gentle and low—

An excellent thing in woman
And the Wilson's thrush, or veery—
But there are maddening moments
When I wish I had wed a Valkyrie.

Whenever her talk is restricted
To topics inconsequential
She utters it face to face,
With clarity reverential.

Then why, when there's something important to say,
Does she always say it going away?
She'll remark, as she mounts the stairs to bed,
"Oh, some FBI man called and said . . ."
Then her words, like birds too swift for banding,
Vanish with her upon the landing.
"Don't you think we ought . . ." Then she's gone, whereat
The conclusion fades out like the Cheshire Cat.
Yes, her words when weighty with joy or dread
Seem to emerge from the back of her head;
The dénouement supreme, the point of the joke,
Is forever drifting away like smoke.
Knowing her custom, knowing the wont of her,
I spend my life circling to get in front of her.

I'll bet that the poet Herrick
With Corinna gone a-Maying,
Had to run like a rabbit
To catch what she was saying.

A WORD TO HUSBANDS

To keep your marriage brimming,
With love in the loving cup,
Whenever you're wrong, admit it;
Whenever you're right, shut up.

THE JOYOUS MALINGERER

Who is the happy husband? Why, indeed,
'Tis he who's useless in the time of need;
Who, asked to unclasp a bracelet or a necklace,
Contrives to be utterly futile, fumbling, feckless,
Or when a zipper nips his loved one's back
Cannot restore the zipper to its track.
Another time, not wishing to be flayed,
She will not use him as a lady's maid.

Stove-wise he's the perpetual backward learner
Who can't turn on or off the proper burner.
If faced with washing up he never gripes,
But simply drops more dishes than he wipes.
She finds his absence preferable to his aid,
And thus all mealtime chores doth he evade.

He can, attempting to replace a fuse,
Black out the coast from Boston to Newport News,
Or, hanging pictures, be the rookie wizard
Who fills the parlor with a plaster blizzard.
He'll not again be called to competition
With decorator or with electrician.

At last it dawns upon his patient spouse
He's better at his desk than round the house.

THE STILLY NIGHT: A SOPORIFIC REFLECTION

There is one source of marital discord so delicate that I approach
it on tiptoe,

And it reveals itself when the partners whose melancholy boast is
that they are insomniacs are really somniacs, only not overt but
crypto-.

He unwinds himself from the bedclothes each morn and piteously
proclaims that he didn't sleep a wink, and she gives him a glance
savage and murderous

And replies that it was she who didn't close an eye until cockcrow
because of his swinish slumber as evidenced by his snores con-
tinuous and stertorous,

And his indignation is unconcealed,

He says she must have dreamed that one up during her night-long
sweet repose, which he was fully conscious of because for eight
solid hours he had listened to her breathing not quite so gentle
as a zephyr on a flowery field.

Such is the genesis of many a myth,

Because her statement is a falsehood that is akin to truth, and his
a truth that is to falsehood akith.

The fact is that she did awaken twice for brief intervals and he was
indeed asleep and snoring, and he did awaken similarly and she
was indeed unconscious and breathing miscellaneously,

But they were never both awake simultaneously.

Oh, sleep it is a blessed thing, but not to those wakeful ones who
watch their mates luxuriating in it when they feel that their
own is sorely in arrears.

I am certain that the first words of the Sleeping Beauty to her prince
were, "You *would* have to kiss me just when I had dropped off
after tossing and turning for a hundred years."

FOR FRANCES, APRIL 12, 1968

My wife
Was a girl from the foaming seas of twilight lore,
On a lucent shell by Nereids borne ashore.
Such being her birth,
She found swift joy in the common things of earth.
She exulted in simple scent and sound and sight,
And her unfeigned delight gave me delight.
She carelessly gathered my heart like a daffodil.
She has it still.

My wife
Is a woman who walks with the inborn pride of a queen,
After turbulent decades of marriage still serene.
Through death and birth
She has learned that the world is not all grief, all mirth.
Steadfast beside me when ventures and spirits fail
Her courage flies as brave as a flag in the gale.
I marvel at her loveliness, her grace—
But not to her face.

My wife
Will be an old lady mischievous and flighty,
Will shake her gold-headed cane in the face of God Almighty.
She will be revered,
Be pampered, be boasted of, be adored and feared.
She will love a surprise, and a dry martini as well,
She will still be the girl who was borne ashore on a shell,
And I'll shout, as the ivy on my stone advances,
Go to it, Frances!

Traveling with Nash

GEOGRAPHICAL REFLECTION

The Bronx?
No, thonx!

SONG OF THE OPEN ROAD

I think that I shall never see
A billboard lovely as a tree.
Indeed, unless the billboards fall
I'll never see a tree at all.

RIDING ON A RAILROAD TRAIN

Some people like to hitch and hike;
They are fond of highway travel;
Their nostrils toil through gas and oil,
They choke on dust and gravel.
Unless they stop for the traffic cop
Their road is a fine-or-jail road,

But wise old I go rocketing by;
I'm riding on the railroad.

I love to loll like a limp rag doll
In a peripatetic salon;
To think and think of a long cool drink
And cry to the porter, *Allons!*
Now the clickety clack of wheel on track
Grows clickety clackety clicker:
The line is clear for the engineer
And it mounts to his head like liquor.

With a farewell scream of escaping steam
The boiler bows to the Diesel;
The Iron Horse has run its course
And we ride a chromium weasel;
We draw our power from the harnessed shower,
The lightning without the thunder,
But a train is a train and will so remain
While the rails glide glistening under.

Oh, some like trips in luxury ships,
And some in gasoline wagons,
And others swear by the upper air
And the wings of flying dragons.
Let each make haste to indulge his taste,
Be it beer, champagne, or cider;
My private joy, both man and boy,
Is being a railroad rider.

A BRIEF GUIDE TO NEW YORK

In New York beautiful girls can become more beautiful by going
   to Elizabeth Arden
And getting stuff put on their faces and waiting for it to harden,
And poor girls with nothing to their names but a letter or two can
   get rich and joyous
From a brief trip to their loyous.
So I can say with impunity

That New York is a city of opportunity.
It also has many fine theaters and hotels,
And a lot of taxis, buses, subways and els,
Best of all, if you don't show up at the office or at a tea nobody
    will bother their head,
They will just think you are dead.
That's why I really think New York is exquisite,
And even nicer to live in than to visit.

LETTER FROM OMAHA

Darling Isabel, Sweet Linell,
This is the tale I have to tell.
I travelled to Buffalo, New York,
And there I delivered a humorous tork,
But I found the audience rather dreary,
And would rather have trudgeoned in Lake Erie.
Rochester next, on Lake Ontario
High-ho the Kodak, high-ho the dairy-o!
Rochester, dears, and your daddy, who's me.
Somehow or other just couldn't agree,
And then the next morning to cap the clim-*ax,*
I couldn't depart, as my train left the tracks;
But *I* was not on it, to Rochester's fury,
And that night I arrived at St. Louis, Missouri.
I travelled from there on a train named Will Rogers,
Who was loved in the West like your ma loves the Dodgers!
I wakened in Tulsa, where folk do not toil,
As everyone there owns a well full of oil.
Think sweetly of Tulsa, if not too much bother,
Since the whole population was kind to your father.
They harked to his words and they purchased his books.
And they laughed at his jests instead of his looks,
And asked for poems about Linell,
And sent their love to Isabel.
I found only one flaw in Oklahoma,
Their water has a chlorine aroma;
Though clear and plenteous, pure and cool,

It's rather like drinking a swimming pool.
Now to continue my lilting ditty,
I went from Tulsa to Kansas City,
And then to here, on a train called the Zephyr,
Whose cowcatcher caught not even a heifer.
So now I sit in the state of Nebraska,
On the way from Salisbury to Alaska,
And I tell you, darlings, that here in Omaha,
The water *still* has a chlorine aromaha.
How different the water in our abode
At 4300 Rugby Road!
So now I'm wondering what on earth
The water will taste like in Fort Worth.
Darling Isabel, sweet Linell,
I hope you're happy, I hope you're well.
When I am away from you, I miss you.
This row of x-es . . . xxxxxxxxxxxxxxxx
    means I kiss you.

Lots of love—
Daddy

P.S. Don't whisper it, even to your Didey-babies,
    But with luck, I will see you on Friday, babies.

THE CITY

Here men walk alone
For most of their lives,
What with hydrants for dogs,
And windows for wives.

DR. FELL AND POINTS WEST

Your train leaves at eleven-forty-five and it is now but eleven-
    thirty-nine and a half,
And there is only one man ahead of you at the ticket window so
    you have plenty of time, haven't you, well I hope you enjoy a
    hearty laugh,

Because he is Dr. Fell, and he is engaged in an intricate maneuver,
He wants to go to Sioux City with stopovers at Plymouth Rock,
  Stone Mountain, Yellowstone Park, Lake Louise and Vancouver,
And he would like some information about an alternate route,
One that would include New Orleans and Detroit, with possibly a
  day or two in Minneapolis and Butte,
And when the agent has compiled the data with the aid of a slug
  of aromatic spirits and a moist bandanna,
He says that settles it, he'll spend his vacation canoeing up and
  down the Susquehanna,
And oh yes, which way is the bus terminal and what's playing at
  the Rivoli,
And how do the railroads expect to stay in business when their em-
  ployees are incapable of answering a simple question accurately
  or civilly?
He then demands and receives change for twenty dollars and saun-
  ters off leaving everybody's jaw with a sag on it,
And when you finally get to buy your ticket not only has your train
  gone but you also discover that your porter has efficiently man-
  aged to get your bag on it.

MARTHA'S VINEYARD

I live at the top of old West Chop
In a house with a cranky stove,
And when I swim I risk life and limb
On the pebbles that line the cove—
Where the waves wish-wash, and the foghorn blows,
And the blowfish nibble at your toes-oes-oes,
The blowfish nibble at your toes.

I lunch and sup on scrod and scup,
And once in a while on beans,
And the only news that I get to peruse
Is in the last year's magazines—
Where the waves wish-wash, and the foghorn blows,
And the blowfish nibble at your toes-oes-oes,
The blowfish nibble at your toes.

When the sea gulls shout the lights go out,
And whenever the lights go on
I pursue the moth with a dusting cloth
Till the Bob White brings the dawn—
Where the waves wish-wash, and the foghorn blows,
And the blowfish nibble at your toes-oes-oes,
The blowfish nibble at your toes.

But when the breeze creeps through the trees
And the small waves shiver and shake,
Oh, I wouldn't swap my old West Chop
For a sizzling Western steak—
I want to wish-wash where the foghorn blows,
And the blowfish nibble at your toes-oes-oes,
The blowfish nibble at your toes.

MY TRIP DAORBA

I have just returned from a foreign tour,
But ask me not what I saw, because I am not sure.
Not being a disciplinarian like Father Day,
I saw everything the wrong way,
Because of one thing about Father Day I am sure,
Which is that he would not have ridden backwards so that the little
Days could ride forwards on their foreign tour.
Indeed I am perhaps the only parent to be found
Who saw Europe, or eporuE, as I think of it, the wrong way round.
I added little to my knowledge of the countryside but much to my
    reputation for docility
Riding backwards through ecnarF and ylatI.
I am not quite certain,
But I think in siraP I saw the ervuoL, the rewoT leffiE, and the
    Cathedral of emaD ertoN.
I shall remember ecnerolF forever,
For that is where I backed past the house where etnaD wrote the
    "onrefnI," or ydemoC eniviD, and twisted my neck admiring
    the bridges across the onrA reviR.
In emoR I glimpsed the muroF and the nacitaV as in a mirror in
    the fog.

While in ecineV I admired the ecalaP s'egoD as beheld from the
steerage of an alodnoG.
So I find conditions overseas a little hard to judge,
Because all I know is what I saw retreating from me as I rode back-
wards in compartments in the niart and in carriages sitting on
the taes-pmuj.

I'LL TAKE THE HIGH ROAD COMMISSION

In between the route marks
And the shaving rhymes,
Black and yellow markers
Comment on the times.

All along the highway
Hear the signs discourse:

MEN
SLOW
WORKING

;

SADDLE
CROSSING
HORSE

.

Cryptic crossroad preachers
Proffer good advice,
Helping wary drivers
Keep out of Paradise.

Transcontinental sermons,
Transcendental talk:

SOFT
CAUTION
SHOULDERS

;

CROSS
CHILDREN
WALK

·

Wisest of their proverbs,
Truest of their talk,
Have I found that dictum:

CROSS
CHILDREN
WALK

·

When Adam took the highway
He left his sons a guide:

CROSS
CHILDREN
WALK

;

CHEERFUL
CHILDREN
RIDE

·

GRIN AND BEAR LEFT

I don't want to be classed among the pedantics,
But next time I visit friends who have moved to the country I want
    to get together with them on terminology, or semantics.
When you ask them on the telephone how to get there they smil-
    ingly cry that it is simple,
In fact you can practically see them dimple,
You just drive on Route 402 to Hartley and then bear left a cou-
    ple of miles till you cross a stream,
Which they imply is alive with tench, chub, dace, ide, sturgeon and
    bream,
And you go on till you reach the fourth road on the right,

And you can't miss their house because it is on a rise and it is white.
Well it's a neighborhood of which you have never been a frequenter,
But you start out on 402 and soon find yourself trying to disen-
tangle
Hartley from East Hartley, West Hartley, North and South Hartley,
And Hartley Center,
And you bear left a couple of miles peering through the wind-
shield, which is smattered with gnats and midges,
And suddenly the road is alive with bridges,
And your tires begin to scream
As you try to decide which bridge spans a rill, which a run, which
a branch, which a creek, which a brook or river, and which pre-
sumably a stream;
And having passed this test you begin to count roads on the right,
than which no more exhausting test is to be found,
For who is to say which is a road, which a lane, which a driveway
and which just a place where somebody backed in to turn
around?
But anyhow turning around seems a good idea so there is one thing
I don't know still:
Whether that white house where the cocktails are getting warm and
the dinner cold is on a ridge, a ledge, a knoll, a rise, or a hill.

POSTCARD TO MISS ISABEL NASH
FROM ST. LOUIS, MISSOURI

As American towns and cities I wander through,
One landmark is constant everywhere I roam:
The house that the Banker built in nineteen-two,
Dim neon tells me is now a Funeral Home.

2ND POSTCARD TO MISS LINELL NASH
FROM CORPUS CHRISTI, TEXAS

Like others of the forty-eight,
Texas is a Baptist state.
I've been long enough in the Hotel Driscoll
To come home Baptist instead of Episcal.

POSTCARD TO MISS ISABEL NASH
FROM NEW ORLEANS, LOUISIANA

If this weather continues, New Orleans
Will be eating codfish cakes, and beans.
I will not heed the Mayor's excuse; it's
Just like Boston, Massachusetts.

POSTCARD TO MISS LINELL NASH
FROM DES MOINES, IOWA

I talked on the local radio
But no one ever mentioned dough.
Somewhere I'll find a stack of coin
But not, I fancy, in Des Moines.

POSTCARD TO MISS LINELL NASH
FROM ROCKFORD, ILLINOIS

Here I sit, in Rockford, Ill.,
My elbows on the windowsill,
Watching traffic, even in Rockford,
Move one foot forward and two feet bockford.

POSTCARD TO MISS LINELL NASH
FROM OKLAHOMA CITY, OKLAHOMA

The citizens of Oklahoma
Adore this oily, rich aroma.
There seems to be a well for each,
But I've got nothing but a speech.

KIPLING'S VERMONT

The summer like a rajah dies,
And every widowed tree
Kindles for Congregational eyes
An alien suttee.

IS IT TRUE WHAT THEY SAY ABOUT DIXIE
OR
IS IT JUST THE WAY THEY SAY IT?

Our country, south and west of Hatteras,
Abounds in charming feminine flatteras.
Sweet talk is scant by Lake Cayuga,
But in Tennessee, they chatta nougat.

TUNE FOR AN ILL-TEMPERED CLAVICHORD

Oh, once there lived in Kankakee
A handy dandy Yankakee,
A lone and lean and lankakee
Cantankakerous Yankakee.
He slept without a blankaket,
And whiskikey, how he drankaket,
This rough and ready Yankakee,
The bachelor of Kankakee.
He never used a hankakee,
He jeered at hanky-pankakee;
Indeed, to give a frank account,
He didn't have a bank account.
And yet at times he hankakered
In marriage to be anchachored.
When celibacy rankakles,
One dreams of pretty ankakles.
He took a trip to Waikiki
And wooed a girl name Psycheche,
And now this rugged Yankakee
'S a married man in Kankakee.
Good night, dear friends, and thankekee.

THE UNWINGED ONES

I don't travel on planes.
I travel on trains.
Once in a while, on trains,
I see people who travel on planes.

Every once in a while I'm surrounded
By people whose planes have been grounded.
I'm enthralled by their air-minded snobbery,
Their exclusive hobnobbery.
They feel that they have to explain
How they happen to be on a train,
For even in Drawing Room A
They seem to feel déclassé.
So they sit with portentous faces
Clutching their attaché cases.
They grumble and fume about how
They'd have been in Miami by now.
By the time that they're passing through Rahway
They should be in Havana or Norway,
And they strongly imply that perhaps,
Since they're late, the world will collapse.
Sometimes on the train I'm surrounded
By people whose planes have been grounded.
That's the only trouble with trains;
When it fogs, when it smogs, when it rains,
You get people from planes.

HAVE A SEAT BEHIND
THE POTTED PALM, SIR

I'm just an untutored traveling man,
And I only know as much as I can,
But ask me about itineraries,
And I'll tell you one factor that never varies:
All of the overnight trains arrive
In the dim-lit neighborhood of five.
Wherever you come, from wherever you've gone,
You always get into town at dawn.
You're reluctant to sway to the washroom once more
Between quivering curtain and quavering snore;
Why should one, when one in one's pocket hath
A hotel reservation for room and bath?

Detroit, Seattle, Dubuque, New Haven,
You descend at sunrise unbuttoned, unshaven,
In yesterday's socks and yesterday's shirt,
And yesterday's city's pervasive dirt,
But only a jiffy, you fondly suppose,
From a bath and a nap and a change of clothes,
Seeing you hold what is laughingly termed
A hotel reservation, confirmed.
You approach the desk with footstep glad,
And your reservation ironclad.
The clerk offhandedly waves you aside;
Your room is there, but it's occupied.
No use to wheedle, nobody to placate;
You're marooned till the squatter decides to vacate.
You retire to a crowded bench in the lobby,
And pretend that your beard is a lovable hobby.
By noon you're a vagrant, offensive and jailable;
You're finally told that your room is available.
You ascend to your castle among the stars,
And what do you find? Four dead cigars,
Towels and sheets in a crumpled bunch,
And word that the maid is out to lunch.
By confirmed reservations I'm stymied and bunkered;
I'd just as soon trust a confirmed drunkard.

MANHATTAN PREVIEWS

WELCOME STRANGER
New York is a fortress whose ambient moats
Still defy all your tunnels and bridges and boats.
Fling up a new bridge or bore a new tunnel,
The flow is forever too great for the funnel.
Manhattan repulses the out-of-town rover;
He is trapped on a ramp, growing mauver and mauver,
While his battery dies and his water boils over.
The only sure way to get into New York
Is, I venture to say, to be brought by the stork.

THE GOLD COAST

High up along Park Avenue
A bit of Moscow comes in view.
Here, after a day at United Nations
Of dutiful denunciations,
Reside the bluebloods of the Reds,
True dialectic thoroughbreds.
A group my tiresome Cousin Emlyn
Refers to as la crème de la Kremlin.

THEATER HOUR

The hotel doorman's frantic whistle
Makes rugged taxi drivers bristle.
The doormen chittering like grackles
Only raise the hacky's hackles.
Contemptuously stares the cabby
Like a bobcat at a tabby,
Then with derisive farewell honks
Heads happily homeward to the Bronx.
That's why, my children, I'm afraidy
That you'll be late for "My Fair Lady."

ALL AROUND THE TOWN

Within myself I lately find
A tendency to glance behind.
This son of Father Knickerbocker's
Now shies away from luggage lockers;
Before a cinematic treat
I stoop and peak beneath the seat.
Only Dione Lucas can make an omelet,
But any fool can make a bomblet.

CITY GREENERY

If you should happen after dark
To find yourself in Central Park,
Ignore the paths that beckon you
And hurry, hurry to the zoo,
And creep into the tiger's lair.
Frankly, you'll be safer there.

AND NOW, LIVE FROM NEW YORK
In N.Y., individuals.
In L.A., it's residuals.

THE AMPUTATORS
There's one I care for even less
Than him who toasts me with "God bless!"
The TV weather maiden snappy
Who waves good night with "Have a happy!"

THE VILLAGE
What walls them from the world of men
These unkempt anthropoids?
Though fifty sages call it Zen,
I plump for adenoids.

PARADISE FOR SALE

DORSET—8 miles Dorchester
In the valley of the River Piddle.
Kiddles Farm, Piddletrenthide
A Small Mixed Farm
With Small Period Farmhouse
Dining/Living Room, Kitchen
3 Bed Rooms, Bathroom.
                —Adv. in *Country Life*

Had I the shillings, pounds, and pence,
I'd pull up stakes and hie me hence;
I'd buy that small mixed farm in Dorset,
Which has an inglenook and faucet—
Kiddles Farm,
Piddletrenthide,
In the valley of the River Piddle.

I'd quit these vehement environs
Of diesel fumes and horns and sirens,
This manic, fulminating ruction
Of demolition and construction,
For Kiddles Farm

Piddletrenthide,
In the valley of the River Piddle.

Yes, quit for quietude seraphic
Con Edison's embrangled traffic,
To sit reflecting that the skylark,
Which once was Shelley's, now is my lark,
At Kiddles Farm
Piddletrenthide,
In the valley of the River Piddle.

I'm sure the gods could not but bless
The man who lives at that address,
And revenue agents would wash their hands
And cease to forward their demands
To Kiddles Farm
Piddletrenthide,
In the valley of the River Piddle.

Oh, the fiddles I'd fiddle,
The riddles I'd riddle,
The skittles I'd scatter,
The winks I would tiddle!
Then hey diddle diddle!
I'll jump from the griddle
And live out my days
To the end from the middle
On Kiddles Farm,
Piddletrenthide,
In the valley of the River Piddle.

THE BACK OF MINE HAND TO MINE HOST

Once there was a pawnbroker who got stuck with a batch of unre-
    deemed slots for used razor blades, and he said, "Well,
I guess I've got the beginnings of a hotel.
So far as I am aware of,
All I need now is no hooks and some dummy taps marked 'Ice Wa-
    ter' and the bathrooms are taken care of."

He also didn't need any bureaus—just those combination desk and
dressing tables that your knees won't fit under, so you can nei-
ther write nor primp, and they have another feature equally
fell:
You have to leave your shirts in your suitcase, because the two
lower drawers are filled with blankets and the top one with
telegraph forms and picture postcards of the hotel.
He got a mad inventor to invent a bedside lamp with a three-way
switch so that when you finish your paperback thriller, either
American or Britannian,
Why, you can't turn out your light without turning on that of your
slumbering companion.
He employed one maid for bedmaking and fifty maids who excel
at the sole duty he assigned them,
Which is to wait until you are in a state of extreme dishabille and
then burst into your room and cry "Just checking!" and vanish
in a puff of smoke, leaving a smell of sulphur behind them.
I would recommend this hotel to you if you have a lot of old razor
blades you have been meaning to get rid of because you can't
afford to have them gold-plated or silverized,
Particularly if you regard the cardboard bosoms with which your
same-day laundered shirts are stuffed as an adequate substitute
for the buttons which have been pulverized.

THE REDCAP

The hunted redcap knows not peace;
His mother was frightened by a valise.
The sight of luggage seems to stun him,
And if you force a bag upon him,
Like a wary doe concealing a fawn,
He hides it till all the cabs have gone.

LONDON

The London taxi is a relic
For which my zeal is evangelic.
It's designed for people wearing hats,
And not for racing on Bonneville Flats.
A man can get out, or a lady in;
When you sit, your knees don't bump your chin.
The driver so deep in the past is sunk
That he'll help you with your bags and trunk;
Indeed, he is such a fuddy-duddy
That he calls you Sir instead of Buddy.

MOSCOW

Over the Volga and through the snow
Away to Babushka's house we go,
Party members aboard a troika,
Whistling Beethoven's Eroica,
Or chattering gaily in a droshky,
While chewing blinis and piroshki,
And eschewing Molotov melancholia
And morbid thoughts of Outer Mongolia.

THE AZORES

An Azore is an isle volcanic
Whose drivers put me in a panic.
The English expression "Slow down, please"
Means "Step on the gas!" in Portuguese.
An Azore is a beauty spot?
I don't know whether it is or not.
While racing round it hell-for-leather,
My eyelids were always jammed together.

MADEIRA

Madeira is the home of wineries
And extremely expensive embroidered fineries.
I seem to sense a relation tender
Between vintner and embroidery vender.
Free sample sippings of the grape
Inflate the tourist to a shape
In which, by the time he's embroiled in the embroidery imbroglio,
He will pay for a dozen doilies the price of an authentic First Folio.

MOROCCO

The bus to Marrakech, Morocco,
Traverses landscapes simply socko.
The agricultural economy
Suggests the Book of Deuteronomy.
The machine has not replaced the mammal,
And everything is done by camel.
I hope I never learn what flesh
I ate that day in Marrakech,
But after struggling with a jawful
I thought it tasted humpthing awful.

PARIS

The independent Parisian hackie
Is bent on proving he's no man's lackey.
As railroads feel about commuters,
As Odysseus felt toward Penelope's suitors,
As landlords feel about repairs,
That's how he feels toward potential fares.
They inspire him with horrendous hates
Which into hunger he sublimates,
So when you hail him he's pleased as Punch
To spit in your eye and go to lunch.

AS GAUGUIN SAID TO SADIE THOMPSON,
YOU PRONOUNCE IT, I'LL PAINT IT

It was not really stout Cortez who stood silent upon a peak in
Darien, it was stout Balboa;
It was a misty day, and he couldn't see Samoa.
Nowadays Samoa can be seen by anybody with the price of a ship
or a plane ticket, or who can build his own raft,
As can Tahiti, Pago Pago, Bali, Fiji and other Pacific paradises over
which tourists go daft.
At the prospect of visiting these oft-visited garden spots I am not
one jot or whit elated;
Rather would I seek out those strange-sounding geographical pin-
points by which the ear as well as the eye is titillated.
In the course of titillating my ears
I have been cruising through the Hydrographic Office of the
United States Navy Department's *Gazetteers*.
Who that revels in lingual judo
Could resist the challenge of the rocks of Mudogomuburamaru-
davemudo?
Doesn't it fill you with euphoria
To think of Pukapuka, where the sahib sahibs gather to drink the
health of Queen Victoria?
You can rest your tongue with Yap and Bam and Kuku,
Then work up through Mog Mog and Kwamkwam and Bora
Bora to Bohigumaguma and Bonglelongdango and
Anigigichairukku.
If you couldn't get a redcap wouldn't you be happy to drag a bag
Through Blupblup or Bum Bum or Bagabag?
Finally, with the golden sand below and the golden moon above
you,
You could relax among the golden girls of Songsong or Luvuluvu,
Which conclusion leads me to believe, on the whole,
That the garden spots of the Pacific were named by those who
write the lyrics for rock and roll,
Or perhaps they simply seem somewhat out of focus
Because I come from a land of conventional names, such as Walla
Walla, Oshkosh, Skaneateles and Hohokus.

YOU STEER AND I'LL TOOT
OR
ALL'S SLICK THAT ENDS SLICK

Henry Henley had a hero, Henry the Navigator, that maritime-
minded Portuguese prince,
Whom he wished to be the greatest navigator since.
Perhaps from this decision he might have divagated
Had he known, as you and I know, that Henry the Navigator never
navigated.
Not only had he never navigated, he never even made a voyage.
He just had a lot of navigators in his employage.
Of the truth I am not an extravagator
When I reckon that had he ever tried to navigate he would not
have been called Henry the Navigator.
Thus it is obvious that if Henry wished to earn that sobriquet it
was foolish of him to want to navigate;
He had no more sense of direction than a crab, or indeed a crab
ravigote.
None could deny his pluck,
But while yet a babe in the bath he couldn't correct the course of
a yawing celluloid duck.
As a courting swain on the lake in Central Park he attempted si-
multaneously to row and woo,
Thereby achieving temporary fame as the only adult unaccompa-
nied by a child to ground his boat in the Children's Zoo.
The day he was appointed to the Steering Committee of his boat
club his heart was light as a perfect chicken vol-au-vent,
But after a year of Henry's steering the club was hopelessly insol-
vent.
You might suppose that at this point he would have ceased to
dream of being known as Henry the Navigator II and quietly
dropped anchor,
But he didn't, and now he is captain of a spanking new 70,000-ton
tanker.

The Sporting Life

TURNS IN A WORM'S LANE

I've never bet on a so-called horse
That the horse didn't lose a leg.
I've never putted on a golfing course
But the ball behaved like an egg.
I've never possessed three royal kings
But somebody held three aces;
In short, I'm a lad whose presence brings
The joy to bankers' faces.

And everybody says, "What a splendid loser!"
Everybody says, "What a thoroughgoing sport!"
And I smile my smile like an amiable Duse,
I leer like a lawyer in the presence of a tort.
And I crack my lips,
And I grin my grin,
While someone else
Rakes my money in.
Yes, I smile a smile like the Mona Lisa,
Though my spirits droop like the Tower of Pisa.
Yes, I chortle like a military march by Sousa
And everybody says, "What a splendid loser!"

I'll buy a tome, an expensive tome,
On the art of double dealing,
And I'll wrap it up and I'll take it home,
While the bells of Hell are pealing.
I'll stealthily study the ebony arts
Of men like the great Houdini,
Till both in foreign and local parts
I'm known as a darned old meany.

And everyone will say, "What a nasty winner!"
And everyone will say, "What a dreadful sport!"
And they'll all stop inviting me to come to dinner,
For I used to be a dimple and I want to be a wart.
But I won't care,
And I'll win with a scowl,
Foul means or fair,
But preferably foul.
I'll jeer my victims every time I vanquish,
And if I lose I shall scream with anguish.
And people will say, "What a dreadful sport!"
And I'll say, "Phooie!" or something of the sort.

ROULETTE US BE GAY

The trouble with games of chance is that they don't do much to
    stimulate your pulse
Unless you risk some money on the results,
And the trouble with playing for money is not that it is a sin,
But that you have got either to lose or win,
And the trouble with losing is not only that you need the money,
    which is an important point, very true,
But also that you never lose it except to somebody who is very
    much richer than you,
And the trouble with winning, if you can bring yourself to imag-
    ine any trouble with winning, is that except in the most glam-
    orous fiction
You never win except from somebody to whom you know that the
    money that they pay over to you is all that stands between
    them and eviction.

Another thing about games of chance
Is a thing at which I look askance,
And that is that no matter how far at any time you may be ahead,
You are always well behind when it is time for bed,
While on the other hand if you start out by losing as steadily and
    heavily as if you were afflicted with Tutankhamen's curse
You finish up even worse,
So you can take it as understood
That your luck changes only if it's good.
And this, my friends, is a brief history of the major troubles with
    gambling but I feel that no improving lesson from it will be
    learned
As long as there is nothing so delightful in the world as money you
    haven't earned.

THE STRANGE CASE OF THE AMBITIOUS CADDY

Once upon a time there was a boy named Robin Bideawee.

≈

He had chronic hiccups.

≈

He had hay fever, too.

≈

Also he was learning to whistle through his teeth.

≈

Oh yes, and his shoes squeaked.

≈

The scoutmaster told him he had better be a caddy.

≈

He said, Robin, you aren't cut out for a scout, you're cut out for a
    caddy.

≈

At the end of Robin's first day as a caddy, the caddymaster asked
    him how he got along.

≈

Robin said, I got along fine but my man lost six balls, am I ready
    yet?

≈

The caddymaster said No, he wasn't ready yet.

≈

At the end of the second day the caddymaster asked him again how he got along.

≈

Robin said, My man left me behind to look for a ball on the fourth hole and I didn't catch up to him till the eighteenth, am I ready yet?

≈

The caddymaster said No, he wasn't ready yet.

≈

Next day Robin said, I only remembered twice to take the flag on the greens and when I did take it I wiggled it, am I ready yet?

≈

The caddymaster said No, he wasn't ready yet.

≈

Next day Robin said, My man asked me whether he had a seven or an eight on the waterhole and I said an eight, am I ready yet?

≈

The caddymaster said No, he wasn't ready yet.

≈

Next day Robin said, Every time my man's ball stopped on the edge of a bunker I kicked it in, am I ready yet?

≈

The caddymaster said No, he wasn't ready yet.

≈

Next day Robin said, I never once handed my man the club he asked for, am I ready yet?

≈

The caddymaster said No, he wasn't ready yet.

≈

Next day Robin said, I bet a quarter my man would lose and told him so, am I ready yet?

≈

The caddymaster said, Not quite.

≈

Next day Robin said, I laughed at my man all the way round, am I ready yet?

≈

The caddymaster said, Have you still got hiccups, and have you still got hay fever, and are you still learning how to whistle through your teeth and do your shoes still squeak?

≈

Robin said, Yes, yes, a thousand times yes.

≈

Then you are indeed ready, said the caddymaster.

≈

Tomorrow you shall caddy for Ogden Nash.

HOW LONG HAS THIS BEEN GOING ON?
OH, QUITE LONG

Some people think that they can beat three two's with a pair of aces,
And other people think they can wind up ahead of the races,
And lest we forget,
The people who think they can wind up ahead of the races are everybody who has ever won a bet.
Yes, when you first get back five-sixty for two, oh what a rosy-toed future before you looms,
But actually your doom is sealed by whoever it is that goes around sealing people's dooms,
And you are lost forever
Because you think you won not because you were lucky but because you were clever.
You think the race ended as it did, not because you hoped it,
But because you doped it,
And from then on you withdraw your savings from the bank in ever-waxing wads
Because you are convinced that having figured out one winner you can figure out many other winners at even more impressive odds,
And pretty soon overdrawing your account or not betting at all is the dilemma which you are betwixt

And certainly you're not going to not bet at all because you are
     sure you will eventually wind up ahead because the only rea-
     son the races haven't run true to form, by which you mean
     your form, is because they have been fixed,
So all you need to be a heavy gainer
Is to bet on one honest race or make friends with one dishonest
     trainer.
And I don't know for which this situation is worse,
Your character or your purse.
I don't say that racetracks are centers of sin,
I only say that they are only safe to go to as long as you fail to be-
     gin to win.

SLOW DOWN, MR. GANDERDONK, YOU'RE LATE

Do you know Mr. Ganderdonk, he is no Einstein, he has no theo-
     ries of Time and Space,
But he is the only man I know can be both the hare and the tor-
     toise in the same race.
Mr. Ganderdonk's proclivity
Is divoty Relativity.
Put him behind you in a twosome or a foursome,
His speed is awesome.
His relationship to your rear
Is that of a catamount to a deer,
And while you are still reaching for your putter
He is standing on the edge of the green going mutter mutter,
But once through you in his foursome or twosome,
His torpor is gruesome.
He is a golfer that the thought of other golfers simply hasn't oc-
     curred to;
He has three swings for every shot, the one he hopes to use, the one
     he does use, and finally the one he would have preferred to.
His world from tee to cup
Consists of those behind him pressing him and those in front of
     him holding him up,
Wherefore the rest of the world is his foe
Because the rest of the world is either too fast or too slow.

For Mr. Ganderdonk there is only one correct pace and that is his,
Whatever it is.

WHO TAUGHT CADDIES TO COUNT?
OR
A BURNT GOLFER FEARS THE CHILD

I have never beheld you, O pawky Scot,
And I only guess your name,
Who first propounded the popular rot
That golf is a humbling game.
You putted perhaps with a mutton bone,
And hammered a gutty ball;
But I think that you sat in the bar alone,
And never played at all.

Ye hae spoken a braw bricht mouthfu', Jamie,
Ye didna ken ye erred;
Ye're richt that golf is a something gamie,
But humble is not the word.
Try arrogant, insolent, supercilious,
And if invention fades,
Add uppity, hoity-toity, bilious,
And double them all in spades.

Oh pride of rank is a fearsome thing,
And pride of riches a bore;
But both of them bow on lea and ling
To the Prussian pride of score.
Better the beggar with fleas to scratch
Than the unassuming dub
Trying to pick up a Saturday match
In the locker room of the club.

The Hollywood snob will look you through
And stalk back into his clique,
For he knows that he is better than you
By so many grand a week;
And the high-caste Hindu's fangs are bared

If a low-caste Hindu blinks;
But they're just like one of the boys, compared
To the nabobs of the links.

Oh where this side of the River Styx
Will you find an equal mate
To the scorn of a man with a seventy-six
For a man with a seventy-eight?
I will tell you a scorn that mates it fine
As the welkin mates the sun:
The scorn of him with a ninety-nine
For him with a hundred and one.

And that is why I wander alone
From tee to green to tee,
For every golfer I've ever known
Is too good or too bad for me.
Indeed I have often wondered, Jamie,
Hooking into the heather,
In such an unhumble, contemptful gamie
How anyone plays together.

LINE-UP FOR YESTERDAY

AN ABC OF BASEBALL IMMORTALS

A is for Alex,
The great Alexander;
More goose eggs he pitched
Than a popular gander.

B is for Bresnahan
Back of the plate;
The Cubs were his love,
And McGraw was his hate.

C is for Cobb,
Who grew spikes and not corn,
And made all the basemen
Wish they weren't born.

D is for Dean.
The grammatical Diz,
When they asked, Who's the tops?
Said correctly, I is.

E is for Evers,
His jaw in advance;
Never afraid
To Tinker with Chance.

F is for Fordham
And Frankie and Frisch;
I wish he were back
With the Giants, I wish.

G is for Gehrig,
The pride of the Stadium;
His record pure gold,
His courage, pure radium.

H is for Hornsby;
When pitching to Rog,
The pitcher would pitch,
Then the pitcher would dodge.

I is for Me,
Not a hard-sitting man,
But an outstanding all-time
Incurable fan.

J is for Johnson.
The Big Train in his prime
Was so fast he could throw
Three strikes at a time.

K is for Keeler,
As fresh as green paint,
The fustest and mostest
To hit where they ain't.

L is for Lajoie,
Whom Clevelanders love,

Napoleon himself,
With glue in his glove.

M is for Matty,
Who carried a charm
In the form of an extra
Brain in his arm.

N is for Newsom,
Bobo's favorite kin.
If you ask how he's here,
He talked himself in.

O is for Ott
Of the restless right foot.
When he leaned on the pellet,
The pellet stayed put.

P is for Plank,
The arm of the A's;
When he tangled with Matty
Games lasted for days.

Q is Don Quixote
Cornelius Mack;
Neither Yankees nor Years
Can halt his attack.

R is for Ruth
To tell you the truth,
There's no more to be said,
Just R is for Ruth.

S is for Speaker,
Swift center-field tender;
When the ball saw him coming,
It yelled "I surrender."

T is for Terry,
The Giant from Memphis,
Whose .400 average
You can't overemphis.

U would be 'Ubbell
If Carl were a cockney;
We say Hubbell and baseball
Like football and Rockne.

V is for Vance,
The Dodgers' own Dazzy;
None of his rivals
Could throw as fast as he.

W, Wagner,
The bowlegged beauty;
Short was closed to all traffic
With Honus on duty.

X is the first
Of two x's in Foxx,
Who was right behind Ruth
With his powerful soxx.

Y is for Young
The magnificent Cy;
People batted against him,
But I never knew why.

Z is for Zenith,
The summit of fame.
These men are up there,
These men are the game.

THE HUNTER

The hunter crouches in his blind,
'Neath camouflage of every kind.
And conjures up a quacking noise
To lend allure to his decoys.
This grown-up man with pluck and luck
Is hoping to outwit a duck.

MEL ALLEN, MEL ALLEN,
LEND ME YOUR CLICHÉ

Let us sing of the unsung hero,
The pitcher too unrenowned,
Who is always in the bull pen,
But never reaches the mound.
It's 3 and 0 on the batter,
The bases are bursting full,
A 4-run lead has vanished,
And the manager signals the bull—
Yes, the manager signals the bull pen
To unlimber another bull.

There's MacTivity, MacTivity,
MacTivity in the bull pen!
He possesses every pitch in the book,
He's got the fast one, he's got the hook,
Slider, glider, sinker and knuckle,
MacTivity's master of many a muckle.
I know he's the lad to save the game,
But when they announce the reliefer's name
I can only guarantee that it's not
MacTivity, the talented Scot.
My hopes descend a deep declivity,
In the right field corner, there's MacTivity,
Subsiding in the bull pen.

He can throw from the port or starboard,
He's a regular pitching machine,
This wizard we all have heard of,
But no one has ever seen.
How the muscles bulge in his sweatshirt,
How his heart with hope is full,
When the manager beckons the bull pen
To send him another bull!
How he mutters a silent prayer,
Lord, let me be that bull!

There's MacTivity, MacTivity,
MacTivity in the bull pen!
And he doesn't warm up for only us,
MacTivity is ubiquitous,
MacTivity really gets around
For a pitcher who never reaches the mound.
Be it Baltimore, Brooklyn or Milwaukee,
There's MacTivity, posed and pawky.
Even in Mudville, when straits are dire
MacTivity's eager to quench the fire.
I know who I'd throw against Musial or Mantle,
But managers' minds are so infantile,
Managers' minds are flivverty-givverty,
In the right field corner, there's MacTivity,
Subsiding in the bull pen.

YOUR LEAD, PARTNER, I HOPE
WE'VE READ THE SAME BOOK

When I was just a youngster,
Hardly bigger than a midge,
I used to join my family
In a game of auction bridge.
We were patient with reneging,
For the light was gas or oil,
And our arguments were settled
By a reference to Hoyle.
Auction bridge was clover;
Then the experts took it over.
You could no longer bid by the seat of your pants,
The experts substituted skill for chance.

The experts captured auction
With their lessons and their books,
And the casual week-end player
Got a lot of nasty looks.
The experts captured auction
And dissected it, and then

Somebody thought up contract,
And we played for fun again.
It was pleasant, lose or win,
But the experts muscled in,
And you couldn't deal cards in your own abode
Without having memorized the latest code.

We turned to simpler pastimes
With our neighbors and our kin;
Oklahoma or canasta,
Or a modest hand of gin.
We were quietly diverted
Before and after meals,
Till the experts scented suckers
And came yapping at our heels.
Behold a conquered province;
I'm a worm, and they are robins.
On the grandchildren's table what books are displayed?
Better Slapjack, and *How to Win at Old Maid.*

In a frantic final effort
To frivol expert-free,
I've invented Amaturo
For just my friends and me.
The deck has seven morkels
Of eleven guzzards each,
The game runs counterclockwise,
With an extra kleg for dreech,
And if you're caught with a gruice,
The score reverts to deuce.
I'll bet that before my cuff links are on the bureau
Some experts will have written *A Guide to Amaturo.*

UNTITLED POEM (on the 1958 Preakness)

At Santa Anita and Hialeah
The horses begin to get the idea.
They loosen their muscles at Tropical Park
And take the baths at Hot Springs, Ark.

They skip the rope at Jamaica and Bowie,
In April going half good, half gooey,
And finish their roadwork
Jogging through the towns
All the way from Keeneland
To Churchill Downs.
They've sworn off smoking,
They've sworn off drinks,
Their condition today is the
Pinkest of pinks.
And for what are they working
Up to the zenith?
For the Preakness, children,
On May seventeenth.

YOU CAN'T KILL AN ORIOLE

Wee Willie Keeler
Runs through the town,
All along Charles Street
In his night gown,
Belling like a hound dog
Gathering the pack:
"Hey, Wilbert Robinson!
"The Orioles are back!
"Hey, Hughey Jennings!
"Hey, John McGraw!
"I got fire in my eye,
"And tobacco in my jaw!
"Hughey, hold my halo,
"I'm sick of being a saint;
"Got to teach the youngsters
"To hit 'em where they ain't!"

MY MIND IS REELING

The fisherman, oh, the fisherman,
That sportsman piscatorial,
Has anesthetized his fellow man
For ages immemorial.
As his ancient prototype was wont
In the days of Hammurabi,
Be the talk of cabbages or kings,
He turns it to his hobby.
When my taxes rise, I blame the lobbyist;
When my eyelids droop, I blame the hobbyist.

The bible of the fisherman tribe
Looms like a rock Gibraltan,
"The Com-pleat Angler" is its name,
Its author, Izaak Walton.
This overlord of fin and gill
Whose dicta they obey yet,
He spelled "complete" compleatly wrong,
And "Isaac" with a K yet.
I heard a little birdie twitter it;
The fisherman's god was semiliterate.

The fisherman's gift of total recall,
His reminiscing chronic,
Make the Ancient Mariner himself
Seem taciturn and laconic.
I do not disbelieve his tales
Of steelhead by the thousand,
I do not tell him to his face
I think I'm being Münchhausened,
But Charles Perrault and the Brothers Grimm
Were amateurs compared to him.

I concede that the fisherman is behooved
By Fate, the Great Behoover,
To pit his wiles against the trout
And the salmon to outmaneuver,
That he played the sailfish dawn to dusk

That hangs o'er his mantel shelf,
But he won't concede that the epic thrills
Nobody but himself.
Once, cornered, button-holed and prodded
By a fisherman, that's when Homer nodded.

The fisherman is a worthy man,
Not given to misprision,
But he washes the scales from off his hands
And not from off his vision.
He may have won a master's degree
From M.I.T. or Fordham,
But he can't perceive that one man's fish
Is another fellow's boredom.
Now let me tell you a real dumfounder—
How my clam got stolen by a flounder.

MR. JUDD AND HIS SNAIL, A SORRY TALE
OR
NEVER UNDERESTIMATE THE WISDOM OF
A SAGE OF THE AGES

I offer one small bit of advice that Billy Graham could write a
   whole column on:
Never ignore any bit of advice offered by King Solomon.
I call your attention to the case of Philander Judd.
His veins were distended with optimism and sporting blood.
His interest in racing was enormous,
But he was by nature nonconformous.
He was not one of those who set their horses or greyhounds
   whirling around the track to their heart's content, or à go go,
He said he knew that something fast could go fast, he was inter-
   ested in how fast could something slow go.
He considered conventional races pallid and stale,
So his entire stable consisted of one thoroughbred gastropod, or
   snail.
The snail, of course, is a mollusk akin to the whelk and the slug,
   and, as is known to every gastropodist,

It moves complacently on one ventral muscular foot, to the bewil-
derment of every biped chiropodist.

Mr. Judd entered his snail in every kind of race but one, for which
he refused to name it,

And that one was a claiming race, because he was afraid that
somebody, perhaps a Gallic gourmet, might claim it.

His snail was beaten in December by a tortoise, so he dropped it
down a couple of classes,

And in January it lost by eight lengths to a jug of molasses.

By now Mr. Judd was deeply indebted to his bookie,

But being an honorable man, he couldn't get out of town or stoop
to any other form of welsher's hookey.

At last he thought he saw a way to settle with his creditors;

He found the perfect spot for his snail, a race in which an amoeba
and a glacier were the other two competitors.

The amoeba posed a real threat, but from the glacier he did not
flinch;

He had clocked it for a full month, during which it had moved
only three-quarters of an inch.

Therefore, although he could not be certain to win the race,

He knew he had a sure thing to place.

Yes, that was what he happily reckoned,

And he bet his remaining roll on the snail for second.

Well, the amoeba outdistanced the snail and the snail outdistanced
the glacier, and then just at the finish line something out of the
ordinary occurred;

The amoeba split apart and finished one two, and the snail ran
third.

Mr. Judd had forgotten what Solomon once told the Queen of
Sheba:

Never trust an Egyptian or an amoeba.

THE ARMCHAIR GOLFER
OR
WHIMPERS OF A SHORTCHANGED VIEWER

It's thirty-five miles from the Chesapeake Bay,
A hundred from Cape Henlopen,
But it's also here on my old TV,
The site of the U.S. Open.

The gallery sways like a primitive throng
At a ceremony pagan,
And murmurs the names of its ancient gods,
Ouimet and Jones and Hagen.

Then swirls around the gods of today
An argumentative chorus:
Can Player match muscle with Nicklaus?
Can Palmer give weight to Boros?

We must wait, my friend, till the drama's end
Unfolds on the magic screen,
So join me here at my nineteenth hole
While they play the first fourteen.

The mysterious first fourteen, my friend,
Which is missing on my screen;
At times I wonder if anyone plays
The invisible first fourteen.

That the Open crown is a kingly crown
Is a statement we all endorse,
But I can't conceal that I sometimes feel
It is won on a four-hole course.

At times I think they have rolled the dice
To decide what their scores will be
As they swing the club for the very first time
When they stand on the fifteenth tee.

But hush! The sponsor is speaking now
The first commercial unrolls
And you settle yourself in your easy chair
To follow the last four holes.

Well, two-ninths of a loaf is better than none
And the picture is sharp and clean;
Just be grateful you're there for the final four,
And the hell with the first fourteen.

COEFFICIENTS OF EXPANSION
(A GUIDE TO THE INFANT SEASON)

What happened in the Hot Stove League last winter?

Well, baseball got a new Commissioner, and the Senators, who are
still the same old Senators although not the original Senators
because the original Senators are now the Twins, got a new
manager, the Splendid Splinter.

Pitchers have been ordered to deliver the ball more allegro and less
adagio,

And if you are wondering about the Royals, well the Royals used
to be Montreal, but now Montreal is the Expos, and Kansas
City, which was the A's, is the Royals, and the A's, which were
first Philadelphia and later Kansas City, are Oakland, under the
partial aegis of Joe DiMaggio.

In lower California, confusion is rife around the pot spots and hot-
rodderies;

No one is able to differentiate between San Diego's twice-born
Padres and the Padres' reborn Johnny Podres.

And, apropos newly launched satellites,

The disappearance of Mickey Mantle was hardly compensated for
by the appearance of something called the Pilots, except per-
haps to a few Seattleites.*

The mound has been lowered because the hitters complained that
the pitchers were too parsimonious and pawky,

And Satchel Paige pitched two scoreless exhibition innings for the Braves of
Atlanta, formerly the Braves of Boston and Milwaukee.

Finally, at least one sportscaster has added a phrase to his cargo of
argot, and I quote him verbatim:

When a batter leaves a runner stranded on third, he has "failed to
plate him."

* Since removed to Milwaukee and renamed the Brewers.

So, that's how it went.

This wrapup has been brought to you through the authority of the
undersigned Lifelong Fan, and is not intended in any way to
express for the aforementioned expansion said Lifelong Fan's
enthusiasm, approval, or written consent.

FROM AN ANTIQUE LAND—I

When I was ten I didn't want to be president,
Or a woman-wary cowboy like William S. Hart;
I didn't even want to be a fireman.
I wanted to drive a racer a mile a minute.
Where is the sound-effects man to give me the cobble-clop of the
milkman's horse on Charlton Street,
The lighting expert to capture the glow in the grate,
The wavering kobold dance of shadows on the ceiling?
I sniff again the fringes of smoke from the shifting, sifting coals,
Soft and insidious, skunk-like sweet, furring the tongue and throat.
Savannah in 1912 hadn't heard of air pollution.
Gulp breakfast now and bundle
Into the bathtub tonneau of the splendid Royal Tourist,
It's almost time for the start of the fabulous Grand Prize.
The sun has unraveled the mist, but it's cold in the wooden stands,
Cold and hard on the bottom.
The mechanics below in the pits pause to blow on their fingers.
How vast the machines in the eyes of a little boy!
Strange as gorgons or minotaurs each with its magic name:
Mercedes, Apperson Jackrabbit, Blitzen Benz, Fiat and Lozier;
Fiat devil-red, Mercedes and Benz fog-gray,
Apperson blue, and Lozier insipid white,
And for every monster a master, Perseus in helmet and goggles.
Their names roar by in my mind:
Spenser Wishart, Ralph DePalma,
Bruce Brown and Caleb Bragg
And perhaps another half-dozen of mythopoeic heroes.
Only Barney Oldfield missing;
He never came to Savannah, and we reckoned we hadn't missed
much.

The flag drops, they are off like panicking razorback hogs,
Under their wheels crushed oyster shell explodes.
Red, blue, gray and white they streak to the first of the turns in the
　　highway
Wearily banked for this moment by black men in black and white
　　stripes.
The driver crowds for position, the spare tire racked behind him,
At his side his trusty mechanic, pumping oil in a fury;
They vanish around the turn.
How long is the course? Five miles? Ten miles?
It stretches from there to now.

FROM AN ANTIQUE LAND—II

When is a Buick not a Buick?
When it's a Skylark? A LeSabre? A Wildcat, an Electra, a Riviera?
Is it that a Chevrolet is a Chevrolet is a Chevrolet,
Or that a Chevrolet is a Chevy II is a Chevy II Nova is a Chevelle?
You may know a hawk from a handsaw,
But do you know a Plymouth from a Valiant from a Barracuda
　　from a Satellite from a Fury from a Road Runner?
Fooled again; it's all of them.
You've decided to buy a Ford, or perhaps an Oldsmobile, a Mer-
　　cury, a Dodge, a Pontiac, a Rambler;
Pick your Rambler, your Pontiac, your Dodge, your Mercury,
　　Oldsmobile, Ford from among the following:
Mustang, Comet, Montego, Firebird, Cougar, Bronco,
Charger, Galaxie, Rebel, Tempest, Falcon, Rogue,
Polara and Toronado.
Go ahead, pick the one you want, assuming you can identify it;
Then tell me who made it.
I remember the one-name cars, the cars you could tell apart.
I remember the Panhard, with a sort of lid on legs on top of the
　　hood;
Pierce Arrow, its headlights spraddled on the mudguards.
They didn't look like the Mercer, nor the Mercer the Marmon,
The Hupp like the Franklin nor the Franklin like the Reo.
You knew the Pope-Hartford from the Pope-Toledo,

The Simplex from the Stanley, and all from the black Tin Lizzie.
Some were steamers, some air-cooled and some chain-driven.
But each as individual as a fingerprint.
You strained the gas through a chamois rag,
And half the grown-ups had broken wrists from the kick of the
　　crank,
And the roadsters looked fine with a collie on the running board.
I see where a fellow paid $45,000 for a 1913 Mercer Runabout.
I wonder how old he was . . .

The Year in Review

DECEMBER—NEW ENGLAND COAST

The gray sea reaches out to grasp the shore
Shuddering back before the icy touch.
The tumbling breakers add their hollow roar
And vainly strive to make secure their clutch
Upon the dreary sands; the flying spray
Drenches the beach, then futile melts away.

Gloomy and damp the dark sky overhangs,
Mirrored below upon the shifting waves.
Rejoicing as they bare their whitecap fangs
Snapping at every lonely gull who braves
Their dripping jaws upon his wheeling course,
And shrieks disdainful at their measured force.

The west wind hurtles past the bushy dunes
Whistling fiercely through the yellow sedge
Dragging the winter in its cheerless tunes.
The conquered sun withdraws its feeble edge
And sinking through the sullen evening light
Commits the ocean to the shroud of night.

Ogden Nash—aged 17 at St. George's School

PRETTY HALCYON DAYS

How pleasant to sit on the beach,
On the beach, on the sand, in the sun,
With ocean galore within reach,
And nothing at all to be done!
No letters to answer,
No bills to be burned,
No work to be shirked,
No cash to be earned.
It is pleasant to sit on the beach
With nothing at all to be done.

How pleasant to look at the ocean,
Democratic and damp; indiscriminate;
It fills me with noble emotion
To think I am able to swim in it.
To lave in the wave,
Majestic and chilly,
Tomorrow I crave;
But today it is silly.
It is pleasant to look at the ocean;
Tomorrow, perhaps, I shall swim in it.

How pleasant to gaze at the sailors,
As their sailboats they manfully sail
With the vigor of vikings and whalers
In the days of the viking and whale.
They sport on the brink
Of the shad and the shark;
If it's windy they sink;
If it isn't, they park.
It's pleasant to gaze at the sailors,
To gaze without having to sail.

How pleasant the salt anaesthetic
Of the air and the sand and the sun;
Leave the earth to the strong and athletic,
And the sea to adventure upon.
But the sun and the sand

No contractor can copy;
We lie in the land
Of the lotus and poppy;
We vegetate, calm and aesthetic,
On the beach, on the sand, in the sun.

SEASIDE SERENADE

It begins when you smell a funny smell,
And it isn't vanilla or caramel,
And it isn't forget-me-nots or lilies,
Or new-mown hay, or daffy-down-dillies,
And it's not what the barber rubs on Father,
And it's awful, and yet you like it rather.
No, it's not what the barber rubs on Daddy,
It's more like an elderly finnan haddie,
Or, shall we say, an electric fan
Blowing over a sardine can.
It smells of seaweed, it smells of clams,
It's as fishy as ready-made telegrams,
It's as fishy as millions of fishy fishes,
In spite of which you find it delishes,
You could do with a second helping, please,
And that, my dears, is the ocean breeze.
And pretty soon you observe a pack
Of people reclining upon their back,
And another sight that is very common
Is people reclining upon their abdomen.
And now you lose the smell of the ocean
In the sweetish vapor of sunburn lotion,
And the sun itself seems paler and colder,
Compared to vermilion face and shoulder.
The beach is peppered with ladies who look
Like pictures out of a medical book.
Last, not least, consider the kiddies,
Chirping like crickets and Katydiddies,
Splashing, squealing, slithering, crawling,
Cheerful, tearful, boisterous, bawling,

Kiddies in clamorous crowds that swarm
Heavily over your prostrate form,
Callous kiddies who gallop in myriads
'Twixt ardent Apollos and eager Nereids,
Kiddies who bring, as a priceless cup,
Something dead that a wave washed up.
Oh, I must go down to the beach, my lass,
And step on a piece of broken glass.

MAN BITES DOG-DAYS

In this fairly temperate clime
Summertime is itchy time.
O'er rocks and stumps and ruined walls
Shiny poison ivy crawls.
Every walk in woods and fields
Its aftermath of itching yields.
Hand me down my rusty hatchet;
Someone murmured, Do not scratch it.

Reason permeates my rhyme:
Summertime is itchy time.
Beneath the orange August moon
Overfed mosquitoes croon.
After sun-up, flies and midges
Raise on people bumps and ridges.
Hand me down my rusty hatchet;
Someone murmured, Do not scratch it.

Lo, the year is in its prime;
Summertime is itchy time.
People loll upon the beaches
Ripening like gaudy peaches.
Friends, the beach is not the orchard,
Nor is the peach by sunburn tortured.
Hand me down my rusty hatchet;
Someone murmured, Do not scratch it.

Now the menu is sublime,
Summertime is itchy time.

Berries, clams, and lobsters tease
Our individual allergies.
Rash in rosy splendor thrives,
Running neck-and-neck with hives.
Hand me down my rusty hatchet;
Someone murmured, Do not scratch it.

The bluebells and the cowbells chime;
Summertime is itchy time.
Despite cold soup, and ice, and thermoses
Garments cling to epidermises.
That fiery-footed centipede,
Prickly heat prowls forth to feed.
Hand me down my rusty hatchet;
Someone murmured, Do not scratch it.

Hatchet-killings ain't a crime:
Summertime is itchy time.

A CAROL FOR CHILDREN

God rest you, merry Innocents,
Let nothing you dismay,
Let nothing wound an eager heart
Upon this Christmas day.

Yours be the genial holly wreaths,
The stockings and the tree;
An aged world to you bequeaths
Its own forgotten glee.

Soon, soon enough come crueler gifts,
The anger and the tears;
Between you now there sparsely drifts
A handful yet of years.

Oh dimly, dimly glows the star
Through the electric throng;
The bidding in temple and bazaar
Drowns out the silver song.

The ancient altars smoke afresh,
The ancient idols stir;
Faint in the reek of burning flesh
Sink frankincense and myrrh.

Gaspar, Balthazar, Melchior!
Where are your offerings now?
What greetings to the Prince of War,
His darkly branded brow?

Two ultimate laws alone we know.
The ledger and the sword—
So far away, so long ago,
We lost the infant Lord.

Only the children clasp his hand:
His voice speaks low to them,
And still for them the shining band
Wings over Bethlehem.

God rest you, merry Innocents,
While innocence endures.
A sweeter Christmas than we to ours
May you bequeath to yours.

THE BOY WHO LAUGHED AT SANTA CLAUS

In Baltimore there lived a boy.
He wasn't anybody's joy.
Although his name was Jabez Dawes,
His character was full of flaws.
In school he never led his classes,
He hid old ladies' reading glasses.
His mouth was open when he chewed,
And elbows to the table glued.

He stole the milk of hungry kittens,
And walked through doors marked NO ADMITTANCE.
He said he acted thus because
There wasn't any Santa Claus.
Another trick that tickled Jabez

Was crying "Boo!" at little babies.
He brushed his teeth, they said in town,
Sideways instead of up and down.

Yet people pardoned every sin,
And viewed his antics with a grin,
Till they were told by Jabez Dawes,
"There isn't any Santa Claus!"
Deploring how he did behave,
His parents swiftly sought their grave.
They hurried through the portals pearly,
And Jabez left the funeral early.

Like whooping cough, from child to child,
He sped to spread the rumor wild:
"Sure as my name is Jabez Dawes
There isn't any Santa Claus!"
Slunk like a weasel or a marten
Through nursery and kindergarten,
Whispering low to every tot,
"There isn't any, no there's not!

"No beard, no pipe, no scarlet clothes,
No twinkling eyes, no cherry nose,
No sleigh, and furthermore, by Jiminy,
Nobody coming down the chimney!"

The children wept all Christmas Eve
And Jabez chortled up his sleeve.
No infant dared to hang up his stocking
For fear of Jabez' ribald mocking.
He sprawled on his untidy bed,
Fresh malice dancing in his head,
When presently with scalp a-tingling,
Jabez heard a distant jingling;
He heard the crunch of sleigh and hoof
Crisply alighting on the roof.

What good to rise and bar the door?
A shower of soot was on the floor.
Jabez beheld, oh, awe of awes,

The fireplace full of Santa Claus!
Then Jabez fell upon his knees
With cries of "Don't," and "Pretty please."
He howled, "I don't know where you read it.
I swear some other fellow said it!"

"Jabez," replied the angry saint,
"It isn't I, it's you that ain't.
Although there is a Santa Claus,
There isn't any Jabez Dawes!"
Said Jabez then with impudent vim,
"Oh, yes there is; and I am him!
Your magic don't scare me, it doesn't"—
And suddenly he found he wasn't!

From grimy feet to unkempt locks
Jabez became a jack-in-the-box,
An ugly toy in Santa's sack,
Mounting the flue on Santa's back.
The neighbors heard his mournful squeal;
They searched for him, but not with zeal.
No trace was found of Jabez Dawes,
Which led to thunderous applause,
And people drank a loving cup
And went and hung their stockings up.

All you who sneer at Santa Claus,
Beware the fate of Jabez Dawes,
The saucy boy who mocked the saint,
Donder and Blitzen licked off his paint.

ONE THIRD OF A CALENDAR

In January everything freezes.
We have two children. Both are she'ses.
This is our January rule:
One girl in bed, and one in school.

In February the blizzard whirls.
We own a pair of little girls.

Blessings upon each of the head—
The one in school and the one in bed.

March is the month of cringe and bluster.
Each of our children has a sister.
They cling together like Hansel and Gretel,
With their noses glued to the benzoin kettle.

April is made of impetuous waters
And doctors looking down throats of daughters.
If we had a son too, and a thoroughbred,
We'd have a horse,
And a boy,
And two girls
In bed.

PUT BACK THOSE WHISKERS, I KNOW YOU

There is one fault I must find with the twentieth century,
And I'll put it in a couple of words: Too advertury.
What I'd like would be some nice dull monotony
If anyone's gotony.
People have gone on for years looking forward hopefully to the be-
    ginning of every fresh Anno Domini,
Full of more hopes than there are grits in hominy,
Because it is their guess that the Old Year has been so bad that the
    New Year cannot help being an improvement, and may I say
    that they would never make a living as guessers,
Because what happens, why the New Year simply combines and
    elaborates on the worst features of its predecessors.
Well, I know what the matter is, it stands out as clear as a chord
    in a symphony of Sibelius's,
The matter is that our recent New Years haven't been New Years
    at all, they have just been the same Old Year, probably 1914 or
    something, under a lot of different aliases.
In my eagerness to encounter a New Year I stand ahead of most,
But only if it's a true New Year, not if it's merely the same Old Year
    with its beard shaved off and wearing a diaper labeled New
    Year just to get on the cover of the *Saturday Evening Post*,

Because there are few spectacles less convincing or more untidy
Than 1914 or something in a didy.
I am in favor of honesty as well as gluttony,
And I don't want a secondhand or repossessed January first any
    more than I want my spring lamb leathery and muttony.
Well anyhow, come on New Year, I may not be able to paint as ca-
    pably as Rembrandt or Dali or El Greco,
But if you are a true New Year I can shout Happy True New Year
    Everybody! quicker than Little Sir Echo.

IT'S A GRAND PARADE IT WILL BE,
MODERN DESIGN

Saint Patrick was a proper man, a man to be admired;
Of numbering his virtues I am never, never tired.
A handsome man, a holy man, a man of mighty deeds,
He walked the lanes of Erin, a-telling of his beads.
A-telling of his beads, he was, and spreading of the word.
I think that of Saint Patrick's Day, Saint Patrick hadn't heard.

The saint was born a subject of the ancient British throne,
But the Irish in their wisdom recognized him as their own.
A raiding party captured him, and carried him away,
And Patrick loved the Irish, and he lived to capture they,
A-walking of the valleys and a-spreading of the word.
I think that of Saint Patrick's Day, Saint Patrick hadn't heard.

He defied the mighty Druids, he spoke them bold and plain,
And he lit the Easter fire on the lofty hill of Shane.
He lit the Easter fire where the hill and heaven met,
And on every hill in Ireland the fire is burning yet.
He lit the Easter fire, a-spreading of the word.
I think that of Saint Patrick's Day, Saint Patrick hadn't heard.

Saint Patrick was a proper man before he was a saint,
He was shaky in his Latin, his orthography was quaint,
But he walked the length of Ireland, her mountains and her lakes,
A-building of his churches and a-driving out the snakes,
A-building of his churches and a-spreading of the word.
I think that of Saint Patrick's Day, Saint Patrick hadn't heard.

But the silver-tongued announcer is a coy, facetious rogue;
He ushers in Saint Patrick with a fine synthetic brogue,
He spatters his commercials with machushlas and colleens,
Begorras, worra-worras, and spurious spalpeens.
I hope one day Saint Patrick will lean down from Heaven's arch,
And jam the bloody airwaves on the Seventeenth of March.

SEPTEMBER IS SUMMER, TOO

OR

IT'S NEVER TOO LATE TO BE UNCOMFORTABLE

Well, well, well, so this is summer, isn't that *mirabile dictu,*
And these are the days when whatever you sit down on you stick to.
These are the days when those who sell four ounces of synthetic
   lemonade concocted in a theater basement for a quarter enter
   into their inheritance,
And Rum Collinses soak through paper napkins onto people's
   Hepplewhites and Sheratons,
And progressive-minded citizens don their most porous finery and
   frippery.
But it doesn't help, because underneath they are simultaneously
   sticky and slippery.
And some insomniacs woo insomnia plus pajamas and others mi-
   nus,
And everybody patronizes air-conditioned shops and movies to get
   cool and then complains that the difference in temperature
   gives them lumbago and sinus,
And people trapped in doorways by thunderstorms console them-
   selves by saying, Well, anyway this will cool it off while we
   wait,
So during the storm the mercury plunges from ninety-four to ninety-
   three and afterwards climbs immediately to ninety-eight,
And marriages break up over such momentous questions as Who
   ran against Harding—Davis or Cox?
And when you go to strike a match the head dissolves on the box,
But these estival phenomena amaze me not,
What does amaze me is how every year people are amazed to dis-
   cover that summer is hot.

TRICK OR TREK

If my face is white as a newmade sail,
It's not that it's clean, it's simply pale.
The reason it's pale as well as clean:
I'm a shaken survivor of Halloween.
The little ones of our community
This year passed up no opportunity;
You should have seen the goblins and witches;
At our expense, they were all in stitches.
They shook with snickers from warp to woof
When our doormat landed on the roof.
And take a look at our garden's format—
It now resembles the missing doormat.
The doorbell got torn out by the roots,
So our guests announce themselves tooting flutes.
Don't blame me if I wince or flinch,
They tore the fence down inch by inch.
Forgive me if I flinch or wince,
We haven't seen our mailbox since,
And we can't get into our own garage
Since they gave the door that Swedish massage.
All this perhaps I could forgive,
In loving kindness I might live,
But on every window they scrawled in soap
Those deathless lines, *Mr. Nash is a dope.*
At the very glimpse of a Jack-o'-lantern
I've got one foot on the bus to Scranton.
When Halloween next delivers the goods,
You may duck for apples—I'll duck for the woods.

A WORD ABOUT WINTER

Now the frost is on the pane,
Rugs upon the floor again,
Now the screens are in the cellar,
Now the student cons the speller,
Lengthy summer noon is gone,

Twilight treads the heels of dawn,
Round-eyed sun is now a squinter,
Tiptoe breeze a panting sprinter,
Every cloud a blizzard hinter,
Squirrel on the snow a printer,
Rain spout sprouteth icy splinter,
Willy-nilly, this is winter.

Summer-swollen doorjambs settle,
Ponds and puddles turn to metal,
Skater whoops in frisky fettle,
Golf club stingeth like a nettle,
Radiator sings like kettle,
Hearth is Popocatapetl.

Runneth nose and chappeth lip,
Draft evadeth weather strip,
Doctor wrestleth with grippe
In never-ending rivalship.
Rosebush droops in garden shoddy,
Blood is cold and thin in body,
Weary postman dreams of toddy,
Head before the hearth grows noddy.

On the hearth the embers gleam,
Glowing like a maiden's dream,
Now the apple and the oak
Paint the sky with chimney smoke,
Husband now, without disgrace,
Dumps ashtrays in the fireplace.

I REMEMBER YULE

I guess I am just an old fogey
I guess I am headed for the last roundup, so come along little dogey.
I can remember when winter was wintery and summer was estival;
I can even remember when Christmas was a family festival.
I can even remember when Christmas was an occasion for fireside
    rejoicing and general good will,

And now it is just the day that it's only X shopping days until.
What, five times a week at 8:15 p.m., do the herald angels sing?
That a small deposit now will buy you an option on a genuine diamond ring.
What is the message we receive with Good King Wenceslaus?
That if we rush to the corner of Ninth and Main we can get that pink mink housecoat very inexpenceslaus.
I know what came upon a midnight clear to our backward parents, but what comes to us?
A choir imploring us to Come all ye faithful and steal a 1939 convertible at psychoneurotic prices from Grinning Gus.
Christmas is a sitting duck for sponsors, it's so commercial,
And yet so noncontroversial.
Well, you reverent sponsors redolent of frankincense and myrrh, come smear me with bear-grease and call me an un-American hellion,
This is my declaration of independence and rebellion.
This year I'm going to disconnect everything electrical in the house and spend the Christmas season like Tiny Tim and Mr. Pickwick;
You make me sickwick.

I ALWAYS SAY THERE'S NO PLACE
LIKE NEW YORK IN THE SUMMER
OR
THAT COTTAGE SMALL BY THE WATERFALL WAS
SNAPPED UP LAST FEBRUARY

Estivation means passing the summer in a torpid condition, which is why I love to estivate,
But I find that planning my estivation is as chaotic as the nightmares caused by that fried lobster with garlic sauce which I when restive and indigestive ate,
When icicles hang by the wall and people smear Chap Stick on their faces
I can't seem to take it in that the hounds of Spring are actually on Winter's traces.
The subfreezing months are what my wits are frozen and subhuman in;

Sing cuccu never so lhude, cuccu cannot convince me that Sumer
is icumen in.
Consequently, on my Sumer plans I do not embark
Until the first crocus has ventured into Central Park.
But come the first crocus,
You can't locate a desirable Sumer location even with the aid of
abracadabra, open sesame, hanky panky and hocus pocus.
By the time you start pleading with rural realtors estival,
Why, they have had themselves a financial festival.
Be it seaside or lakeside, they have rented every habitable tent and
bungalow,
Presumably to foresighted tenants who must have stood in line
since the days of Jean Ingelow or even Michelangelo.
The only properties left are such as were despised by Thoreau be-
fore he departed for Walden,
With President Pierce plumbing and the kind of lighting under
which Priscilla almost got Miles Standish mixed up with John
Alden.
This coming Sumer I must remind myself to remember
That the time to arrange for the Sumer after this is before this com-
ing September.
Meanwhile I guess I'll just sit in the city sipping gin and tonics,
Nibbling those tasty garden-fresh vegetables raised in a twelfth-
floor dining alcove by hydroponics.

SCROOGE RIDES AGAIN
OR
A CHRISTMAS POEM

Backward, turn backward, O Time, you old ghoul,
Make me a child again just for one Yule;
Reverse, an if please you, the flow of the river,
Let me be a receiver instead of a giver;
Tuck me cozily into a wee trundle bed
As visions of sugarplums dance through my head,
Which would be a superior substitute for
The seasonal nightmare of yore and Dior.
Please provide for this Christmas alternative symbols

To replace Lord and Taylor, and Macy's and Gimbel's;
Christmases past are a goulash of memory,
Saksy and Schwarzy and Hammacher Schlemmery.
I can name the great musical B's without qualms,
Paying homage to Bach and Beethoven and Brahms,
It's the charge account B's that ruin my rest,
Such as Bergdorf and Bonwit, and Bendel and Best,
While hard on their heels, like a menacing zombie,
Treads the shadowy figure they call Abercrombie,
And if Tiffany's not on this roster extensive,
Well, even my nightmares don't run that expensive.
Oh, this is the gist if my annual battle logs,
If you fight off their windows, they shell you with catalogues.
The Avenue blooms like a fabulous orchid
Which wealthy collectors have called The New Yorkid,
Who, who can afford this carnivorous plant?
Though the young Aga Khan, I'm afraid that I khan't.
I will flee from Manhattan, the gay tantalizer,
No place for a glum, impecunious miser;
But what overland journeys, what overseas hops,
Will provide sanctuary from luxury shops?
When the pilot takes off, when the captain has anchor-upped,
You are already well on your way to go bankrupt.
With thrift for your armor and prudence your shield,
You race through Chicago and miss Marshall Field.
You tighten your belt and hitch up your braces
And hopefully head for the great open spaces.
But the plain where coyotes fought over the carcass
Of the obsolete Longhorn, that's now Neiman-Marcus,
Where Texans as well as inferior breeds
Go hog-wild over baubles and bangles and beads.
You conquer temptation and fly to Los Angeles,
Arriving there baubleless, beadless and bangleless.
But here is no haven for him with a mate,
For Bullock's and Magnin's like mantrap await.
You're up and away as the jackrabbit jumps,
You reach San Francisco and bump into Gump's.
You feel doomed, like a character out of Euripides,

Perhaps you'll find peace in the simple Antipodes.
Well, in Sydney, my boy, you step out of the clouds
To the great House of Curzon, the great House of Prouds,
Which sound like tiaras and ermine and swords
And a seat in the equally great House of Lords.
Next, you lie to your wife like the naughty Pinocchio,
You deny there are pearls to be purchased in Tokyo;
You lie like Munchausen, like your own passport photo,
You blandly dismiss Mikimoto *in toto*,
And go winging to Rome, taking care on the way
To avoid Lilaram and his Son in Bombay.
Not a lira more dear than a trip to Las Vegas
Are Gucci's and Cucci's seductive bottegas.
It's Cucci for clothing and Gucci for leather,
It's a thrifty device to link them together;
Leer slyly, and hint to your wife in advance
Gucci-Cucci's a kind of provocative dance.
In Paris prolong your penurious saga
By sneaking past Hermès and Balenciaga;
You must hoard self-control to the point of redundance
To resist the temptations of London's abundance;
What with Fortnum and Mason, and Harrod's, and Liberty,
It's a pit for the feet of the flibbertigibberty,
But you hold yourself down to a tuppenny card
Of Buckingham Palace or Changing the Guard.
Then it's home again, home again, jiggety-jog,
You have outdone Magellan and Phileas Fogg,
You trot through the Customs as brisk as a pony,
With naught to declare but your own parsimony.
You've observed the round earth with deliberate strabismus,
And thus triumphed over the spirit of Christmas.
But that old human nature, though often perverse,
Is most of the time rather better than worse.
Having splintered the target at which you had aimed,
You suddenly find you're not pleased, but ashamed.
There is only one way to regain your euphoria;
Head straight for the city's most costly emporia.
Buy the stars for the grown-ups, the moon for the tots,

Buy fripperies foolish in fine carload lots,
And you'll think when the family encircles the tree,
"God has blessed every one, but especially me."

HALLOWEEN HOODLUMS: GO HOME!

There is one old hymn that now arouses my curiosity as well as my
zest,
Which is the one that begins, "For all the saints who from their
labors rest."
Heaven knows all the saints have earned a good rest after their
hardships on this earthly scene,
But I wonder how much rest they actually get on the
Eve of All Saints' Day, generally known as Halloween.
Despite nostalgia that increases with age, I don't insist that new
ways are decadent and only the old ways are fit to venerate,
But I do feel that the celebration of Halloween has tended to de-
generate.
I can remember when children got an adequate thrill from ringing
doorbells and running away, or rigging ticktacks on the win-
dow, or even bobbing for apples,
While they now amuse themselves by upsetting gravestones and
desecrating chapels.
I try to refrain from crabbedness and contentiousness and general
fly-off-the-handleism,
But I find it difficult when the young have ceased to distinguish be-
tween mischief and vandalism.
What has become of the old-fashioned urchin who terrified his co-
operative relatives with the aid of an old sheet and a lighted
pumpkin?
He has given way to a savage and malicious breed compounded of
country slicker and city bumpkin.
These yahoos are driven by some senseless compulsion for de-
struction, not even their court-assigned psychiatrist can put a
curb on it;
If they see a tire, they slash it; if they see a window, they either
break it or soap a dirty noun or verb on it.

On Halloween it's not the ghoulies and ghosties and long-legged
   beasties that put my peace of mind to flight,
It's the things that go bump in the night.
I am by now something of a cynic;
I suspect that any bumps in the night of Halloween are less likely
   to be caused by hobgoblins or bogles than by juvenile humans
   rolling a full garbage pail over a fence and into a swimming
   pool, or tossing a cherry bomb into the ambulance carrying an
   emergency patient to the clinic.
I say humans, but their divorce from the human race seems ab-
   solute and utter,
Although they will on occasion help an old lady to cross the street
   by propelling her with their elbows off the sidewalk and into
   the gutter.
Then, of course, no Halloween would be complete without Trick
   or Treat.
This is a system of extortion that has grown even beyond the in-
   credible and the preposterous.
It equals the Mafia in ruthlessness and arrogance, it is altogether
   Cosa Nosterous.
These are my glummer thoughts, but I have others that are not so
   glum,
One of which is that too often the only visible part of the pond of
   youth is the scum.
My hope continues undimmed
That inevitably the scum will be skimmed.
With such thoughts in mind I firmly expect that on some future All
   Saints' Eve all the saints will enjoy undisturbed rest from their
   labors,
And so, I selfishly add, will I and my neighbors.

CHRISTMAS HASH

"Tiny reindeer hooves are drumming,
Listen, Santa Claus is coming!
See his tummy bulge and billow!
That is Mother's favorite pillow.
All her cotton, as she feared,
Has been purloined to make his beard.
Her lipstick sets his cheeks a-glowing,
His chest expands with Ho Ho Ho-ing.
That last Ho Ho was not too smart—
Santa Claus has come apart."

Persons of Interest

LOOK WHAT YOU DID, CHRISTOPHER!

In fourteen hundred and ninety-two,
Somebody sailed the ocean blue.
Somebody borrowed the fare in Spain
For a business trip on the bounding main,
And to prove to people, by actual test,
You could get to the East by traveling West.
Somebody said, Sail on! Sail on!
And studied China and China's lingo,
And cried from the bow, There's China now!
And promptly bumped into Santo Domingo.
Somebody murmured, Oh dear, Oh dear!
I've discovered the Western Hemisphere.

And that, you may think, my friends, was that.
But it wasn't. Not by a fireman's hat.
Well enough wasn't left alone,
And Columbus was only a cornerstone.
There came the Spaniards,
There came the Greeks,
There came the Pilgrims in leather breeks.

There came the Dutch,
And the Poles and Swedes,
The Persians, too,
And perhaps the Medes,
The Letts, the Lapps and the Lithuanians,
Regal Russians, and ripe Roumanians.
There came the French
And there came the Finns,
And the Japanese
With their formal grins.
The Tartars came,
And the Terrible Turks—
In a word, humanity shot the works.
And the country that should have been Cathay
Decided to be
The U.S.A.

And that, you may think, my friends, was that.
But it wasn't. Not by a fireman's hat.
Christopher C. was the cornerstone,
And well enough wasn't left alone.
For those who followed
When he was through,
They burned to discover something, too.
Somebody, bored with rural scenery,
Went to work and invented machinery,
While a couple of other mental giants
Got together
And thought up Science.
Platinum blondes
(They were once peroxide),
Peruvian bonds
And carbon monoxide,
Tax evaders
And Vitamin A,
Vice crusaders,
And tattle-tale gray—
These, with many another phobia,

We owe to that famous Twelfth of Octobia.
O misery, misery, mumble and moan!
Someone invented the telephone,
And interrupted a nation's slumbers,
Ringing wrong but similar numbers.
Someone devised the silver screen
And the intimate Hollywood magazine,
And life is a Hades
Of clicking cameras,
And foreign ladies
Behaving amorous.
Gags have erased
Amusing dialog,
As gas replaced
The crackling firelog.
All that glitters is sold as gold,
And our daily diet grows odder and odder,
And breakfast foods are dusty and cold—
It's a wise child
That know's its fodder.
Someone invented the automobile,
And good Americans took the wheel
To view American rivers and rills
And justly famous forests and hills—
But somebody equally enterprising
Had invented billboard advertising.
You linger at home
In dark despair,
And wistfully try the electric air.
You hope for a program controversial,
And what do they give you?
A beer commercial.
Oh, Columbus was only a cornerstone,
And well enough wasn't left alone,
For the Inquisition was less tyrannical
Than the iron rules of an age mechanical,
Which, because of an error in '92,
Are clamped like corsets on me and you,

While Children of Nature we'd be today
If San Domingo
Had been Cathay.

And that, you may think, my friends, is that.
But it isn't—not by a fireman's hat.
The American people,
With grins jocose,
Always survive the fatal dose.
And though our systems are slightly wobbly,
We'll fool the doctor this time, probly.

CAPTAIN JOHN SMITH

Captain John Smith was a full-blooded Briton,
The same as Boadicea and Bulwer-Lytton,
But his problem and theirs were not quite the same,
Because they didn't have to go around assuring everybody that that
    was their real name,
And finally he said, This business of everybody raising their eye-
    brows when I register at an inn is getting very boring,
So I guess I'll go exploring,
So he went and explored the River James,
Where they weren't as particular then as they are now about
    names,
And he went for a walk in the forest,
And the Indians caught him and my goodness wasn't he embor-
    rassed!
And he was too Early-American to write for advice from Emily
    Post,
So he prepared to give up the ghost,
And he prayed a prayer but I don't know whether it was a silent
    one or a vocal one,
Because the Indians were going to dash his brains out and they
    weren't going to give him an anaesthetic, not even a local one,
But along came Pocahantas and she called off her father's savage
    minions,
Because she was one of the most prominent Virginians,
And her eyes went flash flash,

And she said, Scat, you po' red trash,
And she begged Captain John Smith's pardon,
And she took him for a walk in the gyarden,
And she said, Ah reckon Ah sho' would have felt bad if anything
    had happened to you-all,
And she told him about her great-uncle Hiawatha and her cousin
    Sittin' Bull and her kissin' cousin King Philip, and I don't know
    who-all,
And he said you'd better not marry me, you'd better marry John
    Rolfe.
So he bade her farewell and went back to England, which adjoins
    Scotland, where they invented golf.

DRAGONS ARE TOO SELDOM

To actually see an actual marine monster
Is one of the things that do before I die I wonster.
Should you ask me if I desire to meet the bashful inhabitant of
    Loch Ness,
I could only say yes.
Often my eye with moisture dims
When I think that it has never been my good fortune to gaze on
    one of Nature's whims.
Far from ever having seen a Gorgon
I haven't even seen the midget that sat in the lap of Mr. Morgan.
Indeed it is my further ill fortune or mishap
That far from having seen the midget that sat in it I have never
    even seen Mr. Morgan's lap.
Indeed I never thought much about Mr. Morgan's having a lap be-
    cause just the way you go into churches and notice the stained
    glass more than the apses
When you think about multi-millionaires you don't think about
    their laps as much as their lapses;
But it seems that they do have laps which is one human touch that
    brings them a little closer to me and you,
And maybe they even go so far as to sometimes have hiccups too.
But regular monsters like sea serpents don't have laps or hiccups
    or any other characteristic that is human,

And I would rather see a second-rate monster such as a mermaid
    than a first-rate genius such as John Bunyan or Schiaparelli or
    Schubert or Schumann;
Yes, I would rather see one of the sirens
Than two Lord Byrons,
And if I knew that when I got there I could see Cyclops or Scylla
    and Charybdis or Pegasus
I would willingly walk on my hands from here to Dallas, Tegasus,
Because I don't mean to be satirical,
But where there's a monster there's a miracle,
And after a thorough study of current affairs, I have concluded
    with regret
That the world can profitably use all the miracles it can get,
And I think life would be a lot less demoralizing
If instead of sitting around in front of the radio listening to torture
    singers sing torture songs we sat around listening to the Lorelei
    loreleising.

COLUMBUS

Once upon a time there was an Italian,
And some people thought he was a rapscallion,
But he wasn't offended,
Because other people thought he was splendid,
And he said the world was round,
And everybody made an uncomplimentary sound,
But his only reply was Pooh,
He replied, Isn't this fourteen ninety-two?
It's time for me to discover America if I know my chronology,
And if I discover America you owe me an apology,
So he went and tried to borrow some money from Ferdinand
But Ferdinand said America was a bird in the bush and he'd rather
    have a berdinand,
But Columbus' brain was fertile, it wasn't arid,
And he remembered that Ferdinand was unhappily married,
And he thought, there is no wife like a misunderstood one,
Because her husband thinks something is a terrible idea she is
    bound to think it a good one,

So he perfumed his handkerchief with bay rum and citronella,
And he went to see Isabella,
And he looked wonderful but he had never felt sillier,
And she said, I can't place the face but the aroma is familiar,
And Columbus didn't say a word,
All he said was, I am Columbus, the fifteenth-century Admiral Byrd,
And just as he thought, her disposition was very malleable,
And she said, Here are my jewels, and she wasn't penurious like Cornelia the mother of the Gracchi, she wasn't referring to her children, no, she was referring to her jewels, which were very very valuable,
So Columbus said, Somebody show me the sunset and somebody did and he set sail for it,
And he discovered America and they put him in jail for it,
And the fetters gave him welts,
And they named America after somebody else,
So the sad fate of Columbus ought to be pointed out to every child and every voter,
Because it has a very important moral, which is, Don't be a discoverer,
Be a promoter.

TWO AND ONE ARE A PROBLEM

Dear Miss Dix, I am a young man of half-past thirty-seven.
My friends say I am not unattractive, though to be kind and true is what I have always striven.
I have brown hair, green eyes, a sensitive mouth and a winning natural exuberance,
And, at the waist, a barely noticeable protuberance.
I am open-minded about beverages so long as they are grape, brandy or malt,
And I am generous to practically any fault.
Well, Miss Dix not to beat around the bush, there is a certain someone who thinks I am pretty nice,
And I turn to you for advice.
You see, it started when I was away on the road

And returned to find a pair of lovebirds had taken up their abode
in my abode.
Well I am not crazy about lovebirds, but I must say they looked
very sweet in their gilded cage,
And their friendship had reached an advanced stage,
And I had just forgiven her who of the feathered fiancés was the
donor of
When the houseboy caught a lost lovebird in the yard that he
couldn't locate the owner of.
So then we had three, and it was no time for flippancy,
Because everybody knows that a lovebird without his own love-
bird to love will pine away and die of the discrepancy,
So we bought a fourth lovebird for the third lovebird and they sat
around very cozily beak to beak
And then the third lovebird that we had provided the fourth love-
bird for to keep it from dying died at the end of the week,
So we were left with an odd lovebird and it was no time for flip-
pancy,
Because a lovebird without is own lovebird to love will pine away
and die of the discrepancy,
So we had to buy a fifth lovebird to console the fourth lovebird
that we had bought to keep the third lovebird contented,
And now the fourth lovebird has lost its appetite, and Miss Dix, I
am going demented.
I don't want to break any hearts, but I got to know where I'm at;
Must I keep on buying lovebirds, Miss Dix, or do you think it
would be all right to buy a cat?

UNTITLED

(Place card for a cousin at a dinner party, 1945)

Mary labors, heart and soul,
Preaching golf, and birth control.
She pleads both causes from door to door,
Helping people cut down their score.

UNTITLED

O Hedda Parsons, Louella Hopper,
I hope you never get things proper,
I hope you never read a grammar
And lose that breathless girlish glamor,
I hope your chatty cataracts
Are never clogged by stodgy facts
I hope no Washington subpoena
E'er draws you East of Pasadena
I hope you never know or care
Which was Jane Austen, which Jane Eyre.

MAX SCHLING, MAX SCHLING,
LEND ME YOUR GREEN THUMB—
A TRAVELOGUE
OF FLOWERY CATALOGUES

Bobolink!
Bobolink!
Spink!
Spank!
Spink!
Bobbink!
Atkink!
Sprink!

Burpee.

THE STRANGE CASE OF THE
LOVELORN LETTER WRITER

Dear Miss Dix, I am a young lady of Scandinavian origin, and I am
   in a quandary.
I am not exactly broody, but I am kind of pondery.
I got a twenty-five waist and a thirty-five bust,
And I am going with a chap whose folks are very uppercrust.
He is the intellectual type, which I wouldn't want to disparage,

Because I understand they often ripen into love after marriage,
But here I am all set
For dalliance,
And what do I get?
Shilly-shalliance.
Just when I think he's going to disrobe me with his eyes,
He gets up off of the davenport and sighs.
Every time I let down my hair,
He starts talking to himself or the little man who isn't there.
Every time he ought to be worrying about me,
Why, he's worrying about his mother, that's my mother-in-law to be,
And I say let's burn that bridge when we come to it, and he says
    don't I have any sin sense,
His uncle and her live in incense,
Well, with me that's fine,
Let them go to their church and I'll go to mine.
But no, that's not good enough for Mr. Conscience and his mental
    indigestion,
He's got to find two answers for every question.
If a man is a man, a girl to him is a girl, if I correctly rememma,
But to him I am just a high pathetical dilemma.
What I love him in spite of
Is, a girl wants a fellow to go straight ahead like a locomotive and
    he is more like a loco-might-of.
Dear Miss Dix, I surely need your advice and solace,
It's like I was in love with Henry Wallace.
Well, while I eagerly await your reply I'm going down to the river
    to pick flowers. I'll get some rosemary if I can't find a camellia.
Yours truly, Ophelia.

FABLES BULFINCH FORGOT:
THE THIRTEENTH LABOR OF HERCULES

Some people think the nose of the Sphinx was flattened by
    Napoleon's cannoneers,
But it wasn't, not by several thousand years.
Credit should go to a person who dressed like Adam and talked
    like Pericles,

This person being known to us as Hercules and to the illiterate
    Greeks as Heracles,
And Hercules performed twelve fabulous labors,
Which caused all the inhabitants of Ultima Thule to exclaim Be-
    gorra and Bejabers,
And just when he thought he was through with labors he was told
    by the gods, several of whom were his cousin,
That he must make it a baker's dozen.
They said that all brawn and no brain makes a dull demigod, so
    on immortality it was no dice
Unless he stumped the Sphinx thrice,
And Hercules said, Well I'll be a duck-billed platypus,
Here is a chance to avenge my friend Oedipus,
And he assumed an expression deceptively pleasant,
And he asked the Sphinx, Who is the heavyweight champion? and
    she said, Ezzard Charles, and he said, No it ezzant,
And he said, I'll give you another bone to pick at,
Why did Orpheus give up conducting and throw away his baton?
    and she said, I bet you don't know, either, and he said, Because
    there were more Bacchantes than he could shake a stick at,
And the Sphinx said, You can't stump me three times in a row, and
    he said, A house full, a hole full, you cannot catch a bowlful
    can you riddle me that without straining?
And she said, Smoke? And Hercules said, No thank you, I'm in
    training.
From that point
The Sphinx's nose has been out of joint.

FABLES BULFINCH FORGOT:
MEDUSA AND THE MOT JUSTE

Once there was a Greek divinity of the sea named Ceto and she
    married a man named Phorcus,
And the marriage must have been pretty raucous;
Their remarks about which child took after which parent must
    have been full of asperities,
Because they were the parents of the Gorgons, the Graeae, and Scylla,
    and the dragon that guarded the apples of the Hesperides.

Bad blood somewhere.

Today the Gorgons are our topic, and as all schoolboys including you and me know,

They were three horrid sisters named Medusa and Euryale and Stheno,

But what most schoolboys don't know because they never get beyond their Silas Marners and their Hiawathas,

The Gorgons were not only monsters, they were also highly talented authors.

Medusa began it;

She wrote *Forever Granite.*

But soon Stheno and Euryale were writing, too, and they addressed her in daily choruses,

Saying, We are three literary sisters just like the Brontës so instead of Gorgons why can't we be brontësauruses?

Well, Medusa may have been mythical but she wasn't mystical,

She was selfish and egotistical.

She saw wider vistas

Than simply being the sister of her sisters.

She replied, tossing away a petrified Argonaut on whom she had chipped a molar,

You two can be what you like, but since I am the big *fromage* in this family, I prefer to think of myself as the Gorgon Zola.

FABLES BULFINCH FORGOT:
CHLOË AND THE ROUÉ

When Lord Byron wrote so glowingly of the isles of Greece

It was not mere coincidence or caprice.

Nobody than Lord Byron could have been sorrier

About the death of a heroic Grecian warrior,

But nobody after so short a period

Could find consolation in the company of a nymph or a Nereid,

So all praise to the nymphs of the isles of Greece.

May their tribe increase.

But their tribe won't increase if they all behave like a nymph named Chloë,

Who lived on the southernmost isle of Greece where it is swampy,
not snowy.

Chloë caught the attention of Zeus,

And he slipped away from the banquet hall mumbling some ridicu-
lous excuse,

And when Hera called after him to come back, she knew what it
meant when he got all skittish and scampery,

He said he'd be back for breakfast, he just had to see a mortal
about a lamprey,

And he didn't want to tell a lie so he disguised himself as a lam-
prey fisherman but couldn't find his lamprey-fishing clothes,

So aside from his lamprey-spear he was as naked as a narcissus or
a rose,

And he tracked Chloë through the swamp and offered her his heart
and a golden chariot, a dandy four-wheeler,

But she refused because she was a Southern nymph, a Hellenic
Dixiecrat, and she had been taught never to trust a nude
eeler.

LEDA'S FORTUNATE GAFFE

The Greeks called the king of gods Zeus and the Romans called
him Jupiter.

Not that the Romans were stupider,

Jupiter being Roman for Zeus Pater, or Zeus the Father,

Which was appropriate, rather.

Zeus Pater is not to be confused with Walter Pater,

Who flourished later.

I don't even know if Walter Pater had a wife,

But I bet he never poured into a lady's room disguised as a shower
of gold in his life.

Zeus Pater, on the other hand, was so eager to escape the restraint
of his jealous queen that once he nearly killed a guard,

And in order to forward his unsavory amours he impersonated just
about everybody except Hildegarde.

One day he tiptoed out through heaven's portal

And picked up the handkerchief of a succulent mortal,

But when he wished to continue the acquaintance, he had run out
    of impersonations, he had nothing new to go as.
Juno always recognized him and followed him like Ruth after Boaz.
But this mortal happened to be Leda
And she was a great reader,
And when they were the equivalent of introduced,
Instead of Zeus, she thought the name was Proust,
And hey, hey!
The perplexing problem of what to impersonate was solved when
    she told him how much she admired *Swann's Way.*

MS. FOUND UNDER A SERVIETTE
IN A LOVELY HOME

. . . Our outlook is totally different from that of our American cousins, who
have never had an aristocracy. Americans relate all effort, all work, and all of
life itself to the dollar. Their talk is of nothing but dollars. The English seldom
sit happily chatting for hours on end about pounds.
              —Nancy Mitford in *Noblesse Oblige*

Dear Cousin Nancy:
You probably never heard of me or Cousin Beauregard or Cousin
    Yancey,
But since you're claiming kin all the way across the ocean, we fig-
    ure you must be at least partwise Southern,
So we consider you not only our kith and kin but also our kithin'
    couthern.
I want to tell you, when Cousin Emmy Lou showed us your piece
    it stopped the conversation flat,
Because I had twenty dollars I wanted to talk about, and Cousin
    Beauregard had ten dollars he wanted to talk about, and
    Cousin Yancey didn't have any dollars at all, and he wanted to
    talk about that.
But Cousin Emmy Lou looked over her spectacles, which the com-
    mon people call glasses,
And she offered us a dollar to stop talking about dollars and start
    talking about the English upper classes.

Cousin Beauregard wanted to know why the English aristocracy
was called English when most of their names were French to
begin with,
And now anybody with an English name like Hobbs or Stobbs has
to accumulate several million of those pounds they seldom chat
about, to buy his way in with.
Cousin Yancey said he could understand that—the St. Aubyns beat
the hell out of the Hobbses in 1066—but there was a more im-
portant point that he could not determine,
Which is why the really aristocratic English aristocrats have names
that are translated from the German.
Cousin Emmy Lou is pretty aristocratic herself; in spite of her
weakness for hog jowl and potlikker, she is noted for her high-
born pale and wan flesh,
And where most people get gooseflesh she gets swan flesh,
And she said she thought you ought to know that she had been
over the royal roster
And she had spotted at least one impostor.
She noticed that the Wicked Queen said "Mirror, mirror on the
wall" instead of "Looking glass, looking glass on the wall,"
which is perfectly true,
So the Wicked Queen exposed herself as not only wicked but def-
initely non-U,
After that we all loosened our collars
And resumed our conversation about dollars.

BRIEF LIVES IN NOT SO BRIEF—I

I yawn at the daily gossip columns,
A circling procession of tawdry names,
Publicity puffs and malicious hints,
And furtive games.

Where, then, shall I turn for honest gossip?
(I am one who on gossip thrives.)
Well, hand me over that sprightly volume,
John Aubrey's *Brief Lies*.

Here are noble foibles and durable crotchets,
Odd trifles passed over by Pepys and Evelyn,
Old bachelors' tales that outstretch old wives';
Here's gossip to revel in.

So lively they leap from Aubrey's notebooks,
Scholar and soldier, poet and peer,
That when they sneeze you cry "God bless you!"
After three hundred year.

Have ever you heard of James Bovey?
Neither had I, neither had I.
Yet he was unique among his fellows;
Aubrey tells why:
"Red-haired men never had any kindnesse for him. In all his Trav-
    ills he was never robbed."

Have ever you heard of Sir Mathew Hale,
Fountain of legalistic lore?
He was Lord Chief Justice in Charles's England,
And furthermore,
"He was a great Cuckold."

Have you heard of the libel on Ben Jonson?
Neither had I, neither had I,
Till I read a remark parenthetically dropped
By my favorite spy:
"He killed Mr. Marlow, the Poet, on Bunhill, comeing from the
    Green-curtain play-house."

When I doubt the genius of Edmund Waller,
Fellow-feeling banishes doubts;
I picture him with his laurels bedraggled,
A butt for louts:
"He haz but a tender weake body, but was always very temperate.
    They made him damnable drunke at Somersethouse, where, at
    the water stayres, he fell downe, and had a cruell fall. 'Twas
    pitty to use such a sweet swan so inhumanely."

Thomas Hobbes had his day in court,
The philosopher had his dazzling day;

His friend recorded it, loyally risking
Lèse-majesté:
"The witts at Court were wont to bayte him. . . . The King would
call him the Beare: Here comes the Beare to be bayted: (this is
too low witt to be published)."

Credulous Aubrey with spaniel ears,
Friskily ranged a gamy century,
Dismissed himself and his guileless art
In a humble entry:
"How these curiosities would be quite forgott, did not such idle
fellowes as I am putt them downe!"

BRIEF LIVES IN NOT SO BRIEF—II

I am fond of the late poet Sir John Suckling,
He may have been no Swan of Avon, but he was a pretty talented
    Twickenham Duckling.
Along with a gift for poesy, he was possessed of ingenuity and ef-
    frontery;
John Aubrey tells us that he *"invented the game of Cribbidge. He*
    sent his Cards to all the Gameing places in the countrey,
Which were marked with private markes of his; he gott twenty
    thousand pounds by this way."
Which was not then nor is now, hay.
I suspect that sometimes the poet Suckling and the poet Herrick
    used to meet
To exchange ideas about ladies' feet.
Herrick took the first leap;
He said that Mistress Susanna Southwell's pretty feet crept out and
    drew in again like snails playing at bopeep,
As I have said, Suckling was no Shakespeare or Housman;
Neither was he a snail man: he was a mouse man.
So he looked up from his marked cards and loaded dice,
And said he knew a bride whose feet stole in and out beneath her
    petticoat like little mice.
As he plucked a fifth ace from under the seat,
He might have added that this bride was afraid of mice, and suc-
    cumbed to the vapours trying to run away from her own feet.

Aubrey says of Suckling, *"He died a Batchelour,"*
Than which, considering his callous attitude toward brides, nothing could be natchelour.

THE ENTRAPMENT OF JOHN ALDEN
OR
WE PAINT THE LILY,
WE BEARD MR. LONGFELLOW

Once there was a Pilgrim Father named Miles Standish,
Because despite many misconceptions few Pilgrim Fathers were named Praise-God Barebones or something equally outlandish.
Miles Standish was ordinarily a direct man, but in affairs of the heart he was inclined to crawfish,
Indeed, he might have been termed Standish-offish.
He had moved from Plymouth to Duxbury and he had a friend who was a born bachelor named John Alden
Who had also moved to Duxbury, though he might have done better to plump for Nahant or Saugus or Malden.
Well, Miles Standish fell in love with a Pilgrim maiden named Priscilla Mullens,
But whenever he approached her she fell into a fit of the sulks or sullens,
And he was afraid that if he offered her marriage in person she would grow even acider,
So the upshot was that he persuaded John Alden to be his ambassador,
And the offshoot of the upshot was that Priscilla welcomed John Alden as Penelope might have welcomed Odysseus
And she baked him a pumpkin pie that was simply delysseus,
And she evinced a frightening tendency to mingle
And when he transmitted Miles Standish's proposal to her she asked him why he didn't speak for himself, but he really had nothing to say for himself except that he enjoyed being single.
Had he been a Method actor preparing for a play set in Greenpoint he could have told himself, "I can ad lib dis,"

But now with the image of Miles Standish looking over one shoulder and an amorous maiden snuggling against the other he stood silent between Priscilla and Charybdis.

This silence resulted in a union which eventually produced eleven children, several of them born in August,

And a recently discovered diary of John Alden's reveals that he often wished that instead of joining Miles Standish in Duxbury he had Nahanted or even Saugused.

WHILE HOMER NODDED:
A FOOTNOTE TO THE ILIAD

In the days when the hollow ships of the well-greaved Achaeans were beached off Priam's city there was a two-faced Achaean named Antiscrupulos,

And he was so two-faced that his duplicity was doubled, it was quadrupulous.

He was owner of a mighty fleet which was not under Achaean registry, it flew the flag of the Hesperides,

And his ships were never hollow, they were always full of costly cargoes such as maidens available for sacrifice, and lotus, the predecessor of L.S.D., and cantharides.

He was far too busy to spend any time hurling insults at Hector on the ringing plains of windy Troy,

He was always furrowing the wine-dark sea in search of costlier cargoes, and nearly always accompanied by a fascinating hetaera, which was the contemporary term for a daughter of joy.

But once he didn't take her with him and he got home a day early and what did he behold?

There was his hetaera in a compromising situation with a shower of gold,

And he said How do you excuse such misconduct? And she said, I don't need any excuse,

This really isn't a shower of gold, it's aegis-bearing Zeus.

Well, Antiscrupulos was very moral about other people's morals, anent which he was a veritable bluenose,

And he was also jealous as a dozen Heras or Junos,

So, after precautiously sacrificing a surplus maiden to aegis-bearing
     Zeus he accused aegis-bearing Zeus of being a compulsive se-
     ducer and a menace to Achaean womanhood both mortal and
     immortal,
And Zeus did not incinerate him with a thunderbolt, he just gave
     a thunderous self-satisfied lecherous chortle.
Antiscrupulos grew even more indignant and ventured on further
     prods,
He said, How can you chortle off your licentious behavior, you
     who should set an example of marital fidelity for us humans,
     you who bear the dread responsibility of being monarch of
     Olympus and king of all the gods?
He said, Tell me, O king of all the gods, for your godless philan-
     dering can you offer the shadow of an excuse, the ghost of an
     excuse, the wraith of an excuse, even the wraithiest?
And Zeus said, Yes, I'm an atheist.

THE SLIPSHOD SCHOLAR
GETS AROUND TO GREECE

I sing of the ancient Greeks.
They had magnificent physiques.
They were also intellectual Titans,
And wore chlamyses and chitons.
Their minds were serene unless too much success induced hubris,
In which case the gods rendered them lugubrous.
They were preeminent in art and science,
And in their pottery they anticipated faïence.
Indeed they were our precursors in many ways; just think how
     their man Homer did Milton and Tennyson precurse:
Because he could not think of a rhyme for orange he invented
     blank verse.
Even the Stock Exchange reflects their far-off light;
Had the Greeks not bequeathed us their language, brokers would
     be trading not in AT&T but in American DistantSound & Dis-
     tantwrite.
If the Greeks had never existed who would have been the most an-
     noyed?

Freud.

Without their drama where would he have uncovered all those complexes,

His pop-plexes and mom-plexes?

The path of Oedipus into the annals of analysis was straight, Electra's rather more tortuous.

I shall try to map it for you though I may evoke offended cries of *De mortuis*.

Electra persuaded her brother, Orestes, to murder their mother, Clytemnestra, who had persuaded her lover, Aegisthus, to murder Agamemnon, their father, whom Electra loved like billy-o,

And Orestes did in fact murder Clytemnestra and her lover with classic punctilio.

Thus was Agamemnon avenged and his adulterous slayers eradicated.

The Greek words for Electra were Accessory Before The Fact, but Dr. Freud and I think of her simply as a daughter who was over-daddycated.

THREE LITTLE MAIDS FROM SCHOOL

Here is the curious history of three adventurous ladies, each of whom was named Françoise.

They all had mastered the art of mistress-ship under the tutelage of their ambitious mammas.

They showed themselves eager students,

And at an early age could distinguish prudishness from prudence.

Like heliotropes their faces turned towards the Sun King, Louis Quatorze,

Who they thought was entitled to a little relaxation between wars.

First to feel the glow was Françoise Louise de la Baume le Blanc, Duchesse de la Vallière.

She relaxed Louis to the extent of four children, none of whom got to be his heir,

And after the appearance at court of Françoise Athénaïs Rochechouart, Marquise de Montespan, Louis did not give her a fifth look,

So she retired to a convent and wrote a religious book.

Then Françoise de Montespan relaxed Louis to the extent of several more children, but unwisely entrusted their education to Françoise d'Aubigné, Marquise de Maintenon, formerly the impoverished widow Scarron,

For whom unwittingly she thus drew from the fire the jackpot *marrons*,

Because Françoise de Maintenon became queen and Françoise de Montespan retired to a convent which she herself had foresightedly founded,

And she didn't write a book but she started a rumor which proved that she could still fight even though permanently grounded.

There may have been some truth in it, but I myself think she went a bit too far;

She whispered that Mme. De Maintenon owed her success to the fact that her real name was Mme. de Pas-Maintenant-Louis-Mais-Plus-Tard.

BUT I COULD NOT LOVE THEE, ANN, SO MUCH, LOVED I NOT HONORÉ MORE

Some find the world in a grain of sand, I in the correspondence of Ann Landers.

I eavesdrop unabashed as she spoons out her acerb sauce with even hand on lachrymose geese and truculent ganders.

Her desk is positively formicating, which means swarming with moving beings, although I might well employ the other word that sounds like unto it,

Because her mail consists mostly of letters from those embittered ones who have discovered about illicit sex that often there are more headaches than fun to it.

A present-day Emma Lazarus, she cries, Give me your huddled problems, the wretched refuse of your wrongs, unwrap for me your festering sores and stigmas;

Your poison is my meat, be it alcoholism, infidelity, frigidity, satyriasis, premarital pregnancy or borborygmus.

Yes, if anyone's Gordian love-knot requires a blade more cutting than Alexander's,

Let them call on Ann Landers.

No pussy-footer she, no purveyor of admonitions soothing or po-
 lite;
It's, Tell the bum to jump in the lake, tell the old bag to go fly a
 kite.
If Anne of Cleves could have written to Ann Landers
I bet Henry would have thought twice before calling her the mare
 of Flanders.
From a human comedy as varied as Balzac's I choose for you one
 except, the ultimate in wails of poignant woe,
The plaint of a teenager who doubted the affection of her boyfriend
 because the only compliment he ever paid her was, You sweat
 less than any fat girl I know.

A Nashional Menagerie

THE OYSTER

The oyster's a confusing suitor;
It's masc., and fem., and even neuter.
But whether husband, pal or wife
It leads a painless sort of life.
I'd like to be any oyster, say,
In August, June, July, or May.

THE PHOENIX

Deep in the study
Of eugenics
We find that fabled
Fowl, the Phoenix.
The wisest bird
As ever was,
Rejecting other
Mas and Pas,
It lays one egg,
Not ten or twelve,

And when it's hatched
Out pops itselve.

THE COBRA

This creature fills its mouth with venum
And walks upon its duodenum.
He who attempts to tease the cobra
Is soon a sadder he, and sobra.

THE LAMA

The one-l lama,
He's a priest.
The two-l llama,
He's a beast.
And I will bet
A silk pajama
There isn't any
Three-l lllama.*

* The author's attention has been called to a type of conflagration known as the three-alarmer. Pooh.

THE COW

The cow is of the bovine ilk;
One end is moo, the other, milk.

THE FISH

The fish, when he's exposed to air,
Displays no trace of savoir faire,
But in the sea regains his balance
And exploits all his manly talents.
The chastest of the vertebrates.
He never even sees his mates,

But when they've finished, he appears
And O.K.'s all their bright ideas.

THE TURTLE

The turtle lives twixt plated decks
Which practically conceal its sex.
I think it clever of the turtle
In such a fix to be so fertile.

THE PIG

The pig, if I am not mistaken,
Supplies us sausage, ham, and bacon.
Let others say his heart is big—
I call it stupid of the pig.

THE RHINOCEROS

The rhino is a homely beast,
For human eyes he's not a feast.
Farewell, farewell, you old rhinoceros,
I'll stare at something less prepoceros.

THE STORK

From long descriptions I have heard
I guess this creature is a bird.
I've nothing else of him to say,
Except I wish he'd go away.

THE WAPITI

There goes the Wapiti,
Hippety-hoppity!

HOW TO TELL A QUAIL FROM A PARTRIDGE

You all know the story of the insomniac who got into such a state
Because the man upstairs dropped one shoe on the floor at eleven
o'clock and the unhappy insomniac sat up until breakfast time
waiting for him to drop the mate.
Well, here I lie in the interval between the beginning of day and the
end of night,
Waiting for a Bob White to finish saying Bob White,
And as much as I should like to be one who prayeth best because
he loveth best all things both great and small,
I am afraid my feeling about Bob Whites will cause my ranking to
be reduced considerably below that of St. Francis and St. Paul,
Which seems a shame, because my affection would remain undi-
minished
If he'd only say Bob White right out and get it finished.
But this particular Bob White just says Bob,
And then goes off on some other job,
And there are you in your resentful plight,
Waiting around for him to come back and say White.
Now nobody wants to be a slave driver or a Cossack or a Hessian,
But you would think it possible to get through a simple sentence
like Bob White in one session.
If he had to cope with some complicated speech like Cuckoo,
pu-wee, to-witta-woo, jug-jug,
Why there'd be some excuse for remembering in the middle of it
that he had to go see a man about a bug.
You could possibly sympathize with him, you think,
For hesitating over something silly like Spink spank spink;
And yes, you say to yourself as you toss on your sleepless pillow,
No self-respecting bird could be expected not to break down
halfway through such a humiliating speech as willow tit-willow
tit-willow,
But this isn't at all the same.
What are you going to do with a bird that can't even remember its
own name?
If you were the King of Italy and you asked a man his name and
he said Benito and then came back half an hour later and added
Mussolini,

Would you ask him please to go ahead and form a Fascist State or
    would you tell him to tell it to Sweeney?
Well, I hope these bitter words of mine will have some effect in in-
    ducing Bob Whites to memorize their parts with all their might,
Or at least that from now on they'll go out only in couples, one to
    remember to say Bob and the other to remember to say White.

THE GIRAFFE

I beg you, children, do not laugh
When you survey the tall giraffe.
It's hardly sporting to attack
A beast that cannot answer back.
Now you and I have shorter necks,
But we can chant of gin and sex;
He has a trumpet for a throat,
And cannot blow a single note.
It isn't that his voice he hoards;
He hasn't any vocal cords.
I wish for him, and for his wife,
A voluble girafter life.

THE CAMEL

The camel has a single hump;
The dromedary, two:
Or else the other way around.
I'm never sure. Are you?

THE TURKEY

There is nothing more perky
Than a masculine turkey.
When he struts he struts
With no ifs or buts.
When his face is apoplectic

His harem grows hectic,
And when he gobbles
Their universe wobbles.

THE DUCK

Behold the duck.
It does not cluck.
A cluck it lacks.
It quacks.
It is specially fond
Of a puddle or pond.
When it dines or sups,
It bottoms ups.

LOCUST-LOVERS, ATTENTION!

My attention has been recently focussed
Upon the seventeen-year locust.
This is the year
When the seventeen-year locusts are here,
Which is the chief reason my attention has been focussed
Upon the seventeen-year locust.
Overhead, underfoot, they abound,
And they have been seventeen years in the ground,
For seventeen years they were immune to politics and class war
    and capital taunts and labor taunts,
And now they have come out like billions of insect debutantes,
Because they think that after such a long wait,
Why they are entitled to a rich and handsome mate,
But like many another hopeful debutante they have been hoaxed
    and hocus-pocussed,
Because all they get is another seventeen-year locust.
Girl locusts don't make any noise,
But you ought to hear the boys.
Boy locusts don't eat, but it is very probable that they take a drink
    now and again, and not out of a spring or fountain,

Because they certainly do put their heads together in the treetops
and render Sweet Adeline and She'll Be Comin' Round the
Mountain.
I for one get bewildered and go all hot and cold
Every time I look at a locust and realize that it is seventeen years
old;
It is as fantastic as something out of H. G. Wells or Jules Verne or
G. A. Henty
To watch a creature that has been underground ever since it
hatched shortly previous to 1920.
Because locusts also get bewildered and go hot and cold because
they naturally expected to find Jess Willard still the champion
And Nita Naldi the vampion,
And Woodrow Wilson on his way to Paris to promote the perpet-
ually not-yet-but-soon League,
And Washington under the thumb of Wayne B. Wheeler and the
Anti-Saloon League.
Indeed I saw one locust which reminded me of a godmotherless
Cinderella,
Because when it emerged from the ground it was whistling Dard-
anella.
Dear locusts, my sympathy for you is intense,
Because by the time you get adjusted you will be defunct, leaving
nothing behind you but a lot of descendants who in turn will
be defunct just as they get adjusted seventeen years hence.

THE CENTIPEDE

I objurgate the centipede,
A bug we do not really need.
At sleepy-time he beats a path
Straight to the bedroom or the bath.
You always wallop where he's not,
Or, if he is, he makes a spot.

THE ANT

The ant has made himself illustrious
Through constant industry industrious.
So what?
Would you be calm and placid
If you were full of formic acid?

THE HIPPOPOTAMUS

Behold the hippopotamus!
We laugh at how he looks to us,
And yet in moments dank and grim
I wonder how we look to him.
Peace, peace, thou hippopotamus!
We really look all right to us,
As you no doubt delight the eye
Of other hippopotami.

THE PURIST

I give you now Professor Twist,
A conscientious scientist.
Trustees exclaimed, "He never bungles!"
And sent him off to distant jungles.
Camped on a tropic riverside,
One day he missed his loving bride.
She had, the guide informed him later,
Been eaten by an alligator.
Professor Twist could not but smile,
"You mean," he said, "a crocodile."

THE SHREW

Strange as it seems, the smallest mammal
Is the shrew, and not the camel.
And that is all I ever knew,
Or wish to know, about the shrew.

THE ROOSTER

The rooster has a soul more bellicose
Than all your Ludendorffs and Jellicoes,
His step is prouder than Davy Crockett's,
As he swaggers by with his hands in his pockets.

THE SEA GULL

Hark to the whimper of the sea-gull;
He weeps because he's not an ea-gull.
Suppose you were, you silly sea-gull;
Could you explain it to your she-gull?

THE EGG

Let's think of eggs.
They have no legs.
Chickens come from eggs
But they have legs.
The plot thickens;
Eggs come from chickens,
But have no legs under 'em.
What a conundrum!

THE PANTHER

The panther is like a leopard,
Except it hasn't been peppered.
Should you behold a panther crouch,
Prepare to say Ouch.
Better yet, if called by a panther,
Don't anther.

THE KITTEN

The trouble with a kitten is
THAT
Eventually it becomes a
CAT.

THE SQUIRREL

A squirrel to some is a squirrel,
To others, a squirrel's a squirl.
Since freedom of speech is the birthright of each,
I can only this fable unfurl:
A virile young squirrel named Cyril,
In an argument over a girl,
Was lambasted from here to the Tyrol
By a churl of a squirl named Earl.

GLOSSINA MORSITANS
OR
THE TSETSE

A *Glossina morsitans* bit rich Aunt Betsy.
Tsk, tsk, tsetse.

THE PANDA

I love the Baby Giant Panda;
I'd welcome one to my veranda.
I never worry, wondering maybe
Whether it isn't Giant Baby;
I leave such matters to the scientists:
The Giant Baby—and Baby Giantists.
I simply wish a julep and a
Giant Baby Giant Panda.

THE PORPOISE

I kind of like the playful porpoise,
A healthy mind in a healthy corpus.
He and his cousin, the playful dolphin,
Why they like swimmin like I like golphin.

CREEPS AND CRAWLS

The insect world appealed to Fabre.
I find the insect world macabre.
In every hill of ants I see
A governed glimpse of what shall be,
And sense in every web contriver
Man's predecessor and survivor.
Someday, perhaps, my citronella
Will rank with Chamberlain's umbrella.

TWO DOGS HAVE I

For years we've had a little dog,
Last year we acquired a big dog;
He wasn't big when we got him,
He was littler than the dog we had.
We thought our little dog would love him,
Would help him to become a trig dog,
But the new little dog got bigger,
And the old little dog got mad.

Now the big dog loves the little dog,
But the little dog hates the big dog,
The little dog is eleven years old,
And the big dog only one;
The little dog calls him *Schweinhund*,
The little dog calls him Pig-dog,
She grumbles broken curses
As she dreams in the August sun.

The big dog's teeth are terrible,
But he wouldn't bite the little dog;
The little dog wants to grind his bones,
But the little dog has no teeth;
The big dog is acrobatic,
The little dog is a brittle dog;
She leaps to grip his jugular,
And passes underneath.

The big dog clings to the little dog
Like glue and cement and mortar;
The little dog is his own true love;
But the big dog is to her
Like a scarlet rag to a Longhorn,
Or a suitcase to a porter;
The day he sat on the hornet
I distinctly heard her purr.

Well, how can you blame the little dog,
Who was once the household darling?
He romps like a young Adonis,
She droops like an old mustache;
No wonder she steals his corner,
No wonder she comes out snarling,
No wonder she calls him *Cochon*
And even *Espèce de vache.*

Yet once I wanted a sandwich,
Either caviar or cucumber,
When the sun had not yet risen
And the moon had not yet sank;
As I tiptoed through the hallway
The big dog lay in slumber,
And the little dog slept by the big dog,
And her head was on his flank.

PLEASE PASS THE BISCUIT

I have a little dog,
Her name is Spangle,
And when she eats,
I think she'll strangle.

She's darker than Hamlet,
Lighter than Porgy;
Her heart is gold,
Her odor, dorgy.

Her claws click-click
Across the floor,
Her nose is always
Against a door.

Like liquid gems,
Her eyes burn clearly;
She's five years old,
And house-trained nearly.

Her shame is deep
When she has erred;
She dreads the blow
Less than the word.

I marvel that such
Small ribs as these
Can cage such vast
Desire to please.

She's as much a part
Of the house as the mortgage;
Spangle, I wish you
A ripe old dortgage.

THE OCTOPUS

Tell me, O Octopus, I begs,
Is those things arms, or is they legs?
I marvel at thee, Octopus;
If I were thou, I'd call me Us.

THE FLY

God in His wisdom made the fly
And then forgot to tell us why.

THE CANARY

The song of canaries
Never varies,
And when they're moulting
They're pretty revolting.

THE TERMITE

Some primal termite knocked on wood
And tasted it and found it good,
And that is why your Cousin May
Fell through the parlor floor today.

THE JELLYFISH

Who wants my jellyfish?
I'm not sellyfish!

THE KANGAROO

O Kangaroo, O Kangaroo,
Be grateful that you're in the zoo,
And not transmuted by a boomerang
To zestful tangy Kangaroo meringue.

THE EEL

I don't mind eels
Except as meals.
And the way they feels.

THE GRACKLE

The grackle's voice is less than mellow,
His heart is black, his eye is yellow,
He bullies more attractive birds
With hoodlum deeds and vulgar words,
And should a human interfere,
Attacks that human in the rear.
I cannot help but deem the grackle
An ornithological debacle.

THE SKINK

Let us do justice to the skink
Who isn't what so many think.
On consultation with a wizard
I find the skink a kind of lizard.
Since he is not a printer's whim,
Don't sniff and back away from him,
Or you may be adjudged too drunk
To tell a lizard from a skunk.

I HAPPEN TO KNOW

Hark to the locusts in their shrill armadas.
Locusts aren't locusts. Locusts are cicadas.

To seals in circuses I travel on bee lines.
Seals aren't seals. Seals are sea lions.

I'm a buffalo hunter. Want to see my license?
Buffaloes aren't buffaloes. Buffaloes are bisons.

I'm too old to be pedantically hocus-pocussed.
I'll stand on the buffalo, the seal and the locust.

THE SHARK

How many scientists have written
The shark is gentle as a kitten!
Yet this I know about the shark:
His bite is worser than his bark.

THE MERMAID

Say not the mermaid is a myth,
I knew one once named Mrs. Smith.
She stood while playing cards or knitting;
Mermaids are not equipped for sitting.

THE GANDER

Be careful not to cross the gander,
A bird composed of beak and dander.
His heart is filled with prideful hate
Of all the world except his mate,
And if the neighbors do not err
He's overfond of beating her.
Is she happy? What's the use
Of trying to psychoanalyze a goose?

THE WASP

The wasp and all his numerous family
I look upon as a major calamily.
He throws open his nest with prodigality,
But I distrust his waspitality.

THE FROG

The frog is slick,
The frog is slippery,
The frog's career is hoppity-hippery.
He catches flies through hocus-pokery,
His tights are green, his song is croakery.
The little frog goes Pinkle-tink.
The big frog goes Ker-chonk, I think.

THE ASP

Whenever I behold an asp
I can't suppress a startled gasp.
I do not charge the asp with matricide,
But what about his Cleopatricide?

THE AMOEBA

I have no marriage problems
For I am an amoeba
And half of me is Romeo
And half, the Queen of Sheba.

When he-me goes upon the town
She-me does not sit up,
When we are mad we live as one
But when in love we split up.

PASTORAL

Two cows
In a marsh,
Mildly munching
Fodder harsh.
Cow's mother,
Cow's daughter,
Mildly edging

Brackish water.
Mildly munching,
While heron,
Brackish-minded,
Waits like Charon.
Two cows,
Mildly mooing;
No bull;
Nothing doing.

THE LION

Oh, weep for Mr. and Mrs. Bryan!
He was eaten by a lion;
Following which, the lion's lioness
Up and swallowed Bryan's Bryaness.

THE GUPPY

Whales have calves,
Cats have kittens,
Bears have cubs,
Bats have bittens.
Swans have cygnets,
Seals have puppies,
But guppies just have little guppies.

THE PORCUPINE

Any hound a porcupine nudges
Can't be blamed for harboring grudges.
I know one hound that laughed all winter
At a porcupine that sat on a splinter.

FOR A GOOD DOG

My little dog ten years ago
Was arrogant and spry,
Her backbone was a bended bow
For arrows in her eye.
Her step was proud, her bark was loud,
Her nose was in the sky,
But she was ten years younger then,
And so, by God, was I.

Small birds on stilts along the beach
Rose up with piping cry,
And as they flashed beyond her reach
I thought to see her fly.
If natural law refused her wings,
That law she would defy,
For she could do unheard-of things,
And so, at times, could I.

Ten years ago she split the air
To seize what she could spy;
Tonight she bumps against a chair,
Betrayed by milky eye.
She seems to pant, Time up, time up!
My little dog must die,
And lie in dust with Hector's pup;
So, presently, must I

WHO CALLED THAT ROBIN
A PICCOLO PLAYER?

ROBINS GETTING LAZY—Robins, now usually half tame and preferring
suburban to forest life, have become stupid and lazy in many cases.
—*New York Daily Mirror*

Hark hark the lark, no it is not a lark, it is a robin singing like a lark,
He is in disguise because he is now the target of a newspaper cru-
sade like dirty books and vivisection and the man-eating shark.
He has been termed lethargic and fat,

It is said of him that he would rather live in Greenwich or Great Neck than in Medicine Hat,

It is rumored that at the Garden Club his wife once met an author,

And that he himself prefers a California Colonial bungalow to the tepee of Hiawatha,

And wears nylon instead of buckskin hosen,

And buys his worms at a supermarket, cellophane-wrapped, and frozen.

In fact, the implication couldn't be clearer

That he is the spit and image of a reader of the *Mirror*.

Well for heaven's sake, how far can this scurrilous name-calling degenerate?

They are now attempting to besmirch a bird that I venerate.

His breast may be red, that is true,

But his heart is red, white and blue;

And as for being lazy, I know one robin that held down two jobs at once just so his younger brother (their parents had passed away uninsured) could get to be a transport pilot,

But if you mentioned it he was modest as a butter cup or vilot,

And the only reason he himself wasn't making those selfsame flights,

He had a bad head for heights.

If these editorial scandalmongers have to mong scandal about birds, let them leave the robin alone and turn their attention to the pelican;

It has an Oriental background and a triangular horny excrescence developed on the male's bill in the breeding season which later falls off without leaving trace of its existence, which for my money is suspicious and un-Amelican.

NEXT!

I thought that I would like to see
The early world that used to be,
That mastodonic mausoleum,
The Natural History Museum.
At midnight in the vasty hall
The fossils gathered for a ball.

High above notices and bulletins
Loomed up the Mesozoic skeletons.
Aroused by who knows what elixirs,
They ground along like concrete mixers.
They bowed and scraped in reptile pleasure,
And then began to tread the measure.
There were no drums or saxophones,
But just the clatter of their bones,
A rolling, rattling carefree circus
Of mammoth polkas and mazurkas.
Pterodactyls and brontosauruses
Sang ghostly prehistoric choruses.
Amid the megalosauric wassail
I caught the eye of one small fossil.
Cheer up, old man, he said, and winked—
It's kind of fun to be extinct.

A CAUTION TO EVERYBODY

Consider the auk;
Becoming extinct because he forgot how to fly, and could only walk.
Consider man, who may well become extinct
Because he forgot how to walk and learned how to fly before he thinked.

A DOG'S BEST FRIEND IS HIS ILLITERACY

It has been well said that quietness is what a Grecian urn is the still unravished bride of,
And that a door is what a dog is perpetually on the wrong side of.
I may add that a sachet is what many a housewife's linen is fragrantly entrusted to,
But that a cliché is what a dog owner must eventually get adjusted to.
What does the visitor say when your dog greets him with Southern hospitality and salutes him all kissin-cousiny?

He says, He smells my dog on me, doesn't he?
And he asks, How old is he, and you say Twelve, and he appraises
    Spot with the eye of an antiquarian,
And says, Seven twelves are eighty something, why Spot in human
    terms you're an octogenarian,
But these two bromides are just the rattle before the strike,
Because then he says it's funny but he's noticed how often dogs and
    their masters look alike.
Such are the comments faced by dog owners from Peoria to Pe-
    shawar,
And frequently from a man who in canine terms is 322 years old,
    and he is the spit and image of his own Chihuahua.
The only escape is to have something instead of dogs but whatever
    I substituted I should probably err,
And if I ended up with raccoons every guest would turn out to be
    a raccoonteur.

THE CATERPILLAR

I find among the poems of Schiller
No mention of the caterpillar,
Nor can I find one anywhere
In Petrarch or in Baudelaire,
So here I sit in extra session
To give my personal impression.
The caterpillar, as it's called,
Is often hairy, seldom bald;
It looks as if it never shaves;
When as it walks, it walks in waves;
And from the cradle to the chrysalis
It's utterly speechless, songless, whistleless.

THE CHIPMUNK

My friends all know that I am shy,
But the chipmunk is twice as shy as I.
He moves with flickering indecision
Like stripes across the television.

He's like the shadow of a cloud,
Or Emily Dickinson read aloud.
Yet his ultimate purpose is obvious, very:
To get back to his chipmonastery.

THE PLATYPUS

I like the duck-billed platypus
Because it is anomalous.
I like the way it raises its family.
Partly birdly, partly mammaly.
I like its independent attitude.
Let no one call it a duck-billed platitude.

THE BAT

Myself, I rather like the bat,
It's not a mouse, it's not a rat.
It has no feathers, yet has wings,
It's quite inaudible when it sings.
It zigzags through the evening air
And never lands on ladies' hair,
A fact of which men spend their lives
Attempting to convince their wives.

THE SQUID

What happy appellations these
Of birds and beasts in companies!
A shrewdness of apes, a sloth of bears.
A skulk of foxes, a huske of hares.
An exaltation 'tis of larks,
And possibly a grin of sharks,
But I declare a squirt of squid
I should not like to be amid,
Though bachelors claim that a cloud of sepia
Makes a splendid hiding place in Leap Year.

THE SQUAB

Toward a better world I contribute my modest smidgin;
I eat the squab, lest it become a pigeon.

THE PRAYING MANTIS

From whence arrived the praying mantis?
From outer space, or lost Atlantis?
I glimpse the grim, green metal mug
That masks this pseudo-saintly bug,
Orthopterous, also carnivorous,
And faintly whisper, Lord deliver us.

THE MANATEE

The manatee is harmless
And conspicuously charmless.
Luckily the manatee
Is quite devoid of vanity.

UP FROM THE EGG: THE CONFESSIONS OF A NUTHATCH AVOIDER

Bird watchers top my honors list,
I aimed to be one, but I missed.
Since I'm both myopic and astigmatic,
My aim turned out to be erratic,
And I, bespectacled and binocular,
Exposed myself to comment jocular.
We don't need too much birdlore, do we,
To tell a flamingo from a towhee;
Yet I cannot, and never will,
Unless the silly birds stand still.
And there's no enlightenment so obscure
As ornithological literature.
Is yon strange creature a common chickadee,

Or a migrant *alouette* from Picardy?
You rush to consult your nature guide
And inspect the gallery inside,
But a bird in the open never looks
Like its picture in the birdie books—
Or if it once did, it has changed its plumage,
And plunges you back into ignorant gloomage.
That is why I sit here growing old by inches,
Watching the clock instead of finches,
But I sometimes visualize in my gin
The Audubon that I audubin.

THE SNARK WAS A BOOJUM WAS A PRAWN

A giant new prawn has been dredged up near Santiago, Chile
. . . it is succulent and mysterious. . . . The new prawn has not
been named, a fact that is causing no concern in Chile.—*Times*

Could some descending escalator
Deposit me below the equator,
I'd hunt me a quiet Chilean haunt,
Some Santiago restaurant;
The fact I speak no *Español*
Would handicap me not at all,
Since any language would be aimless
In ordering a tidbit nameless;
I'd simply tie my napkin on
And gesture like a giant prawn,
Then, served the dish for which I yearned,
Proceed to munch it, unconcerned.
Happy crustacean, anonymous prawn,
From distant Latin waters drawn,
Hadst thou in Yankee seas appeared,
Account executives would have cheered,
Vice-presidents in paroxysms
Accorded thee multiple baptisms;
Yea, shouldst thou hit our markets now,
Soon, prawn, wouldst thou be named—and how!
I see the bright ideas drawn:

Prawno, Prawnex, and Vitaprawn;
And, should upper-bracket dreamers wake,
Squab o'Neptune, and Plankton Steak.
Small wonder thou headest for Santiago,
Where gourmets ignore such frantic farrago;
That's exactly where I myself would have went if I'd
Been mysterious, succulent, and unidentified.

THE OSTRICH

The ostrich roams the great Sahara.
Its mouth is wide, its neck is narra.
It has such long and lofty legs,
I'm glad it sits to lay its eggs.

THE SHRIMP

A shrimp who sought his lady shrimp
Could catch no glimpse,
Not even a glimp.
At times, translucence
Is rather a nuisance.

THE EMMET

The emmet is an ant (archaic),
The ant is just a pest (prosaic).
The modern ant, when trod upon,
Exclaims, "I'll be a son-of-a-gun!"
Not so its ancestor, the emmet,
Which perished crying "Zounds!" or "Demmit!"

CAPERCAILLIE, AVE ATQUE VAILLIE

One letter from a long correspondence on the capercaillie in the English magazine *Country Life* is headed "How to Outwit the Capercaillie" and reads, in part: ". . . the cock capercaillie is blind and deaf during the last part of each 'verse' of his love song, the part described by Mr. Richmond as sounding 'like a polar bear splashing into a swimming pool.' . . . Between verses and during the first two parts of them (the 'kek kek kek' and 'whoosh'), however, the cock is most alert. . . ."

Spring, the sweet Spring, is the year's pleasant king;
Then blooms each thing, then maids dance in a ring,
Cold doth not sting, capercaillie then doth sing—
Kek kek kek, whoosh, kek kek kek, whoosh!

Sings he no cuckoo, jug-jug, pu-we, to-witta-woo,
Trills doth he eschew, lark song and tereu,
Hen doth he woo with wild Highland cockadoo—
Kek kek kek, whoosh, kek kek kek, whoosh!

The truant from school doth think to hear a ghoul,
Bee-stung bear in pool, or scold on ducking stool.
Nay, nay, young fool! Here cries a ravished soul—
Kek kek kek, whoosh, kek kek kek, whoosh!

To bird of caution rid, with rival now outbid,
Comes, as to Duncan did, stop't ear and closèd lid,
And archer, slyly hid, transfixes him amid
Kek kek kek, whoosh, and kek kek kek, whoosh.

Farewell, poor cock, which died a laughingstock—
Yet thy pibroch doth lately run amok,
While chicks of strange flock chant, as they roll and rock,
Kek kek kek, whoosh, kek kek kek, whoosh!

THE KIPPER

For half a century, man and nipper,
I've doted on a tasty kipper,
But since I am no Jack the Ripper
I wish the kipper had a zipper.

THE DOG

The truth I do not stretch or shove
When I state the dog is full of love.
I've also proved, by actual test,
A wet dog is the lovingest.

HARK, HARK, THE LARKS DO BARK

Every schoolboy knows a wallaby from a wombat,
But only bright schoolboys know that the lark fight and not the
   dog fight is the most personal form of aerial combat.
Take the duel between those two rivals for the heart of a frivolous
   lady lark who to each had beckoned:
Percy B. Shelley's lark and the lark celebrated in *Sound of Music*
   by Oscar Hammerstein II.
The Shelley lark was from heaven or near it amorously pouring its
   full heart,
And the comments of the Hammerstein lark were jealous and tart.
Its very salutation was pert:
"Hail to thee, whatever thou mayst be, because it's on record that
   bird thou never wert.
Thou wert never even a gnatcatcher or a goatsucker or a godwit or
   yet a skua bird."
And the Shelley lark said, "I am too a bird!"
And the Hammerstein lark said, "I will argue to and fro not,
Shelley himself admits that what thou art we know not.
He said that maybe thou wast a highborn maiden in a palace
   tower, or perhaps a glowworm golden in a bed of dew.
Does that sound like a bird to you?"
And the Shelley lark said, "Shelley says, what says Shelley, let Shel-
   ley say!
What says Oscar Hammerstein II? He says only that you are still
   learning to pray.
A fine claim you have to be famous!
At your age I not only knew all of 'Now I Lay Me,' but also I could
   whistle 'Lead Kindly Light' and 'Venite Adoremus.'"
Here the lady lark, who had been yawning, exclaimed, "Oh, skip it!"
And went off with a tone-deaf pipit.

HIGH, LOW THE COMEDY: A WINTER'S TALE

Ice from the leaking hill glints on the terrace below.
My sunflower seed speckles the crusty snow.
High-perched on the white-topped wall, cardinal aflame,
Like one of Braddock's redcoats, easy game,
Come-kill-me target for all his absurd disguise,
Sun-fielder's sooty smudge around defensive eyes.
Vulnerable is cautious; timid, severe;
He orders mate to alight, prove the coast clear.
Hungry he watches, first pecks no lurking peril reveal.
Down he flutters, drives her off, approaches his meal.
Behind frozen azalea cat crouches, twitches,
Pupil and teacher of a hundred witches,
Here's insolence and ancient arrogance; he's sleek
With confidence, fierce whiskers boasting from each cheek.
Low-bellied he tenses muscles, springs in beauty hateful.
Balefire he fears not, knows not ice to footing fateful.
Cardinal flies away, saved by skidding cat-fall.
I shudder, as watching Lucifer do a pratfall.

COMPLAINT TO THE MANAGEMENT
OF CROSS KEYS

I wish to scotch the rumor that
I am an enemy of the cat.
I guess that no one on this globe
Is less of an ailurophobe,
In spite of which I hate the feline
That for my warblers makes a bee-line,
Whose owner turns it loose to prey
On nuthatch, cardinal, junco, jay,
Whose ancient hunting urge is stirred
By sight of dove and mocking bird,
Who spurns its Puss-in-Boots to speed
To where I've scattered sunflower seed.
Three cats there are which mar the scene
At number 30 Olmstead Green;

One gray, one black, one black and white,
All insolence and appetite.
Like witches at Walpurgis' party
To them "Scat!" simply means "Eat hearty!"
Here cats walk wild, but dogs on leashes.
Are cats a special privileged species?

THE WHALE

Behold the sulphur-bottom whale,
Some 25 yards from nose to tail.
I find it somewhat ludicrous
That whales are mammals, just like us,
And basking where the plankton teems
They dream their sweet cetacean dreams.
One dreaming sulphur-bottom chick
In her Maidenform bra met Moby Dick.

TO A FOOLISH DOG

Joxer, bouncing harlequin,
All ingratiating grin,
Which begat thee, jolly Joxer?
Airedale, poodle, beagle, boxer?
Scottie braw or Irish terrier?
Never mind, the more the merrier;
A pedigree so heterodox
Perks up thy personality, Jox,
For thou, rambunctious residual,
Wert whelped unique and individual,
A blithe buffoon, a jester pampered,
Nor by the Ten Commandments hampered,
(I know thou triflest with the Seventh)
But Joxer, mind the stern Eleventh,
Or learn from choking leash and baffling tether
Thy neighbor's Leghorns thou shalt not de-feather.

THE HYENA

Hyena is the kind of beast
I'd not sit down with to a feast.
He is appetite undiscriminating
And mindless laughter unabating.
Slavering in the plush arena,
The studio audience is mostly hyena.

THE PYTHON

The python has, and I fib no fibs,
318 pairs of ribs.
In stating this I place reliance
On a séance with one who died for science.
This figure is sworn to and attested;
He counted them while being digested.

THE COELACANTH

Consider now the Coelacanth,
Our only living fossil,
Persistent as the amaranth,
And status quo apostle.
It jeers at fish unfossilized
As intellectual snobs elite;
Old Coelacanth, so unrevised
It doesn't know it's obsolete.

THE ELK

Moose makes me think of caribou,
And caribou, of moose,
With, even from their point of view,
Legitimate excuse.
Why then, when I behold an elk,
Can I but think of Lawrence Welk?

TYRANNOSAURUS REX

Tiny tots of either sex
Adore Tyrannosaurus Rex.
Indeed all little ones adore
Any savage carnivore,
Of which, O Rex, thou rightly boastest,
Thou art not only first, but mostest.

What's in a Word?

VERY LIKE A WHALE

One thing that literature would be greatly the better for
Would be a more restricted employment by authors of simile and
  metaphor.
Authors of all races, be they Greeks, Romans, Teutons or Celts,
Can't seem just to say that anything is the thing it is but have to go
  out of their way to say that it is like something else.
What does it mean when we are told
That the Assyrian came down like a wolf on the fold?
In the first place, George Gordon Byron had had enough experience
To know that it probably wasn't just one Assyrian, it was a lot of
  Assyrians.
However, as too many arguments are apt to induce apoplexy and
  thus hinder longevity,
We'll let it pass as one Assyrian for the sake of brevity.
Now then, this particular Assyrian, the one whose cohorts were
  gleaming in purple and gold,
Just what does the poet mean when he says he came down like a
  wolf on the fold?
In heaven and earth more than is dreamed of in our philosophy
  there are a great many things,

But I don't imagine that among them there is a wolf with purple and gold cohorts or purple and gold anythings.

No, no, Lord Byron, before I'll believe that this Assyrian was actually like a wolf I must have some kind of proof;

Did he run on all fours and did he have a hairy tail and a big red mouth and big white teeth and did he say Woof woof?

Frankly I think it very unlikely, and all you were entitled to say, at the very most,

Was that the Assyrian cohorts came down like a lot of Assyrian cohorts about to destroy the Hebrew host.

But that wasn't fancy enough for Lord Byron, oh dear me no, he had to invent a lot of figures of speech and then interpolate them,

With the result that whenever you mention Old Testament soldiers to people they say Oh yes, they're the ones that a lot of wolves dressed up in gold and purple ate them.

That's the kind of thing that's being done all the time by poets, from Homer to Tennyson;

They're always comparing ladies to lilies and veal to venison,

And they always say things like that the snow is a white blanket after a winter storm.

Oh it is, is it all right then, you sleep under a six-inch blanket of snow and I'll sleep under a half-inch blanket of unpoetical blanket material and we'll see which one keeps warm,

And after that maybe you'll begin to comprehend dimly

What I mean by too much metaphor and simile.

AN ENTHUSIAST IS A DEVOTEE IS A ROOTER
OR
MR. HEMINGWAY, MEET MR. STENGEL

Into the Grand Canyon of the Colorado
Drop, my boon companion, the word "aficionado."
Brand me as provincial, hoot me for a jingo,
Hint that I'm an Oedipus to love my mother lingo,
On my reputation cast a nasty shadow,
Adamant you'll find me anent "aficionado."

Never may I languish prey to xenophobia.
Sydney Smith admire I, and Luca della Robbia,
And should Fate transport me into regions foreign
I could wear a chlamys, I could wear a sporran;
Yet, gazing at the Parthenon, strolling through the Prado,
Art lover I might be, but no aficionado.

Monosyllabic Master, whither are we heading,
Since you thrust upon us this verbal featherbedding?
You who freed the language of fetters euphemistic,
You who taught us terseness, muscular and fistic,
You whose prose is soldierly, Spartan and Mohican—
Why employ ten letters to do the job that three can?

This reproachful tribute to a first-class writing man
Comes from no aficionado,
Just
A loyal
Fan.

WHAT IS BIBBIDI-BOBBIDI-BOO IN SANSKRIT?

When people tell me French is difficult, I show my dimple.
French is simple.
My pen is cosmopolitan, not parochial.
I am at home in French either classical or collochial.
I can pronounce *filet mignon* even while chewing it,
And I can and will fluently translate popular songs such as "Everybody's Doing It."
Tout le monde est faisant le, faisant le, fasiant le,
Tout le monde est faisant le,
Faisant quoi?
Dindon pas!
Vois ce ragtime couple débonnaire,
Vois-les jeter leurs épaules en air,
C'est un hibou,
Un hibou, un hibou,
Où?

I think that even Mr. Berlin would agree that this has life and movement,
And that the few changes are an improvement.
That ragtime couple, for example, instead of just being vaguely over there,
They are now obviously in some expensive club, they are debonair.
And the substitution of *c'est un hibou, un hibou, un hibou* (it's an owl, it's an owl, it's an owl) for *c'est un ours, c'est un ours, c'est un ours* (it's a bear, it's a bear, it's a bear)—
That is a veritable *coupe de tonnerre,*
That is a truly superior brand of merchandise,
Because in French *ours* (bear) might be confused with *oursin* (sea urchin) and what would a debonair owl-loving ragtime couple want with a fishy batch of sea-urchindise?
I feel that I have built myself a monument of more than bricks and mortar,
And, having gained the gratitude of Mr. Berlin, I am now leafing through the works of Mr. Oscar Hammerstein and Mr. Cole Porter.

EVERYBODY'S MIND TO ME A KINGDOM IS
OR
A GREAT BIG WONDERFUL WORLD IT'S

Some melodies are popular as well as classical, which I suppose makes them popsicles,
And some poems are part William Cullen Bryant and part Nick Kenny which makes them thanatopsicles,
And to some people Wisconsin is what Guinevere was to Launcelot,
And if they are away from it they are Wisconsolate.
Some naturalists know why the sphinx is sphinxlike and the griffin is griffiny,
And some couples are so wealthy that even their tiffs are from Tiffany.
Some Angeleno socialites fine each other a dollar
If they say La Jolla,
And give each other a Picasso or a Goya

For pronouncing it La Hoya.

Why should not I pick up a masterpiece or a coin?

I will no longer say Des Moines,

I shall sail into the C.B. & Q. ticket office like a swan,

And ask for a lower to Day Mwahn.

This I shall do because I am a conscientious man, when I throw rocks at sea birds I leave no tern unstoned,

I am a meticulous man, and when I portray baboons I leave no stern untoned,

I am a man who values the fitness of things above notoriety and pelf,

Which is why I am happy I heard the cockney postmaster say to a doctor who was returning a leprechaun to Gloccamorra in an open envelope, Physician, seal it thy h'elf.

THIS IS MY OWN, MY NATIVE TONGUE

Often I leave my television set to listen to my wireless,

So, often I hear the same song sung by the same singer many times a day, because at repeating itself the wireless is tireless.

There is one such song from which at sleepy time I can hardly bear to part,

A song in which this particular singer, who apparently has offended a nameless character in an undescribed way, states that he apawlogizes from the bawttom of his heart.

I am familiar with various accents—I know that in Indiana you stress the "r" in Carmen,

And that in Georgia if a ladybug's house is on far she sends for the farman,

And I have paaked my caah in Cambridge, and elsewhere spoken with those who raise hawgs and worship strange gawds—but here I am, late in life's autumn,

Suddenly confronted with somebody's apawlogies and bawttom.

I tell you whawt,

Things were different when I was a tawddling tawt.

I may have been an indifferent schawlar,

Lawling around in my blue serge suit and doodling on my Eton cawllar:

In fact, I didn't even pick up much knowledge

In a year at cawllege;
I guess that of normal intelligence I had only about two thirds,
But, by gum, I was taught, or, by gum, was I tot to pronounce my
  words,
And now they've gawt me wondering:
Was it the dawn or the don that from China cross the bay came up
  thundering?
As a tot, was I tawddling or was I toddling?
When I doodled, was I dawdling or was I dodling?
I have forgawtten all I ever knew of English, I find my position as
  an articulate mammal bewildering and awesome.
Would God I were a tender apple blawssom.

THE CLUB CAR

Come, child, while rambling through the nation
Let's practice our pronunciation.
The liquid confluence here we see
Of r-i-b and a-l-d.
When first potato chips he nibbled,
That gentleman was merely ribald,
But now that he is four-rye-highballed,
We may properly pronounce him ribald.

LET'S NOT PLAY LOTTO, LET'S JUST TALK

If anybody says conversation in our day is as good as it was in Dr.
  Johnson's,
Why, that's a lot of nonsense.
The art of conversation has been lost, or at least mislaid,
And no modern phrase-coiner can think of a fresher word for
  spade than spade.
Take the causerie of the most effervescent coterie,
It sounds like something sworn to before a notary.
Where are yesterday's epigrams, banter and badinage?
All you hear is who behaved scandalously at the club dance and
  how hard it is to get a new car into an old garage.

The maxim, the apothegm, yea, even the aphorism, die like echoes
in the distance,
Overwhelmed by such provocative topics as clothes, beauticians,
taxes and the scarcity of competent domestic assistants.
Come, sprinkle ashes and coffee substitutes upon my head,
I weep for the art of conversation, it is dead.
But wait a minute, the art of conversation is not dead, see it arise,
vigorous, stimulating and untroubled,
Just as you start to play six spades, vulnerable, doubled and
redoubled.

GOOD-BY NOW
OR
PARDON MY GAUNTLET

Bring down the moon for genteel Janet;
She's too refined for this gross planet.
She wears garments and you wear clothes,
You buy stockings, she purchases hose.
She says That is correct, and you say Yes,
And she disrobes and you undress.
Confronted by a mouse or moose,
You turn green, she turns chartroose.
Her speech is new-minted, freshly quarried;
She has a fore-head, you have a forehead.
Nor snake nor slowworm draweth nigh her;
You go to bed, she doth retire.
To Janet, births are blessed events,
And odors that you smell she scents.
Replete she feels, when her food is yummy,
Not in the stomach but the tummy.
If urged some novel step to show,
You say Like this, she says Like so.
Her dear ones don't die, but pass away;
Beneath her formal is lonjeray.
Of refinement she's a fount or fountess,
And that is why she's now a countess.
She was asking for the little girls' room
And a flunky thought she said the earl's room.

WHO'LL BUY MY LINGUAL?
OR
YOU PRONOUNCE PLUIE, LOUIE

I wander through a Paris shower,
Off to inspect a flat *à louer.*

The water pours as from a pitcher
On walls inscribed *Défense d'afficher.*

If I have splashed through such a pond,
I don't remember *ou* or *quand.*

With raindrops glistening on my garment,
I reach my goal, I don't know *comment.*

I ring, I do not wish to trespass,
For trespassing is naughty, *n'est-ce pas?*

The stairway irks my fallen arch,
Because one learns *l'ascenseur ne marche.*

I like the flat; with cheerful mien
I murmur to the man, *"Combien?"*

He mentions his idea of payment,
I say that it's exorbitant, *vraiment—*

Have I misunderstood his statement?
I do not speak the French *parfaitement.*

He mentions a reduced emolument,
I cry that it's a deal, *absolument.*

And now I think a glass of wine
Would not be too unpleasant, *hein?*

OAFISHNESS SELLS GOOD,
LIKE AN ADVERTISEMENT SHOULD

I guess it is farewell to grammatical compunction,
I guess a preposition is the same as a conjunction,
I guess an adjective is the same as an adverb,
And "to parse" is a bad verb.

Blow, blow, thou winter wind,
Thou art not that unkind
Like man's ingratitude to his ancestors who left him the English
   language for an inheritance;
This is a chromium world in which even the Copley Plazas and the
   Blackstones and the Book Cadillacs are simplified into Sheratons.
I guess our ancient speech has gone so flat that we have to spike it;
Like the hart panteth for the water brooks I pant for a revival of
   Shakespeare's *Like You Like It.*
I can see the tense draftees relax and purr
When the sergeant barks, "Like you were."
—And don't try to tell me that our well has been defiled by immi-
   gration;
Like goes Madison Avenue, like so goes the nation.

DO YOU PLAN TO SPEAK BANTU?
OR
ABBREVIATION IS THE THIEF OF SANITY

The merchant, as crafty a man is he
As Haughton or Stagg or Zuppke;
He sells his wares by the broad turnpike,
Or, as some would have it, tpke.

The merchant offers us merchandise
Frozen or tinned or sudsy,
And the way that he spells his merchandise,
I have to pronounce it mdse.

Twixt the wholesale price and the retail price
The merchant doth daily hustle,
His mdse he sells at the retail price,
But he buys his mdse whsle.

Let us purchase some whsle mdse, love,
And a shop will we set up
Where the turnpike runs through the township, love,
Where the tpke runs through the twp.

And you shall be as precious, love,
As a mermaidsk from Murmansk,

And I will tend the customers, love,
In a suit with two pr. pantsk.

CHACUN À SON BERLITZ

French is easy.
At speaking French I am the champ of the Champs Elysee,
And since I can speak Parisian without a flaw,
I will tell you why the crows, or les corbeaux, always win their bat-
tle against the scarecrows: it's on account of their esprit de caw.

SHALL WE DANCE?
BEING THE CONFESSIONS OF
A BALLETRAMUS—II

I learned my French by working hard
At listening to Hildegarde.
That's why a word like *"entrechat"*
Is something *je ne comprends pas.*
Is it a stage direction that
Calls for the advent of a cat?
Assume a comma in the center:
Does *"entre, chat"* bid cat to enter?
Let's start again. Does *"entre"* mean
"Among," or possibly "between"?
I find I cannot swallow that;
How do you get between one cat?
Let's forget the tiresome *entrechat*
And watch a *danse du ventrechat.*

LAMENTS FOR A DYING LANGUAGE—III

In the nice-minded Department of Prunes and Prisms,
It's I for you
And euphemisms.
Hence the phrase I would eagerly jettison:
"Senior citizen."

Shall we retranslate
Joel 2:28?
To the sociologist squeamish
The words "Your old men shall dream dreams" are less than
beamish,
So "Your senior citizens shall dream dreams" it shall henceforth
be,
Along with Hemingway's "The Senior Citizen and the Sea."
I, though no Joel, prophecy that someday while the senior citizens
are projecting the image of an age-adjusted social group,
The old men will rise up and knock them for a loop.

LAMENTS FOR A DYING LANGUAGE—IV

Those authors I can never love
Who write, "It fit him like a glove."
Though baseballs may be hit, not "hitted,"
The past of "fit" is always "fitted."
The sole exception worth a *haricot*
Is "Joshua fit de battle ob Jericho."

A MINT OF PHRASES
OR
A TEAM IS AS STRONG AS ITS BENCH

Consider how Time's vasty corridors
Ring with the words of famous orators!
Demosthenes and Billy Graham,
Jeremiah and maybe Nahum,
Patrick Henry and Cicero,
Daniel Webster and Mirabeau,
Burke and William Jennings Bryan,
Pitt the Elder's gifted scion,
The Gracchi, Danton and Disraeli,
Cato fulminating daily,
And other men with names less metric
Who altered history by their rhetoric,

Were their apothegms spontaneous,
Off the cuff, extemporaneous,
Or, soaking in the tub or shaving,
Did they think a thought worth saving,
Roll it on their tongues and smile,
And store it in their future file?
Not even Churchill, without notes,
Could stand and coin such golden quotes
Had he not learned in early days
To hoard each fleeting happy phrase,
And draw on, as he faced the throng,
A bank of jewels five words long.
Eloquence bleeds and weeps and sweats;
Also, eloquence never forgets.

UNTITLED

The tongues of the people are fashioned
On the wheel of an all-wise potter—
Where the natives say "wotter" for "water"
The water tastes like wotter.

THE SAD CASE OF THE EXPATRIATE SOCIALITE
OR
IT'S NEVER IN THE PHRASE BOOK

Once there was a Manhattan socialite named Stella Maris,
And her French was formidable in Manhattan but not in Paris,
Manhattan headwaiters responded to her French with suavity to
    spare.
Not so in *La Ville Lumière.*
At her socially impeccable school she had passed her college
    boards and had read Corneille and Molière,
But in Paris even her request for a glass of water was answered by
    a humiliating stare.
Should she offer a taxi driver a cigarette with a halting *Voulez-
vous fumer* he understands her at once, but should she then ask

to be taken to the Boulevarde Haussmann or even the Champs
    Elysées,
Why he is as stonily uncomprehending as a rock fan listening to
    Les Pêcheurs de Perles by Alexandre César Léopold Bizet.
She grows more and more like Burns's mouse, timid, cowerin' and
    sleekit;
Her schooling has taught her everything about French except how
    to speak it.
What boots her now her term paper on Racine?
When in need of a stimulant she can't remember whether to ask
    for *un fine* or *une fine*.
You'll be glad to know that she has now recognized the problem
    of gender and in a state of mild but permanent inebriety has
    learned to dwell with it;
These days she orders *deux fines,* and the hell with it.
There is a precedent for her action set by Madame de Rambouillet,
Who, I have been told, always demanded a double Drambuie.

ONE MAN'S OPIATE

In the *Affendämmerung*, or twilight of the apes,
What is more fitting than that man should for reassurance turn to
    japes?
In chaos sublunary
What remains but constant buffoonery?
I know of a man named Daniel Deronda
And of buffoonery he is a veritable Golconda.
Once he was sipping a *fine* in a café in Montmartre,
When a man sat down at his table who wanted to discuss Sartre.
Daniel didn't wish to discuss Sartre, whose works filled him with
    ennui;
He told himself, "Dan, we can't put up with ennui, can we?"
So he said, "Frappe, frappe," and the man said, "Qui va là?" and
    he said, "Alençon," and the man said, "Alençon qui?"
And Daniel said, "Alençonfants de la patrie."
The Sartre man, himself a lacemaker, was so taken aback that in-
    stead of exclaiming, "Ma fwah!" ("My faith!"), il s'écria, "Mon
    fwah!" which every goose knows means "My liver!"

And then he threw himself into the Seine, a river.
I'm all for Daniel: In this age penumbrel,
Let the timbrel resound in the tumbrel.

WHAT DO YOU WANT, A MEANINGFUL DIALOGUE OR A SATISFACTORY TALK?

Bad money drives out good.
That's Gresham's law, which I have not until recently understood.
No economist I, to economics I have an incurable allergy,
But now I understand Gresham's law through obvious analogy.
Just as bad money drives the good beyond our reach,
So has the jargon of the hippie, the huckster and the bureaucrat debased the sterling of our once lucid speech.
What's worse, it has induced the amnesia by which I am faced;
I can't recall the original phraseology which the jargon has replaced.
Would that I had the memory of a computer or an elephant!
What used I to say instead of uptight, clout, and thrust, and relevant?
Linguistics becomes an ever eerier area, like I feel like I'm in Oz,
Just trying to tell it like it was.

To Your Health

OH TO BE ODD!

Hypochondriacs
Spend the winter at the bottom of Florida and the summer on top
    of the Adirondriacs.
You go to Paris and live on champagne wine and cognac
If you're a dipsomognac.
If you're a manic-depressive
You don't go anywhere where you won't be cheered up, and peo-
    ple say "There, there!" if your bills are excessive.
But you stick around and work day and night and night and day
    with your nose to the sawmill,
If you're nawmill.

WINTER COMPLAINT

I

Now when *I* have a cold
I am careful with my cold,
I consult my physician
And I do as I am told.

I muffle up my torso
In woolly, woolly garb,
And I quaff great flagons
Of sodium bicarb.
I munch on aspirin,
I lunch on water,
And I wouldn't dream of osculating
Anybody's daughter,
And to anybody's son
I wouldn't say howdy,
For I am a sufferer
Magna cum laude.
I don't like germs,
But I'll keep the germs I've got.
Will I take a chance of spreading them?
Definitely not.
I sneeze out the window
And I cough up the flue,
And I live like a hermit
Till the germs get through.
And because I'm considerate,
Because I'm wary,
I am treated by my friends
Like Typhoid Mary.

II
Now when *you* have a cold
You are careless with your cold,
You are cocky as a gangster
Who has just been paroled.
You ignore your physician,
You eat steaks and oxtails,
You stuff yourself with starches,
You drink a lot of cocktails,
And you claim that gargling
Is of time a waste,
And you won't take soda
For you don't like the taste,
And you prowl around parties

Full of selfish bliss,
And you greet your hostess
With a genial kiss.
You convert yourself
Into a deadly missile,
You exhale Hello's
Like a steamboat whistle.
You sneeze in the subway
And you cough at dances,
And let everybody else
Take their own good chances.
You're a bronchial boor,
A bacterial blighter;
And you get more invitations
Than a gossip writer.

Yes, your throat is froggy,
And your eyes are swimmy,
And your hand is clammy,
And your nose is brimmy,
But you woo my girls
And their hearts you jimmy
While I sit here
With the cold you gimmy.

THE GERM

A mighty creature is the germ,
Though smaller than the pachyderm.
His customary dwelling place
Is deep within the human race.
His childish pride he often pleases
By giving people strange diseases.
Do you, my poppet, feel infirm?
You probably contain a germ.

I'M TERRIBLY SORRY FOR YOU,
BUT I CAN'T HELP LAUGHING

Everybody has a perfect right to do what they please,
But one thing that I advise everybody not to do is to contract a
    laughable disease.
People speak of you respectfully if you catch bubonic,
And if you get typhus they think you have done something posi-
    tively mastodonic;
One touch of leprosy makes the whole world your kin,
And even a slight concussion earns you an anxious inquiry and not
    a leering grin.
Yes, as long as people are pretty sure you have something you are
    going to be removed by,
Why they are very sympathetic, and books and flowers and visits
    and letters are what their sympathy is proved by.
But unfortunately there are other afflictions anatomical,
And people insist on thinking that a lot of them are comical,
And if you are afflicted with this kind of affliction people are
    amused and disdainful,
Because they are not bright enough to realize that an affliction can
    be ludicrous and still be ominous and painful.
Suppose for instance you have a dreadful attack of jaundice, what
    do they do?
They come around and smile and say Well, well, how are you to-
    day, Dr. Fu-Manchu?
The early martyrs thought they knew what it was to be taken over
    the jumps,
But no martyr really ought to get his diploma until he has under-
    gone his friends' witticisms during his mumps.
When you have laryngitis they rejoice,
Because apparently the funniest thing in the world is when you
    can't curse and swear at them for laughing at your lost voice,
    because you have lost your voice.
And as for boils,
Well, my pen recoils.
So I advise you, at the risk of being pedantic,
If you must be sick, by all means choose a sickness that is prefer-
    ably fatal and certainly romantic,

Because it is much better to have that kind of sickness and be sick
    unto death or anyway half to death,
Than to have the other kind and be laughed to death.

THE COMMON COLD

Go hang yourself, you old M.D.!
You shall no longer sneer at me.
Pick up your hat and stethoscope,
Go wash your mouth with laundry soap;
I contemplate a joy exquisite
In never paying you for your visit.
I did not call you to be told
My malady is a common cold.

By pounding brow and swollen lip;
By fever's hot and scaly grip;
By these two red redundant eyes
That weep like woeful April skies;
By racking snuffle, snort, and sniff;
By handkerchief after handkerchief;
This cold you wave away as naught
Is the damnedest cold man ever caught.

Give ear, you scientific fossil!
Here is the genuine Cold Colossal;
The Cold of which researchers dream,
The Perfect Cold, the Cold Supreme.
This honored system humbly holds
The Supercold to end all colds;
The Cold Crusading to end Democracy;
The Führer of the Streptococcracy.

Bacilli swarm within my portals
Such as were ne'er conceived by mortals,
But bred by scientists wise and hoary
In some Olympian laboratory;
Bacteria as large as mice,
With feet of fire and heads of ice,

Who never interrupt for slumber
Their stamping elephantine rumba.

A common cold, forsooth, gadzooks!
Then Venus showed promise of good looks;
Don Juan was a budding gallant,
And Shakespeare's plays show signs of talent;
The Arctic winter is rather coolish,
And your diagnosis is fairly foolish.
Oh what derision history holds
For the man who belittled the Cold of Colds!

THIS IS GOING TO HURT JUST A LITTLE BIT

One thing I like less than most things is sitting in a dentist chair
    with my mouth wide open,
And that I will never have to do it again is a hope that I am against
    hope hopen.
Because some tortures are physical and some are mental,
But the one that is both is dental.
It is hard to be self-possessed
With your jaw digging into your chest,
So hard to retain your calm
When your fingernails are making serious alterations in your life
    line or love line or some other important line in your palm;
So hard to give your usual effect of cheery benignity
When you know your position is one of the two or three in life
    most lacking in dignity,
And your mouth is like a section of road that is being worked on,
And it is all cluttered up with stone crushers and concrete mixers
    and drills and steam rollers and there isn't a nerve in your head
    that you aren't being irked on.
Oh, some people are unfortunate enough to be strung up by thumbs,
And others have things done to their gums,
And your teeth are supposed to be being polished,
But you have reason to believe they are being demolished,
And the circumstance that adds most to your terror
Is that it's all done with a mirror,

Because the dentist may be a bear, or as the Romans used to say, only they were referring to a feminine bear when they said it, an *ursa*,

But all the same how can you be sure when he takes his crowbar in one hand and mirror in the other he won't get mixed up, the way you do when you try to tie a bow tie with the aid of a mirror, and forget that left is right and *vice versa*?

And then at last he says That will be all; but it isn't because he then coats your mouth from cellar to roof

With something that I suspect is generally used to put a shine on a horse's hoof,

And you totter to your feet and think, Well it's all over now and after all it was only this once,

And he says come back in three monce.

And this, O Fate, is I think the most vicious circle that thou ever sentest,

That Man has to go continually to the dentist to keep his teeth in good condition when the chief reason he wants his teeth in good condition is so that he won't have to go to the dentist.

COMPLAINT TO FOUR ANGELS

Every night at sleepy-time
Into bed I gladly climb.
Every night anew I hope
That with the covers I can cope.

Adjust the blanket fore and aft.
Swallow next a soothing draught;
Then a page of Scott or Cooper
May induce a healthful stupor.

Oh the soft luxurious darkness,
Fit for Morgan, or for Harkness!
Traffic dies along the street.
The light is out. So are your feet.

Adjust the blanket aft and fore,
Sigh, and settle down once more.

Behold, a breeze! The curtains puff.
One blanket isn't quite enough.

Yawn and rise and seek your slippers,
Which, by now, are cold as kippers.
Yawn, and stretch, and prod yourself,
And fetch a blanket from the shelf.

And so to bed again, again,
Cozy under blankets twain.
Welcome warmth and sweet nirvana
Till eight o'clock or so mañana.

You sleep as deep as Keats or Bacon;
Then you dream and toss and waken.
Where is the breeze? There isn't any.
Two blankets, boy, are one too many.

O stilly night, why are you not
Consistent in your cold and hot?
O slumber's chains, unlocked so oft
With blankets being donned or doffed!

The angels who should guard my bed
I fear are slumbering instead.
O angels, please resume your hovering;
I'll sleep, and you adjust the covering.

WHEN THE DEVIL WAS SICK, COULD HE PROVE IT?

Few things are duller
Than feeling unspecifically off-color,
Yes, you feel like the fulfillment of a dismal prophecy,
And you don't feel either exercisey or officey,
But still you can't produce a red throat or a white tongue or uneasy respiration or any kind of a symptom,
And it is very embarrassing that whoever was supposed to be passing out the symptoms skymptom,
Because whatever is the matter with you, you can't spot it

But whatever it is, you've got it,

But the question is how to prove it,

And you suck for hours on the thermometer you finally sent out
for and you can't move it,

And your entire system may be pneumococci'd or streptococci'd,

But the looks you get from your loved ones are simply skeptococci'd,

So you unfinger your pulse before Conscience can jeer at you for
a compulsive fingerer,

And you begin to believe that perhaps your loved ones are right,
perhaps you are nothing but a hypochondriacal old malingerer,

And you take a farewell look at the thermometer, and it's as good
as a tonic,

Because you've got as pretty a ninety-nine point one as you'd wish
to see in a month of bubonic.

Some people hold out for a hundred or more before they collapse

But that leaves too many gaps;

As for me,

I can get a very smug Monday, Tuesday, Wednesday, Thursday, or
Friday in bed out of a tenth of a degree.

It is to this trait that I am debtor

For the happy fact that on weekends I generally feel better.

A BULLETIN HAS JUST COME IN

The rabbit's dreamy eyes grow dreamier
As he quietly gives you tularemia.

The parrot clashes his hooked proboscis
And laughs while handing you psittacosis.

In every swamp or wooded area
Mosquito witches brew malaria.

We risk at every jolly picnic
Spotted fever from a tick nick.

People perish of bubonic;
To rats, it's better than a tonic.

The hog converted into pork
Puts trichinosis on your fork.

The dog today that guards your babies
Tomorrow turns and gives them rabies.

The baby, once all milk and spittle,
Grows to a Hitler, and boy, can he hittle!

That's our planet, and we're stuck with it.
I wish its inheritors the best of luck with it.

ALLERGY IN A COUNTRY CHURCHYARD

Once there was a man named Mr. Weaver,
And he had a lot of hay but he didn't have any hay fever,
So he ran an advertisement which he wanted to charge, but for
     which he was compelled to pay,
And he advertised that he would like to meet up with somebody
     who had a lot of hay fever but didn't have any hay,
So along came a man and he said he had seen his ad in the paper,
And was the proposition serious or merely a prankish caper,
And Mr. Weaver said it was as serious as the dickens,
Because to his mind hay fever was to the human race what bum-
     blefoot, limber neck and edema of the wattles were to chickens,
And he said he was the most modest of men,
But never having had hay fever he felt very irked at being outex-
     perienced by any passing bumblefooted hen,
And the man said I can describe hay fever for you so you'll know
     all about it but first how much are you prepared to pay?
And Mr. Weaver said, "Can I charge it?" and the man said No, so
     Mr. Weaver said he would give him all his hay,
So the man said All right and threw pepper in Mr. Weaver's eyes,
And Mr. Weaver said, "What are you doing?" and the man said
     "Never mind, just kindly answer the following questions with
     the correct replies,
What's the kind of nut you put back in the dish at cocktail parties,"
     and Mr. Weaver said "A cashew," and the man said "Gesund-
     heit. What material do politicians say their opponents' lies are

composed of?" and Mr. Weaver said "The whole cloth," and the man said "No no try again," and Mr. Weaver said "A tissue," and the man said "Geshundheit. What's a filmy collar often worn by women?" and Mr. Weaver said "A fichu," and the man said "Gesundheit. Now you know all about hay fever,"
So he went off with Mr. Weaver's hay, but first he telephoned an old schoolmate in Vancouver and charged the call to Mr. Weaver.

SAMSON AGONISTES

I test my bath before I sit,
And I'm always moved to wonderment
That what chills the finger not a bit
Is so frigid upon the fundament.

VISITORS LAUGH AT LOCKSMITHS
OR
HOSPITAL DOORS HAVEN'T GOT LOCKS ANYHOW

Something I should like to know is, which would everybody rather not do:
Be well and visit an unwell friend in the hospital, or be unwell in the hospital and have a well friend visit you?
Take the sight of a visitor trying to entertain a patient or a patient trying to entertain a visitor,
It would bring joy to the heart of the Grand Inquisitor.
The patient either is too ailing to talk or is panting to get back to the chapter where the elderly spinster is just about to reveal to the Inspector that she now thinks she can identify the second voice in that doom-drenched quarrel,
And the visitor either has never had anything to say to the patient anyway or is wondering how soon it would be all right to depart for Belmont or Santa Anita or Laurel,
And besides, even if both parties have ordinarily much to discuss and are far from conversational mediocrities,
Why, the austere hygienic surroundings and the lack of ashtrays would stunt a dialogue between Madam de Staël and Socrates,

And besides, even if anybody did get to chatting glitteringly and
    gaudily,
They would soon be interrupted by the arrival of a nurse or an or-
    derly,
It is a fact that I must chronicle with distress
That the repartee reaches its climax when the visitor finally spots
    the handle on the foot of the bed and cranks the patient's knees
    up and down and says That certainly is ingenious, and the pa-
    tient answers Yes.
How many times a day do I finger my pulse and display my tongue
    to the mirror while waiting for the decision to jell:
Whether to ignore my host of disquieting symptoms and have to
    spend my days visiting friends who have surrendered to theirs,
    or to surrender to my own and spend my days being visited by
    friends who are thereby being punished for being well.

WHAT TO DO UNTIL THE DOCTOR GOES
OR
IT'S TOMORROW THAN YOU THINK

Oh hand me down my old cigar with its Havana wrapper and its
    filling of cubeb,
Fill the little brown jug with bismuth and paregoric, and the pot-
    tle and cannikin with soda and rhubeb,
Lend me a ninety-nine piece orchestra tutored by Koussevitsky,
I don't want the ownership of it, I just want the usevitsky,
Bring me a firkin of Arkansas orators to sing me oratorios,
Remove these calf-clad Spenglers and Prousts and replace them
    with paper-covered Wodehouses and Gaboriaus,
Wrap up and return these secretarial prunes and prisms,
Let me have about me bosoms without isms.
Life and I are not convivial,
Life is real, life is earnest, while I only think I am real, and know
    I am trivial.
In this imponderable world I lose no opportunity
To ponder on picayunity.
I would spend either a round amount or a flat amount
To know either a puma is only tantamount to a catamount or para-
    mount to a catamount,

It is honey in my cup,
When I read of a sprinter sprinting the hundred in ten seconds flat,
    to think: Golly, suppose he stood up!
No, I am not delirious, just aglow with incandescence;
This must be convalescence.

COUSIN EUPHEMIA KNOWS BEST
OR
PHYSICIAN, HEAL SOMEBODY ELSE

Some people don't want to be doctors because they think doctors
    have to work too hard to make a living,
And get called away from their bed at night and from their dinner
    on Christmas and Thanksgiving.
These considerations do not influence me one particle;
I do not want to be a doctor simply because somewhere in the fam-
    ily of every patient is a female who has read an article.
You remove a youngster's tonsils and the result is a triumph of
    medical and surgical science,
He stops coughing and sniffling and gains eleven pounds and gets
    elected captain of the Junior Giants,
But his great-aunt spreads the word that you are a quack,
Because she read an article in the paper last Sunday where some
    Romanian savant stated that tonsillectomy is a thing of the
    past and the Balkan hospitals are bulging with people standing
    in line to have their tonsils put back.
You suggest calamine lotion for the baby's prickly heat,
And you are at once relegated to the back seat,
Because its grandmother's cousin has seen an article in the "House-
    hold Hints" department of *Winning Parcheesi* that says the
    only remedy for prickly heat is homogenized streptomycin,
And somebody's sister-in-law has seen an article where the pathol-
    ogist of *Better Houses and Trailers* says calamine lotion is out,
    a conscientious medicine man wouldn't apply calamine lotion
    to an itching bison.
I once read an unwritten article by a doctor saying there is only
    one cure for a patient's female relative who has read an article
A hatpin in the left ventricle of the hearticle.

THE OLD DR.'S VALENTINE
TO HIS ONLY MILLIONAIRE

I remember the shape you were in when you went
From the ambulance into the oxygen tent.
Your kidneys were clogged, your liver was leather,
I took you apart, then put you together.
I hear that today you're a Trabert at tennis,
A Hogan at golf, and an amorous menace.
There's only one effort too great for you still—
To pick up your pen, and pay my bill.

OLD DR. VALENTINE
TO HIS SON

Your hopeless patients will live,
Your healthy patients will die.
I have only this word to give:
Wonder, and find out why.

PEEKABOO, I ALMOST SEE YOU

Middle-aged life is merry, and I love to lead it,
But there comes a day when your eyes are all right but your arm
    isn't long enough to hold the telephone book where you can
    read it,
And your friends get jocular, so you go to the oculist,
And of all your friends he is the joculist,
So over his facetiousness let us skim,
Only noting that he has been waiting for you ever since you said
    Good evening to his grandfather clock under the impression
    that it was him,
And you look at his chart and it says SHRDLU QWERTYOP, and you
    say Well, why SHRDNTLU QWERTYOP? And he says one set of
    glasses won't do.
You need two,
One for reading Erle Stanley Gardner's Perry Mason and Keats's
    "Endymion" with,

And the other for walking around without saying Hello to strange
   wymion with.
So you spend your time taking off your seeing glasses to put on
   your reading glasses, and then remembering that your reading
   glasses are upstairs or in the car,
And then you can't find your seeing glasses again because without
   them on you can't see where they are.
Enough of such mishaps, they would try the patience of an ox,
I prefer to forget both pairs of glasses and pass my declining years
   saluting strange women and grandfather clocks.

AND HOW KEEN WAS THE VISION
OF SIR LAUNFAL?

Man's earliest pastime, I suppose,
Was to play with his fingers and his toes,
Then later, wearying of himself,
He devised the monster and the elf.
Enlivening his existence drab
With Blunderbore and Puck and Mab.
A modern man, in modern Maryland,
I boast my private gate to fairyland,
My kaleidoscope, my cornucopia,
My own philosopher's stone, myopia.
Except when rationalized by lenses,
My world is not what other men's is;
Unless I have my glasses on,
The postman is a leprechaun,
I can wish on either of two new moons,
Billboards are graven with mystic runes,
Shirts hung to dry are ragtag gypsies,
Mud puddles loom like Mississipsies,
And billiard balls resemble plums,
And street lamps are chrysanthemums.
If my vision were twenty-twenty,
I should miss miracles aplenty.

WHAT, NO SHEEP?

WHAT, NO SHEEP? These are a few of the 600 prod-
ucts sold in the "sleep shop" of a New York depart-
ment store.

—From an advertisement of the
Consolidated Edison Company in the *Times*

I don't need no sleepin' medicine—
I seen a ad by old Con Edison.
Now when I lay me on my mattress
You kin hear me snore from hell to Hatteras,
With muh Sleep Record,
Muh Vaporizer,
Muh Electric Slippers,
Muh Yawn Plaque,
Muh Slumber Buzzer,
Muh miniature Electric Organ,
An' muh wonderful Electric Blanket.

My old woman couldn't eat her hominy—
Too wore out from the durned insominy.
She give insominy quite a larrupin',
Sleeps like a hibernatin' tarrapin,
With her Eye Shade,
Her Clock-Radio,
Her Sinus Mask,
Her Massagin' Pillow,
Her Snore Ball,
Her miniature Electric Organ,
An' her wonderful Electric Blanket.

Evenin's when the sunlight westers
I pity muh pioneer an-cestors.
They rode the wilderness wide and high,
But how did they ever go sleepy-bye
Without their Eye Shade,
Their Clock-Radio,
Their Sleep Record,
Their Vaporizer,
Their Sinus Mask,

Their Electric Slippers,
Their Yawn Plaque,
Their Slumber Buzzer,
Their Massagin' Pillow,
Their Snore Ball,
Their miniature Electric Organ,
An' their wonderful Electric Blanket?

CAN I GET YOU A GLASS OF WATER?
OR
PLEASE CLOSE THE GLOTTIS AFTER YOU

One trouble with a cough,
It never quite comes off.
Just when you think you're through coughing
There's another cough in the offing.
Like the steps of a moving stair
There is always another cough there.
When you think you are through with the spasm
And will plunge into sleep like a chasm,
All of a sudden, quickly,
Your throat gets tickly.
What is this thing called a cough
That never quite comes off?
Well, the dictionary says it's an expulsion of air from the lungs
with violent effort and noise produced by abrupt opening of
the glottis,
To which I can only reply, Glottis—shmottis!
Not that I reject the glottis theory, indeed I pride myself on the
artistry
Of my glottistry,
But there is a simpler definition with which I freely present you:
A cough is something that you yourself can't help, but everybody
else does on purpose just to torment you.

UNTITLED

Enter, breath;
Breath, slip out;
Blood, be channeled,
And wind about.
O, blessèd breath and blood which strive
To keep this body of mine alive!
O gallant breath and blood
Which choose
To wage the battle
They must lose!

UNTITLED

What's the diagnosis?
Mononucleosis?
Influenza Asian?
Contusion or abrasion?
Bronch- or laryngitis?
Hiccups, hepatitis?
Perhaps a fractured tibia?
A bug picked up in Libya?
Demanding treatment surgical,
Or patently allergical?
Whatever be his ailment,
The patient needs regalement,
He's perishing of ennui;
We can't allow that, can we?
Where can we find a medium
To dissipate his tedium?
Why, here it is—BED RIDDANCE!
What a happy co-in-cid-ence!

P.S.
Every epidemic offers
Bullion for the florists' coffers.

*(Verse requested from Nash by Little,
Brown for the publisher's letter to book-
sellers on* Bed Riddance.*)*

The Thirteenth Floor

OLD MEN II

This is the city
Beyond the wood,
These are streets
The old man paces,
These are the crowds
That pass him by
This is the mist
That veils their faces,
These are the eyes
That do not include him,
These are the voices
He cannot hear.
These are the children
Who people the city.
This is the old man—
And this is fear!

(Editor's Note: While this poem is actually untitled and previously unpublished, Nash wrote it as a follow-up to his poem *Old Men*; consequently I have given it the title of *Old Men II*.)

THE PARTY

Come Arabella, fetch the cake,
On a dish with silver handles.
Oh mercy! Feel the table shake!
Lucinda, light the candles.

For Mr. Migg is thir-ty,
Is thir–ty,
Is thir—ty.
The years are crawling over him
Like wee red ants.
Oh, three times ten is thir-ty,
Is for–ty,
Is fif—ty.
The further off from England
The nearer is to France.

The little flames they bob and jig,
The dining hall is breezy.
Quick! puff your candles, Mr. Migg,
The little flames die easy.
For Mr. Migg is fort-ty,
Is for–ty,
Is for—ty.
The years are crawling over him
Like wee red ants.
Oh, four times ten is for-ty,
Is fif–ty,
Is six—ty,
And creeping through the icing,
The other years advance.

Why Arabella, here's a ring!
Lucinda, here a thimble!
For Mr. Migg there's not a thing—
'Tis not, I trust, a symbol!

For Mr. Migg is fif-ty,
Is fif–ty,

Is fif—ty.
The years are crawling over him
Like wee red ants.

Oh, five times ten is fif-ty,
Is six–ty,
Is seven—ty.
Lucinda, put the cake away,
We're going to the dance.

UNTITLED

The eyes are lovely
And the hair,
Gold as sunset
And light as air.
The oval line of cheek and chin—
Perfect! The mouth
A shade too thin.
Of course he'd not
See that at first,
Not till he
Had slaked his thirst.
But he should have looked
Where my gaze lingers—
The throat! The throat!
Foredoomed to fingers.

TIME MARCHES ON

You ask me, brothers, why I flinch.
Well, I will tell you, inch by inch.
Is it not proper cause for fright
That what is day will soon be night?
Evenings I flinch the selfsame way,
For what is night will soon be day.
At five o'clock it chills my gore
Simply to know it isn't four.

How Sunday into Monday melts!
And every month is something else.
If Summer on the ladder lingers,
Autumn tramples upon her fingers,
Fleeing before the jostling train
Of Winter, and Spring, and Summer again.
Year swallows year and licks its lips,
Then down the gullet of next year slips.
We chip at Time with clocks and watches;
We flee him in love and double scotches;
Even as we scatter in alarm
He marches with us, arm in arm;
Though while we sleep, he forward rides,
Yet when we wake, he's at our sides.
Let men walk straight or let them err,
He never leaves them as they were.
While ladies draw their stockings on
The ladies they were are up and gone.
I pen my lines, I finish, I scan them,
I'm not the poet who began them.
Each moment Time, the lord of changers,
Stuffs our skins with ephemeral strangers.
Good heavens, how remote from me
The billion people I used to be!
Flinch with me, brothers, why not flinch,
Shirts caught in the eternal winch?
Come, let us flinch till Time stands still;
Although I do not think he will.
Hark brothers, to the dismal proof:
The seconds spattering on the roof!

UNDER THE FLOOR

Everybody knows how the waters come down at Lodore,
But what about voices coming up through the floor?
Oh yes, every time that into a task you set your teeth
Something starts talking in the room underneath,
And no matter how many authorities you quiz,

You can never find out who or what it is;
You know one thing about it and nothing more,
That it is just something that goes around making noises that come
   up through the floor.
Sometimes it sings the Indian Love Call and sometimes it sings,
   Lead, Kindly Light, by Cardinal Newman,
But even then it doesn't sound human,
And sometimes it just gobbles,
And the sound wibbles and wobbles,
And sometimes it snarls like a ghoul interrupted at its unholy feast,
And sometimes it just mutters like blood going down the drain of
   a tub after a murderer has finished dismembering the deceased;
It cackles, it crackles, it drones, it buzzes, it chortles,
It utters words but in no tongue spoken by mortals,
Yes, its language is a mystery forevermore,
The language of whatever it is that makes the noise that comes up
   through the floor,
And you shiver and quiver and wonder,
What's under?
Is it banshees or goblins or leprechauns, or trolls or something?
Or pixies or vampires or lost souls or something?
What is it below?
Better not, better not know.
Don't let it upset you,
But also don't overlook the possibility that someday whatever it is
   tha makes the noises that come up through the floor may come
   up through the floor and get you.

LISTEN . . .

There is a knocking in the skull,
An endless silent shout
Of something beating on a wall,
And crying, Let me out.

That solitary prisoner
Will never hear reply,
No comrade in eternity
Can hear the frantic cry.

No heart can share the terror
That haunts his monstrous dark;
The light that filters through the chinks
No other eye can mark.

When flesh is linked with eager flesh,
And words run warm and full,
I think that he is loneliest then,
The captive in the skull.

Caught in a mesh of living veins,
In cell of padded bone,
He loneliest is when he pretends
That he is not alone.

We'd free the incarcerate race of man
That such a doom endures
Could only you unlock my skull,
Or I creep into yours.

THE SCREEN WITH THE FACE
WITH THE VOICE

How long
Is a song?
O Lord,
How long?
A second?
A minute?
An hour?
A day?
A decade?
A cycle of Cathay?
Press the ears
With occlusive fingers;
The whining melody
Lingers, lingers;
The mouthing face
Will not be hid,
But leers at the eye

From the inner lid.
With the sure advance of ultimate doom
The moaning adenoids larger loom;
The seven-foot eyebrows fall and rise
In roguish rapture or sad surprise;
Eyeballs roll with fine emotion,
Like buoys rocked by a treacle ocean;
Tugged like the bell above the chapel,
Tosses the giant Adam's apple;
Oozes the voice from the magic screen,
A slow Niagara of Grenadine;
A frenzy of ripe orgiastic pain,
Niagara gurgling down a drain.
How long
Is a song?
O Lord,
How long?
As long as Loew,
And Keith
And Albee;
It Was,
And Is,
And Always Shall Be.
This is the string Time may not sever,
This is the music that lasts forever,
This is the Womb,
This is the Tomb,
This is Alpha, Omega, and Oom!
The eyes, the eyes shall follow you!
The throat, the throat shall swallow you!
Hygienic teeth shall wolf you!
And viscous voice engulf you!
The lolloping tongue itself answer your question!
The Adam's Apple dance at your ingestion!
And you shall never die, but live to nourish the bowels
Of deathless celluloid vowels.

ANY MILLENNIUMS TODAY, LADY?

As I was wandering down the street
With nothing in my head,
A sign in a window spoke to me
And this is what it said:

"Are your pillows a pain in the neck?
Are they lumpy, hard, or torn?
Are they full of old influenza germs?
Are the feathers thin and forlorn?
Bring 'em to us,
We do the trick;
Re-puff,
Replenish,
Re-curl,
Re-tick,
We return your pillows, spanned-and-spicked,
Re-puffed, replenished, re-curled, re-ticked."

As I was wandering down the street
With too much in my head,
The sign became a burning bush,
And this is what it said:

"Is the world a pain in the neck
Is it lumpy, hard, or torn?
Is it full of evil ancestral germs
That were old before you were born?
Bring it to us,
We do the trick;
Re-puff,
Replenish,
Re-curl,
Re-tick,
In twenty-four hours we return the world
Re-puffed, replenished, re-ticked, re-curled."

As I was wandering down the street
I heard the trumpets clearly,
But when I faced the sign again

It spoke of pillows merely.
The world remains a derelict,
Unpuffed, unplenished, uncurled, unticked.

THE WENDIGO*

The Wendigo,
The Wendigo!
Its eyes are ice and indigo!
Its blood is rank and yellowish!
Its voice is hoarse and bellowish!
Its tentacles are slithery,
And scummy,
Slimy,
Leathery!
Its lips are hungry blubbery,
And smacky,
Sucky,
Rubbery!
The Wendigo,
The Wendigo!
I saw it just a friend ago!
Last night it lurked in Canada;
Tonight, on your veranada!
As you are lolling hammockwise
It contemplates you stomachwise.
You loll,
It contemplates,
It lollops.
The rest is merely gulps and gollops.

*Wendigo: In the mythology of the north-
ern Algonquians, an evil spirit; one of a fab-
ulous tribe of cannibals.
     —Webster's unabridged dictionary

TWEEDLEDEE AND TWEEDLEDOOM

Said the Undertaker to the Overtaker,
Thank you for the butcher and the candlestick-maker,
For the polo player and the pretzel-baker,
For the lawyer and the lover and the wife-forsaker,
Thank you for my bulging, verdant acre,
Said the Undertaker to the Overtaker.
Move in, move under, said the Overtaker.

THE BUSES HEADED FOR SCRANTON

The buses headed for Scranton travel in pairs,
The lead bus in the bolder,
With the taut appearance of one who greatly dares;
The driver glances constantly over his shoulder.

The buses headed for Scranton are sturdy craft,
Heavy-chested and chunky;
They have ample vision sideways and fore and aft;
The passengers brave, the pilots artful and spunky.

Children creep hand in hand up gloomy stairs;
The buses headed for Scranton travel in pairs.

They tell of a bus that headed for Scranton alone;
It dwindled into the West.
It was later found near a gasoline pump—moss-grown,
Deserted, abandoned, like the *Mary Celeste.*

Valises snuggled trimly upon the racks,
Lunches in tidy packets,
Twelve *Daily Newses* in neat, pathetic stacks.
Thermoses, Chiclets, and books with paper jackets.

Some say the travelers saw the Wendigo,
Or were eaten by bears.
I know not the horrid answer, I only know
That the buses headed for Scranton travel in pairs.

HOW MANY MILES TO BABYLON?

How many miles to Babylon?
Love-in-a-mist and Bovril.
Are there more Sitwells than one?
Oh yes, there are Sacheverell.

THE BARGAIN

As I was going to St. Ives
I met a man with seven lives;
Seven lives,
In seven sacks,
Like seven beeves
On seven racks.
These seven lives
He offered to sell,
But which was best
He couldn't tell.
He swore that with any
I'd be happy forever;
I bought all seven
And thought I was clever,
But his parting words
I can't forget:
Forever
Isn't over yet.

A TALE OF THE THIRTEENTH FLOOR

The hands of the clock were reaching high
In an old midtown hotel;
I name no name, but its sordid fame
Is table talk in hell.
I name no name, but hell's own flame
Illumes the lobby garish,
A gilded snare just off Times Square
For the maidens of the parish.

The revolving door swept the grimy floor
Like a crinoline grotesque,
And a lowly bum from an ancient slum
Crept furtively past the desk.
His footsteps sift into the lift
As a knife in the sheath is slipped,
Stealthy and swift into the lift
As a vampire into a crypt.

Old Maxie, the elevator boy,
Was reading an ode by Shelley,
But he dropped the ode as it were a toad
When the gun jammed into his belly.
There came a whisper as soft as mud
In the bed of an old canal:
"Take me up to the suite of Pinball Pete,
The rat who betrayed my gal."

The lift doth rise with groans and sighs
Like a duchess for the waltz,
Then in middle shaft, like a duchess daft,
It changes its mind and halts.
The bum bites lip as the landlocked ship
Doth neither fall nor rise,
But Maxie the elevator boy
Regards him with burning eyes.
"First, to explore the thirteenth floor,"
Says Maxie, "would be wise."

Quoth the bum, "There is moss on your double cross,
I have been this way before,
I have cased the joint at every point,
And there is no thirteenth floor.
The architect he skipped direct
From twelve unto fourteen,
There is twelve below and fourteen above,
And nothing in between,
For the vermin who dwell in this hotel
Could never abide thirteen."

Said Max, "Thirteen, that floor obscene,
Is hidden from human sight;
But once a year it doth appear,
On this Walpurgis Night.
Ere you peril your soul in murderer's role,
Heed those who sinned of yore;
The path they trod led away from God,
And onto the thirteenth floor,
Where those they slew, a grisly crew,
Reproach them forevermore."

"We are higher than twelve and below fourteen,"
Said Maxie to the bum,
"And the sickening draft that taints the shaft
Is a whiff of kingdom come.
The sickening draft that taints the shaft
Blows through the devil's door!"
And he squashed the latch like a fungus patch,
And revealed the thirteenth floor.

It was cheap cigars like lurid scars
That glowed in the rancid gloom,
The murk was a-boil with fusel oil
And the reek of stale perfume.
And round and round there dragged and wound
A loathsome conga chain,
The square and the hep in slow lock step,
The slayer and the slain.
(For the souls of the victims ascend on high,
But their bodies below remain.)

The clean souls fly to their home in the sky,
But their bodies remain below
To pursue the Cain who each has slain
And harry him to and fro.
When life is extinct each corpse is linked
To its gibbering murderer,
As a chicken is bound with wire around
The neck of a killer cur.

Handcuffed to Hate come Doctor Waite
(*He* tastes the poison now),
And Ruth and Judd and a head of blood
With horns upon its brow.
Up sashays Nan with her feathery fan
From *Floradora* bright;
She never hung for Caesar Young
But she's dancing with him tonight.

Here's the bulging hip and the foam-flecked lip
Of the mad dog, Vincent Coll,
And over there that ill-met pair,
Becker and Rosenthal,
Here's Legs and Dutch and a dozen such
Of braggart bullies and brutes,
And each one bends 'neath the weight of friends
Who are wearing concrete suits.

Now the damned make way for the double-damned
Who emerge with shuffling pace
From the nightmare zone of persons unknown,
With neither name nor face.
And poor Dot King to one doth cling,
Joined in a ghastly jig,
While Elwell doth jape at a goblin shape
And tickle it with his wig.

See Rothstein pass like breath on a glass,
The original Black Sox kid;
He riffles the pack, riding piggyback
On the killer whose name he hid.
And smeared like brine on a slavering swine,
Starr Faithful, once so fair,
Drawn from the sea to her debauchee,
With the salt sand in her hair.

And still they come, and from the bum
The icy sweat doth spray;
His white lips scream as in a dream,
"For God's sake, let's away!

If ever I meet with Pinball Pete
I will not seek his gore,
Lest a treadmill grim I must trudge with him
On the hideous thirteenth floor."

"For you I rejoice," said Maxie's voice,
"And I bid you go in peace,
But I am late for a dancing date
That nevermore will cease.
So remember, friend, as your way you wend,
That it would have happened to you,
But *I* turned the heat on Pinball Pete;
You see—*I* had a daughter, too!"

The bum reached out and he tried to shout,
But the door in his face was slammed,
And silent as stone he rode down alone
From the floor of the double-damned.

THE ABOMINABLE SNOWMAN

I've never seen an abominable snowman,
I'm hoping not to see one,
I'm also hoping, if I do,
That it will be a wee one.

THE BIRTHDAY THAT NEVER WAS:
A FEBRUARY FANTASY

Washington, eighteen sixty-eight.
The night was cold, and the hour was late.
The dark Potomac, smooth as ice,
Mirrored the moon so you saw it twice—
But for once the moon was vanity-proof
And turned its face to the White House roof
Where the chimney smoke rose thin and slow
And told of a cherry-red hearth below.

The President lolled as much at ease
As ever he could, because of his knees
(Like his wrists and elbows, awkward points;
He seemed a creature composed of joints),
One hand ruffling his rebel hair,
And an arm along the arm of the chair;
Tranquility his again, and mirth,
But he was the tiredest man on earth.

He raised his bearded chin from his breast
And thoughtfully spoke to the waiting guest:
I reckon you're stumped, Mr. Edwin Booth,
As to why you're here, so I'll tell the truth.

Your Brutus tonight had me overawed,
I was listening for Shakespeare to applaud;
But it's not to hang laurels on your brow,
Which must have more than enough by now;
The uncomplimentary fact remains
That I've taken a notion to pick your brains.
I've had reports from politicians,
And ladies returning from earnest missions;
I know there are carpet-bagging cheaters
And unreconstructible ember-eaters,
Extremists ranting upon the scene—
But what of the millions in between?
You're just back from a tour of the South,
Give it me straight from the horse's mouth. . . .

Everywhere, sir, one tale to tell:
Below the Potomac all is well.

What of the wounds from the battle field?

A few still healing, but most are healed.
Thanks to a generous heart and hand
There is hope again in a stricken land.
They may be short of marble and gilding,
But with what they've got they are building.
You have proved that the Gray can blend with the Blue,

And bitterness fades like the summer dew.
A Southern lady, so help me Hannah,
Has married a Yankee in Savannah,
And if I may clinch my humble opinion,
There's talk that Texas approves the Union.

You bring, said the President, standing up,
Oil for my head and a brimming cup.
And thanks again for tonight's performance;
You made Brutus the noblest of murdering varmints.
—I'm a curious man who loves a sequel;
When will the stage present your equal?

Today there would be a finer and other,
John Wilkes Booth, my beloved brother;
But the yellow fever closed that door,
He died in Richmond in sixty-four.
But I talk too much when old memories stir;
Mr. Lincoln, a happy birthday, sir!

THE MIRACULOUS COUNTDOWN

Let me tell you of Dr. Faustus Foster.
Chloë was lost, but he was loster.
He was what the world for so long has missed,
A truly incompetent scientist.
His morals were good and his person cleanly,
He had skied at Peckett's and rowed at Henley.
The only liquor that touched his lips
He drew through pipettes with filter tips.
He could also recite, in his modest manner,
The second verse of the Star-Spangled Banner.
Yet, to his faults we must not be blinded;
He was ineluctably woolly-minded.
When his further deficiencies up are summed,
He was butter fingered and margarine thumbed.
You'd revoke the license of any rhymer
Who ranked him with Teller and Oppenheimer.
It took him, and here your belief I beg,

Twenty minutes to boil a three-minute egg,
Which will give you a hint as to what went on
Whenever he touched a cyclotron.
There wasn't a problem he feared to face,
From smashing atoms to conquering space,
And, should one of his theories expire,
He had other ions in the fire,
Even walking to work to save his carfare
For tackling bacteriological warfare.
For years he went to no end of bother
To explode this planet or reach another.
A more ambitious, industrious savant
You may have encountered; I know I haven't.
One Christmas Eve he was tired and irked,
He had shot the works and nothing worked.
"I'd sell my soul," he cried to the night,
"To have one experiment come out right."
No sooner said than his startled eyes
Saw a ghostly stranger materialize,
Who, refraining from legalistic jargon,
Announced, "You have got yourself a bargain.
Here's a pact with iron-clad guarantees;
Sign here, in the usual fluid, please."
Faustus disdained to quibble or linger,
He merely remarked, as he pricked his finger,
"It had better be good, your *quid pro quo*;
My blood is especially fine type O."
(Always in character, come what may
He was down in his doctor's records as A.)
A snicker was heard from the stranger weird,
Then he snatched the parchment and disappeared.
Faustus was filled with wild surmise
And roseate dreams of the Nobel prize,
Now certain to drop in his lap with awful ease,
He thought, with the aid of Mephistopheles.
Behold him now in his laboratory,
A modern Merlin, hell-bent for glory.
With a flourish worthy of the Lunts

He triggered every project at once.
Intercontinental ballistic missiles
Blasted the air with roars and whistles,
Rockets punctured the midnight clear,
And the atmosphere and the stratosphere.
Before the human eye could absorb it
A giant satellite entered orbit.
With the germ's equivalent of a howl
The bacteria issued forth to prowl.
Faustus shouted with joy hysterical,
And was then struck dumb as he watched a miracle.
He gazed aghast at his handiwork
As every experiment went berserk.
The bacteria, freed from their mother mold,
Settled down to cure the common cold.
Distant islanders sang Hosanna
As nuclear fall-out turned to manna.
Rockets, missiles, and satellite
Formed a flaming legend across the night.
From Cape Canaveral clear to the Isthmus
The monsters spelled out Merry Christmas,
Penitent monsters whose fiery breath
Was rich with hope instead of death.
Faustus, the clumsiest of men,
Had butter-fingered a job again.
I've told you his head was far from level;
He thought he had sold his soul to the devil,
When he'd really sold it, for heaven's sake,
To his guardian angel by mistake.
When geniuses all in every nation
Hasten us towards obliteration,
Perhaps it will take the dolts and geese
To drag us backward into peace.

THE SOLITARY HUNTSMAN

The solitary huntsman
No coat of pink doth wear,
But midnight black from cap to spur
Upon his midnight mare.
He drones a tuneless jingle
In lieu of tally-ho,
"I'll catch a fox
And put him in a box
And never let him go."

The solitary huntsman,
He follows silent hounds,
No horn proclaims his joyless sport,
And never a hoofbeat sounds.
His hundred hounds, his thousands,
Their master's will they know;
To catch a fox
And put him in a box
And never let him go.

For all the fox's doubling
They track him to his den.
The chase may fill a morning,
Of threescore years and ten.
The huntsman never sated
Screaks to his saddlebow,
"I'll catch another fox
And put him in a box
And never let him go."

NOTES FOR THE CHART IN 306

The bubbles soar and die in the sterile bottle
Hanging upside down on the bedside lamppost.
Food and drink
Seep quietly through the needle strapped to the hand.
The arm welcomes the sting of the mosquito hypodermic—

Conveyor of morphia, the comforter.
Here's drowsiness, here's lassitude, here's nothingness,
Sedation *in excelsis*.
The clouded mind would stray into oblivion
But for the grackle-squawk of the box in the hall,
The insistent call for a faceless goblin horde
Of sorcerers, vivisectionists, body-snatchers.
Dr. Polyp is summoned,
Dr. Gobbo and Dr. Prodigy,
Dr. Tortoise, Dr. Sawdust, and Dr. Mary Poppins,
La belle dame sans merci.
Now it's Dr. Bandarlog and Dr. Bacteria,
And last of all, the terrifying one,
Dodger Thomas.
And there is no lock on the door.
On the third day, the goblins are driven off
To the operating room beneath the hill.
Dr. Vandeleur routs gibbering Bandarlog,
Bacteria flees before swarthy Dr. Bagderian,
Sawdust and Polyp yield to Saunders and Pollitt,
And its Porter instead of Tortoise who knocks at the door.
He will test the blood, not drain it.
The eerie imposters are gone, all gone but one—
Dodger Thomas.
I know he is lurking somewhere in a shadow.
Dodger Thomas.
I've never met him, but old friends have.
I know his habit:
He enters without knocking.

A DREAM OF INNOCENT ORGIES
OR
THE MOST UNFORGETTABLE CHARACTERS
I NEVER MET

I'm glad I wasn't ever a Clyde or a Bonnie,
But I'm sorry I wasn't a stage-door Johnny.
I'd love to have driven down the Gay White Way
In a hansom cab with a big bouquet
To share a bottle and a Chicken Kiev
With a Mitzi Hajos or a Fritzi Scheff
Or a Trixie Friganza—
To squire such dames as,
Glittering names as,
Mitzi Hajos,
Fritzi Scheff,
Or Trixie Friganza.

Had I been born just a little bit earlier,
When ladies of the chorus were voluptuously girlier,
I'm sure I could have fostered in a manner deft
A brotherly acquaintance with the second from the left.
But I'd rather have waited for a real bonanza
Like a Fritzi Scheff or a Trixie Friganza
Or a Mitzi Hajos—
To spend my patrimony
Skirting matrimony
With a Fritzi Scheff,
A Mitzi Hajos,
Or a Trixie Friganza.

I'd have overtipped the doormen underneath the canopies
Of elegant cafés from Rector's to Bustanoby's.
They'd warn me when a menace appeared on the premises—
Say, a gentleman name of Harry Thaw or lady name of Nemesis.
When I heard the chimes at midnight with a Mitzi Hajos,
My conduct would have been I hope outrajos . . .
Through all my salad days,
Mardi Gras gala days,
With a Mitzi Hajos,

A Fritzi Scheff,
Or a Trixie Friganza.

Had I only been twenty instead of ten
I'd have been a legend in Manhattan then,
But temptation was thwarted by the simple truth:
I was just too young to misspend my youth
With a Fritzi Scheff,
A Mitzi Hajos,
A Trixie Friganza,
Or even a Floradora girl.

This American Life:
Behind the Scenes

LINES INDITED WITH ALL THE
DEPRAVITY OF POVERTY

One way to be very happy is to be very rich
For then you can buy orchids by quire and bacon by the flitch.
And yet at the same time
People don't mind if you only tip them a dime.
Because it's very funny
But somehow if you're rich enough you can get away with spend-
ing water like money
While if you're not rich you can spend in one evening your salary
for the year
And everybody will just stand around and jeer.
If you are rich you don't have to think twice about buying a judge
or a horse,
Or a lower instead of an upper, or a new suit, or a divorce,
And you never have to say When,
And you can sleep every morning until nine or ten,
All of which
Explains why I should like very, very much to be very, very rich.

INVOCATION

("Smoot Plans Tariff Ban on Improper Books"—
News item)

Senator Smoot (Republican, Ut.)
Is planning a ban on smut.
Oh root-ti-toot for Smoot of Ut.
And his reverent occiput.
Smite, Smoot, smite for Ut.,
Grit your molars and do your dut.,
Gird up your l—ns,
Smite h–p and th–gh,
We'll all be Utah
By and by.

Smite, Smoot, for the Watch and Ward,
For Hiram Johnson and Henry Ford,
For Bishop Cannon and John D., Junior,
For Governor Pinchot of Pennsylvania,
For John S. Sumner and Elder Hays
And possibly Edward D. Bernays,
For Orville Poland and Ella Boole,
For Mother Machree and the Shelton pool.
When smut's to be smitten
Smoot will smite
For G–d, for country,
And Fahrenheit.

Senator Smoot is an institute
Not to be bribed with pelf;
He guards our homes from erotic tomes
By reading them all himself.
Smite, Smoot, smite for Ut.,
They're smuggling smut from Balt. to Butte!
Strongest and sternest
Of your s–x
Scatter the scoundrels
From Can. to Mex.!

Smite, Smoot, for Smedley Butler,
For any good man by the name of Cutler,

Smite for the W.C.T.U.,
For Rockne's team and for Leader's crew,
For Florence Coolidge and Admiral Byrd,
For Billy Sunday and John D., Third,
For Grantland Rice and for Albie Booth,
For the Woman's Auxiliary of Duluth,
Smite, Smoot,
Be rugged and rough,
Smut if smitten
Is front-page stuff.

PEEKABOO, I SEE A RED

The results of the patriotic activities of the D.A.R. might not be so
    minus
Were the ladies not troubled by sinus.
Alas, every time they try to put people who don't agree with them
    on the stand as defendants
They find themselves troubled by the sinus of the Declaration of
    Independence.

THE PULPITEERS HAVE HAIRY EARS

There are too many people who think that just because they have
    parishes or dioceses
It imparts infallibility to all their biaseses.
Just give them a pulpit or two under their belts and they become
    very zealous
In forcing their opinions of everything onto everybody ealous.
I wonder why it is that so many clerics
Must be perpetually in hysterics.
It's odd, but at any hint of gaiety
On the part of the laity
Their furies and rages
Fill pages and pages and pages.
When the American girl was first by Mr. Ziegfeld glorified
They were all violently horrified
And they gave vent to loud jeremiads

Over Mr. White's amorous, clamorous dryads
And I hate to think what would happen if they should get a glimpse
Of one of Mr. Carroll's charming undraped nimpse.
Yet I am sure none of those lovely girls has done anyone any harm,
For who is any the worse for a view of a shapely artistic feminine leg or arm?
Also the clerics are very apt to become bitter at my, and bitter at your
Ideas of what is or is not proper in current literature.
Their speech is luxuriant
With words such as lewd, lascivious, obscene and prurient
(So much so that I often wonder if Mr. John S. Sumner
Is not one of the pulpit's alumner.)
Don't they know that such a loud, nasty noise
Just puts ideas into the heads of little girls and boys?
Neither do clerics like prize fighting, cock fighting, bull fighting or any other kind of fighting
Unless it is a war, in which case they urge people to go out and do a lot of smiting.
In fact the world is so full of a number of amusing things
That twenty-five percent of its ministers seem to be as unhappy as ex-kings
The other seventy-five percent are very nice
But I wish we could dispose of the remainder in a trice
For I think that they are nothing but pulpiteers
And for them I give the opposite of three cheers.

REFLECTION ON THE DEPRESSION— WHAT'S A DEPRESSION?

It's comforting to be assured by Washington that your dollar will buy much more
Than ever before,
But unfortunate that trying to make this year's 99 cents do the work of last year's dollar
Is like trying to get a 16 neck into a 15 collar.

LOVE UNDER THE REPUBLICANS
(OR DEMOCRATS)

Come live with me and be my love
And we will all the pleasures prove
Of a marriage conducted with economy
In the Twentieth Century Anno Donomy.
We'll live in a dear little walk-up flat
With practically room to swing a cat
And a potted cactus to give it hauteur
And a bathtub equipped with dark brown water.
We'll eat, without undue discouragement,
Foods low in cost but high in nouragement
And quaff with pleasure, while chatting wittily,
The peculiar wine of Little Italy.
We'll remind each other it's smart to be thrifty
And buy our clothes for something-fifty.
We'll stand in line on holidays
For seats at unpopular matinees
And every Sunday we'll have a lark
And take a walk in Central Park.
And one of these days not too remote
I'll probably up and cut your throat.

BIRTH COMES TO THE ARCHBISHOP

Ministers
Don't like bar sinisters.
They consider that sort of irregularity
As the height of vulgarity
And go around making remarks
About the need for patrolling the beaches and parks.
They hate to see any deadlock
Between sin and wedlock
And get very nervous
When people omit the marriage service.
They regard as villains
Owners of unauthorized chillains,

A point of view
Which of course doesn't embarrass me or you
But makes things very inconvenient
For many really quite nice girls who may have been just a bit
    lenient.

So although none of us is in danger
Of the arrival of an inexplicable little stranger
Still I think we ought to join with a lot of others
And wish the best of luck to the nation's unmarried mothers.

MONEY IS EVERYTHING

Better a parvenu
Living luxuriously on Park Arvenu
Than a Schuyler or a Van Rensselaer
Living inexpensselaer.

THE TERRIBLE PEOPLE

People who have what they want are very fond of telling people
    who haven't what they want that they really don't want it.
And I wish I could afford to gather all such people into a gloomy
    castle on the Danube and hire half a dozen capable Draculas to
    haunt it.
I don't mind their having a lot of money, and I don't care how they
    employ it,
But I do think that they damn well ought to admit they enjoy it.
But no, they insist on being stealthy
About the pleasures of being wealthy,
And the possession of a handsome annuity
Makes them think that to say how hard it is to make both ends
    meet is their bounden duity.
You cannot conceive of an occasion
Which will find them without some suitable evasion.
Yes indeed, with arguments they are very fecund;
Their first point is that money isn't everything, and that they have
    no money anyhow is their second.

Some people's money is merited,
And other people's is inherited,
But wherever it comes from,
They talk about it as if it were something you got pink gums from.
Perhaps indeed the possession of wealth is constantly distressing,
But I should be quite willing to assume every curse of wealth if I
could at the same time assume every blessing.
The only incurable troubles of the rich are the troubles that money
can't cure,
Which is a kind of trouble that is even more troublesome if you are
poor.
Certainly there are lots of things in life that money won't buy, but
it's very funny—
Have you ever tried to buy them without money?

THE BEGGAR
(AFTER WILLIAM BLAKE)

Beggar, beggar, burning low
In the city's trodden snow,
What immortal hand or eye
Could frame thy dread asymmetry?

In what distant deep of lies
Died the fire of thine eyes?
What the mind that planned the shame?
What the hand dare quench the flame?

And what shoulder and what art
Could rend the sinews of thy heart?
And when thy heart began to fail,
What soft excuse, what easy tale?

What the hammer? What the chain?
What the furnace dulled thy brain?
What the anvil? What the blow
Dare to forge this deadly woe?

When the business cycle ends
In flaming extra dividends,

Will He smile his work to see?
Did He who made the Ford make thee?

DON'T SELL AMERICA SHORT

London Bridge is falling down—
But stocks are going up!
Hunger shuffles through the town—
But stocks are going up!
Tell the farmer in the dell,
Tell the striker in the cell,
Zero hour and all is well—
Stocks are going up!

Sorry, boy, to let you out—
But stocks are going up!
Hear the happy brokers shout
Stocks are going up!
Coffee, buddy? There's the line.
Smile with Doctor Julius Klein.
What's October, 'twenty-nine?
Stocks are going up!

We are wiser now than then—
But stocks are going up!
Never touch the stuff again—
But stocks are going up!
Just a nip to start the day,
And one to drive the blues away—
O.K.! America, O.K.!
Stocks are going up!

YES AND NO

Oh would I were a politician,
Or else a person with a mission.
Heavens, how happy I could be
If only I were sure of me.

How would I strut, could I believe
That, out of all the sons of Eve,
God had granted this former youth
A binding option on His truth.

One side of the moon we've seen alone;
The other she has never shown.
What dreamless sleep, what sound digestion,
Were it the same with every question!

Sometimes with secret pride I sigh
To think how tolerant am I;
Then wonder which is really mine;
Tolerance, or a rubber spine?

ELECTION DAY IS A HOLIDAY

People on whom I do not bother to dote
Are people who do not bother to vote.
Heaven forbid that they should ever be exempt
From contumely, obloquy and various kinds of contempt.
Some of them like Toscanini and some like Rudy Vallee,
But all of them take about as much interest in their right to ballot
    as their right to ballet.
They haven't voted since the heyday of Miss Russell (Lillian)
And excuse themselves by saying What's the difference of one vote
    in fifty million?
They have such refined and delicate palates
That they can discover no one worthy of their ballots,
And then when someone terrible gets elected
They say, There, that's just what I expected!
And they go around for four years spouting discontented criticisms
And contented witticisms,
And then when somebody to oppose the man they oppose gets
    nominated
They say Oh golly golly he's the kind of man I've always abomi-
    nated,
And they have discovered that if you don't take time out to go to
    the polls

You can manage very nicely to get through thirty-six holes.
Oh let us cover these clever people very conspicuously with loathing,
For they are un-citizens in citizens' clothing.
They attempt to justify their negligence
On the grounds that no candidate appeals to people of their in-
tegligence,
But I am quite sure that if Abraham Lincoln (Rep.) ran against
Thomas Jefferson (Dem.)
Neither man would be appealing enough to squeeze a vote out of
them.

THE VERY UNCLUBBABLE MAN

I observe, as I hold my lonely course,
That nothing exists without a source.
Thus, oaks from acorns, lions from cubs,
And health and wealth from the proper clubs.
There are yacht clubs, golf clubs, clubs for luncheon,
Clubs for flowing bowl and puncheon,
Clubs for dancing, clubs for gambling,
Clubs for sociable Sunday ambling,
Clubs for imbibing literature,
And clubs for keeping the cinema pure,
Clubs for friendship, clubs for snobbery,
Clubs for smooth political jobbery.
As civilization onward reels,
It's clubs that grease the speeding wheels.

Alas!

Oh, everybody belongs to something,
But I don't belong to anything;
No, I don't belong to anything, any more than the miller of Dee,
And everything seems to belong
To people who belong to something,
But I don't belong to anything,
So nothing belongs to me.

Racquet, Knickerbocker, Union League,
Shriners parading without fatigue,

Oddfellows, Red Men, Woodmen of the World,
Solvent Moose and Elks dew-pearled,
Tammany tigers, Temperance doves,
Groups of various hates and loves,
Success is the thing they all have an air of,
Theirs are the summonses taken care of,
Theirs are the incomes but not the taxes,
Theirs are the sharpest, best-ground axes;
Millions of members of millions of bands,
Greeting fellow members with helping hands;
Good fellows all in incorporated hordes,
Prosperity is what they are moving towards.

Alas!

Oh, everybody belongs to something,
But I don't belong to anything;
Yes, I belong to nothing at all, from Kiwanis to the R.F.C.,
And everything definitely belongs
To people who belong to lots of things,
But I don't belong to anything,
So nothing belongs to me.

MA, WHAT'S A BANKER?
OR
HUSH, MY CHILD

The North wind doth blow,
And we shall have snow,
And what will the banker do then, poor thing?
Will he go to the barn
To keep himself warm.
And hide his head under his wing?
Is he on the spot, poor thing, poor thing?
Probably not, poor thing.

For when he is good,
He is not very good,
And when he is bad he is horrider,
And the chances are fair

He is taking the air
Beside a cabaña in Florida.
But the wailing investor, mean thing, mean thing,
Disturbs his siesta, poor thing.

He will plunge in the pool,
But he makes it a rule
To plunge with his kith and his kin,
And whisper about
That it's time to get out
When the widows and orphans get in.
He only got out, poor thing, poor thing,
Yet they call him a tout, poor thing.

His heart simply melts
For everyone else;
By love and compassion he's ridden;
The pay of his clerks
To reduce, how it irks!
But he couldn't go South if he didden.
I'm glad there's a drink within reach, poor thing,
As he weeps on the beach, poor thing.

May he someday find peace
In a temple in Greece,
Where the government harbors no rancor;
May Athens and Sparta
Play host to the martyr,
And purchase a bond from the banker.
With the banker in Greece, poor thing, poor thing,
We can cling to our fleece, Hot Cha!

GOODY FOR OUR SIDE AND YOUR SIDE TOO

Foreigners are people somewhere else,
Natives are people at home;
If the place you're at is your habitat,
You're a foreigner, say in Rome.
But the scales of Justice balance true,

And tit only leads to tat,
So the man who's at home when he stays in Rome
Is abroad when he's where you're at.

When we leave the limits of the land in which
Our birth certificates sat us,
It does not mean just a change of scene,
But also a change of status.
The Frenchman with his fetching beard,
The Scot with his kilt and sporran,
One moment he may a native be,
And the next may find him foreign.

There's many a difference quickly found
Between the different races,
But the only essential differential
Is living in different places.
Yet such is the pride of prideful man,
From Austrians to Australians,
That wherever he is, he regards as his,
And the natives there, as aliens.

Oh, I'll be friends if you'll be friends,
The foreigner tells the native,
And we'll work together for our common ends
Like a preposition and a dative.
If our common ends seem mostly mine,
Why not, you ignorant foreigner?
And the native replies, contrariwise,
And hence, my dears, the coroner.

So mind your manners when a native, please,
And doubly when you're not
And Vickers and Krupp will soon fold up,
And Sopwith pawn his yacht.
One simple thought, if you have it pat,
Will eliminate the coroner:
You may be a native in your habitat,
But to foreigners you're just a foreigner.

I YIELD TO MY LEARNED BROTHER
OR
IS THERE A CANDLESTICK MAKER
IN THE HOUSE?

The doctor gets you when you're born,
The preacher, when you marry,
And the lawyer lurks with costly clerks
If too much on you carry.
Professional men, they have no cares;
Whatever happens, they get theirs.

You can't say When
To professional men,
For it's always When to they;
They go out and golf
With the big bad wolf
In the most familiar way.
Hard times for them contain no terrors;
Their income springs from human errors.

The noblest lord is ushered in
By the practicing physician,
And the humblest lout is ushered out
By a certified mortician.
And in between, they find their foyers
Alive with summonses from lawyers.

Oh, would my parents long ago
Had memorized this motto!
For then might I, their offspring, buy
A Rolls or an Isotto.
But now I fear I never can,
For I am no professional man.

You can't say When
To professional men,
For it's always When to they;
They were doing fine
In '29,
And they're doing fine today.

One beacon doth their paths illumine,
To wit: To err is always humine.

ONE FROM ONE LEAVES TWO

Higgledy piggledy, my black hen,
She lays eggs for gentlemen.
Gentlemen come every day
To count what my black hen doth lay.
If perchance she lays too many,
They fine my hen a pretty penny;
If perchance she fails to lay,
The gentlemen a bonus pay.

Mumbledy pumbledy, my red cow,
She's cooperating now.
At first she didn't understand
That milk production must be planned;
She didn't understand at first
She either had to plan or burst,
But now the government reports
She's giving pints instead of quarts.

Fiddle de dee, my next-door neighbors,
They are giggling at their labors.
First they plant the tiny seed,
Then they water, then they weed,
Then they hoe and prune and lop,
Then they raise a record crop,
Then they laugh their sides asunder,
And plow the whole caboodle under.

Abracadabra, thus we learn
The more you create, the less you earn.
The less you earn, the more you're given,
The less you lead, the more you're driven,
The more destroyed, the more they feed,
The more you pay, the more they need,
The more you earn, the less you keep,
And now I lay me down to sleep.

I pray the Lord my soul to take
If the tax-collector hasn't got it before I wake.

LET ME BUY THIS ONE

Solomon said, Stay me with apples for I am sick with l'amour,
But I say, Comfort me with flagons, for I am sick with rich people
    talking and acting poor.
I have never yet met even a minor Croesus
Whose pocketbook didn't have paresis;
I have never yet been out with a tycoon for an evening in Man-
    hattan's glamorous canyons
When the evening's bills weren't paid by the tycoon's impoverished
    but proud companions.
There is one fact of life that no unwealthy child can learn too soon,
Which is that no tycoon ever spends money except on another ty-
    coon.
Rich people are people that you owe something to and take out to
    dinner and the theater and dancing and all the other expensive
    things there are because you know they are accustomed to the
    best and as a result you spend the following month on your up-
    pers,
And it is a big evening to you but just another evening to them and
    they return the hospitality by saying that someday you must
    drop in to one of their cold Sunday suppers.
Rich people are also people who spend most of their time com-
    plaining about the income tax as one of life's greatest and most
    intolerable crosses,
And eventually you find that they haven't even paid any income tax
    since 1929 because their income has shrunk to fifty thousand
    dollars a year and everything has been charged off to losses,
And your own income isn't income at all, it is salary, and stops com-
    ing in as soon as you stop laboring mentally and manually,
But you have been writing out checks for the Government annu-
    ally,
So the tax situation is just the same as the entertainment situation
    because the poor take their little pittance

And pay for the rich's admittance

Because it is a great truth that as soon as people have enough
coupons in the safe-deposit vault or in the cookie jar on the shelf,

Why they don't have to pay anything themself,

No, they can and do just take all their coins and store them,

And other people beg to pay for everything for them,

And they certainly are allowed to,

Because to accept favors is the main thing that the poor are and the
rich aren't too proud to,

So let us counterattack with sangfroid and phlegm,

And I propose a Twenty-second Amendment to the Constitution
providing that the rich must spend as much money on us poor
as we do on them.

BANKERS ARE JUST LIKE ANYBODY ELSE,
EXCEPT RICHER

This is a song to celebrate banks,

Because they are full of money and you go into them and all you
hear is clinks and clanks,

Or maybe a sound like the wind in the trees on the hills,

Which is the rustling of the thousand dollar bills.

Most bankers dwell in marble halls,

Which they get to dwell in because they encourage deposits and
discourage withdralls,

And particularly because they all observe one rule which woe be-
tides the banker who fails to heed it,

Which is you must never lend any money to anybody unless they
don't need it.

I know you, you cautious conservative banks!

If people are worried about their rent it is your duty to deny them
the loan of one nickel, yes, even one copper engraving of the
martyred son of the late Nancy Hanks;

Yes, if they request fifty dollars to pay for a baby you must look at
them like Tarzan looking at an uppity ape in the jungle,

And tell them what do they think a bank is, anyhow, they had bet-
ter go get the money from their wife's aunt or ungle.

But suppose people come in and they have a million and they want
  another million to pile on top of it,
Why, you brim with the milk of human kindness and you urge
  them to accept every drop of it,
And you lend them the million so then they have two million and
  this gives them the idea that they would be better off with four,
So they already have two million as security so you have no hesi-
  tation in lending them two more,
And all the vice-presidents nod their heads in rhythm,
And the only question asked is do the borrowers want the money
  sent or do they want to take it withm.
But please do not think that I am not fond of banks,
Because I think they deserve our appreciation and thanks,
Because they perform a valuable public service in eliminating the
  jackasses who go around saying that health and happiness are
  everything and money isn't essential,
Because as soon as they have to borrow some unimportant money
  to maintain their health and happiness they starve to death so
  they can't go around any more sneering at good old money,
  which is nothing short of providential.

PRAYER AT THE END OF A ROPE

Dear Lord, observe this bended knee,
This visage meek and humble,
And heed this confidential plea,
Voiced in a reverent mumble.

I ask no miracles nor stunts,
No heavenly radiogram;
I only beg for once, just once,
To not be in a jam.

One little moment thy servant craves
Of being his own master;
One placid vale between the waves
Of duty and disaster.

Oh, when the postman's whistle shrills,
Just once, Lord, let me grin:

Let me have settled last month's bills
Before this month's come in.

Let me not bite more off the cob
Than I have teeth to chew;
Please let me finish just one job
Before the next is due.

Consider, too, my social life,
Sporadic though it be;
Why is it only mental strife
That pleasure brings to me?

For months, when people entertain,
Me they do not invite;
Then suddenly invitations rain,
All for the self-same night.

R.S.V.P.'s I pray thee send
Alone and not in bunches,
Or teach me I cannot attend
Two dinners or two lunches.

Let me my hostess not insult,
Not call her diamonds topaz;
Else harden me to the result
Of my fantastic faux pas.

One little lull, Lord, that's my plea,
Then loose the storm again;
Just once, this once, I beg to be
Not in a jam. Amen.

FIRST PAYMENT DEFERRED

Let us look into the matter of debt
Which is something that the longer you live, why the deeper into
    it you get,
Because in the first place every creditor is his debtor's keeper,
And won't let you get into debt in the first place unless you are ca-
    pable of getting in deeper,

Which is an unfortunate coincidence

Because every debtor who is capable of getting deeper into debt is attracted only to creditors who will encourage him to get deeper into debt, which is a most fabulous and unfair You-were-a-creditor-in-Babylon-and-I-was-a-Christian-debtor Elinor Glyn-cidence.

Some debtors start out with debts which are little ones,

Such as board and lodging and victual ones;

Other debtors start out by never demanding that their bills be itemized,

Which means that they are bitten by little creditors upon the backs of bigger creditors and are so on ad infinitumized.

Veteran debtors dabble in stocks,

Or their families get adenoids or appendicitis or pox,

Any of which means that debt is what they get beneather and beneather,

Either to them who told them about the stocks or to them who administer the chloroform and ether.

Some debts are fun while you are acquiring them,

But none are fun when you set about retiring them,

So you think you will reform, you think instead of sinking into debt you will ascend into credit,

So you live on a budget and save twenty-five percent of your salary and cut corners and generally audit and edit,

And that is the soundest idea yet,

Because pretty soon your credit is so good that you can charge anything you want and settle down for eternity into peaceful and utterly irremediable debt.

A PENNY SAVED IS IMPOSSIBLE

The further through life I drift

The more obvious it becomes that I am lacking in thrift.

Now thrift is such a boon to its possessor that years ago they began to tax it,

But it is a bane to him that lacks it

Because if you lack it you will go into a shoppe and pay two dollars for a gifte,

But if you possess it you find something just as good for a dollar
    fifte.
A penny is merely something that you pull several of out of your
    pocket before you find the nickel you need for a telephone call,
    if thriftlessness is in your blood,
Whereas to the thrifty a penny is something to be put out at stud.
Thrifty people put two-cent stamps on letters addressed to a three-
    cent zone,
And thriftless people on the other end pay the postage due and the
    thrifty people chuckle and rub their hands because the saving
    on every six letters represents a year's interest on a dollar loan.
Oh, that I were thrifty, because thrifty people leave estates to de-
    light their next of kin with;
Oh yes that I were thrifty, because then not only would I have
    money in the bank to pay my bills, but I could leave the money
    in the bank because I wouldn't have run up the bills to begin
    with;
Oh that I were not a spendthrift, oh then would my heart indeed
    be gladsome,
Because it is so futile being a spendthrift because I don't know any
    places where thrift could be spent even if I had some.

WHITTLING JOE

Here's a fellow you'd like to know,
A citizen named Whittling Joe.
Joe is whittling in a plant,
Whittling things the Axis can't,
Whittling with his sharp machines
Cargo ships and submarines,
Whittling bombers, whittling tanks,
Whittling shells in shiny ranks—
Shave a sliver off Benito,
Slice a slab off Hirohito,
And Joseph really whets his whittler
Whistling as he whittles Hitler.
That's a job that Joe enjoys,
Whittling down the Axis boys.

Whittling Joe is never through;
He likes to whittle with dollars, too,
So every payday Joe is fond
Of whittling Hitler with a bond.
Multiplied by fifty million,
Whittling Joe is some civilian!

(Editor's Note: This was one of many poems written by Nash to raise money for War Bonds during World War II.)

THE SECOND MONTH IT'S NOT ITEMIZED

I go to my desk to write a letter,
A simple letter without any frills;
I can't find space to write my letter,
My desk is treetop high in bills.

I go to my desk to write a poem
About a child of whom I'm afraid;
I can't get near it to write my poem
For the barrel of bills, and all unpaid.

I go to my desk for an aspirin tablet,
For a handy bottle of syrup of squills,
I reach in the drawer for the trusty bicarbonate;
My fingers fasten on nothing but bills.

I go to my desk to get my checkbook
That checks may blossom like daffodils,
Hundreds of checks to maintain my credit;
I can't get through the bills to pay my bills.

I've got more bills than there are people,
I've got bigger bills than Lincoln in bronze,
I've got older bills than a Bangor & Aroostook day coach,
I've got bills more quintuplicate than Dionnes.

There's a man named Slemp in Lima, Ohio,
Since 1930 he has been constantly ill,
And of all the inhabitants of this glorious nation
He is the only one who has never sent me a bill.

The trouble with bills, it costs money to pay them,
But as long as you don't, your bank is full.
I shall now save some money by opening a charge account
With a fuller, a draper, and a carder of wool.

I CAN'T STOP UNLESS YOU STOP
OR
LINES ADDRESSED TO A MAN MAKING
$5,000 A YEAR WHO OVERTIPS A MAN MAKING
$10,000 A YEAR TO MAKE HIMSELF FEEL
HE'S MAKING $20,000 A YEAR

I do not wish to tiptoe through the tulips to Tipperary,
And I might vote for Tyler too, but about Tippecanoe I am a little
    wary.
The fact is, that at any mention of any form of tips,
My mind goes into an eclipse.
The world of tips has moved too fast for me,
The price of ransoming my hat has become too vast for me.
I have to get used to one thing at a time,
And just as I learn that there is no more such tip as a nickel, I find
    that there is no more such tip as a dime.
If you give a dime to a bellhop,
The skyscrapers buck like broncos, and you can almost feel the ho-
    tel hop.
If you want to talk to bellhops or porters,
You start with baby-talk, which is quarters.
If you want to talk to head waiters, or, as they now style them-
    selves, maitre d's,
You talk in C's or G's,
And the girl with the tray of cigarettes expects the Taj Mahal,
And not a small Mahal, either, but a large Mahal.
This is a sad situation for low and middle income persons,
And when you go abroad, it worsens.
At least on the trains over here
You don't have to tip the conductor and the engineer,
And over here, certainly until recently, it would have been consid-
    ered impudent effrontery

To tip the President of the country.
Whereas, in certain nations that shall be nameless,
The entire citizenry is shameless.
Granted that itching palms
Know no qualms,
Nevertheless people, whether men or mice,
Resent scratching the same palm twice,
Which happens wherever you eat or sleep, on the continent, be-
cause a fat percentage is added to the bill to cover all tips,
But if you think that no further tipping is expected, you'd better
learn to carry your own pemmican and balance your baggage
on your hips.
Oh dear, I think that extravagant tips are an unnecessary menace,
Whether in Valdosta, Georgia, or Valparaiso, or Vancouver, or
Venice.
I think that they are a betrayal of the tipper's unsure ego, or not
quite–quiteness,
I think that they are a vulgar substitute for common politeness.
I think that people could do very well both at home and abroad on
moderate gratuities or fees
If they would just take the trouble to learn and employ the foreign
and domestic terms for Thank you, and Please.

FATHER, DEAR FATHER, GO JUMP IN THE LAKE
OR
YOU'RE COSTLIER THAN YOU THINK

Once there was a man named Mr. Arents,
And he was the severest of parents.
Every time his seven children asked him when they could have a
convertible he answered, bye and bye,
And he confiscated all their phonograph records that had songs
with people singing, Aye yi aye yi.
He complained that they smoked too many cigarettes,
And he would neither feed nor bathe their pets.
He insulted all their friends at 4 A.M.
By standing at the head of the stairs in his pajamas and remarking,
Ahem.

He insisted that they put on their shoes before they ate,
And objected when they scooped the middles out of the rolls and
 deposited the crust on their plate.
That was the erstwhile Mr. Arents,
The most unreasonable of parents.
You ought to see the new Mr. Arents,
He is a veritable model of forbearance.
He feels that whatever his seven children request,
It behooves him to behave at their behest.
Mr. Arents has had a warning,
Wherefore he brings them seven apples and seven convertibles
 each morning;
He is currying favor
Against the day his voice begins to quaver;
Any good will that his children may bear him, he wants to pad it,
He wants them to remember him as a right guy when he had it.
He knows that he is now an asset but he fears that all too soon
He will be an elderly liability in a chimney corner slurping por-
 ridge from a wooden spoon.

Mr. Arents has recently been told by an annuity salesman some-
 thing that makes him feel so singular that he has shrunk to Mr.
 Arent:
Namely, it is easier for one parent to support seven children than
 for seven children to support one parent.

PERIOD PERIOD

PERIOD I
Our fathers claimed, by obvious madness moved,
Man's innocent until his guilt is proved.
They would have known, had they not been confused,
He's innocent until he is accused.

PERIOD II
The catch phrase "Nothing human to me is alien"
Was coined by some South European rapscallion.
This dangerous fallacy I shall now illumine:
To chauvinists, nothing alien is human.

EXIT, PURSUED BY A BEAR

Chipmunk chewing the Chippendale,
Mice on the Meissen shelf,
Pigeon stains the Aubusson,
Spider lace on the delf.

Squirrel climbing the Sheraton,
Skunk on the Duncan Phyfe,
Silverfish in the Gobelins
And the calfbound volumes of *Life*.

Pocks on the pink Picasso,
Dust on the four Cézannes,
Kit on the keys of the Steinway,
Cat on the Louis Quinze.

Rings on the Adam mantel
From a thousand bygone thirsts,
Mold on the Henry Millers
And the Ronald Firbank firsts.

The lion and the lizard
No heavenly harmonies hear
From the high-fidelity speaker
Concealed behind the Vermeer.

Jamshid squats in a cavern
Screened by a waterfall,
Catered by Heinz and Campbell,
And awaits the fireball.

LINES FRAUGHT WITH NAUGHT BUT THOUGHT

If you thirst to know who said, "I think, therefore I am," your
   thirst I will quench;
It was René Descartes, only what he actually said was, "*Je pense,
   donc je suis*," because he was French.
He also said it in Latin, "*Cogito, ergo sum*,"
Just to show that he was a man of culture and not a tennis tramp
   or a cracker barrel philosophy bum.

Descartes was one of the few who think, therefore they are,
Because those who don't think, but are anyhow, outnumber them
   by far.
If of chaos we are on the brink
It is because so many people only think that they think.
In truth, of anything other than thinking they are fonder,
Because thought requires the time and effort to reflect, cogitate,
   contemplate, meditate, ruminate and ponder.
Their minds are exposed to events and ideas but they have never
   pondered or reflected on them
Any more than motion picture screens meditate on the images that
   are projected on them.
Hence, our universal confusion,
The result of the unreasoned, or jumped at, conclusion.
People who just think that they think, they secretly think that
   thinking is grim,
And they excuse themselves with signs reading THIMK, or, as
   Descartes would have said, PEMSEZ, and THINK OR THWIM.
Instead of thoughts, they act on hunches and inklings,
Which are not thoughts at all, only thinklings.
Can it be because we leave to the Russians such dull pursuits as
   thinking that the red star continues to twinkle so?
I thinkle so.

IS THERE AN OCULIST IN THE HOUSE?

How often I would that I were one of those homely philosophical
   old codgers
Like, say, Mr. Dooley or Will Rogers,
Because I could then homelily call people's attention to the fact
   that we didn't see eye to eye with the Italians so we had a war
   with them, after which, to put it succinkly
We and the Italians became as close as Goodson and Todman or
   Huntley and Brinkley,
And we didn't see eye to eye with the Germans and we had to ei-
   ther fight or bootlick,
So we fought, and now everything between us and the Germans is
   gemütlich,

And the Japanese didn't see eye to eye with us, so they fought us
    the soonest,
And today we and the Japanese are of companions the boonest.
Now at the daily boasts of "My retaliation can lick your retalia-
    tion" I am with apprehension stricken,
As one who watches two adolescent hot-rodders careening head-
    long toward each other, each determined to die rather than
    chicken.
Once again there is someone we don't see eye to eye with, and
    maybe I couldn't be dafter,
But I keep wondering if this time we couldn't settle our differences
    before a war instead of after.

LITTLE PRETTY PENNY, LET'S SQUANDER THEE

Why do so many billionaires go in for penuriousness
Instead of luxuriousness?
Why are so many prosperous potential sybarites
Afraid of being termed flibbertigibberites?
Too many tycoons who would relish a display of extravagance
Explore the edges of ostentation in a sort of timid circumnavi-
    gance.
If I were Mr. Onassis do you know what I would do? I would buy
    Neiman-Marcus
And give it for Easter to Mr. Niarchos.
If I were Mr. Niarchos I might buy the Parthenon
And present it to the Huntington Hartford Museum after chang-
    ing its name to the General MacArthurnon.
Were I the favorite customer of Harry Winston
I might well acquire the Green Bay Packers and give them to Rut-
    gers for use in the game with Princeton.
Or were I a Nizam counting my rubies and emeralds and wives in
    my Oriental palace
I'd find it a change of pace to present Dallas to Madame Callas, or
    even Madame Callas to Dallas.
Were I an Aga or a Khan fond of a friend despite his gross addic-
    tion to food and drink who might therefore be described as cra-
    pulous,

I would give him a deed to Le Pavillon and Lüchow's and La Tour
   D'Argent and all the Indian pudding in Indianapulous.
I'd like to say to a Gulbenkian or a Rockefeller, why don't you
   show in what league you are?
Why don't you transport the Taj Mahal and use it as a guesthouse
   in Antigua?
Had I the wells of an H. L. Hunt I would be openhanded like Car-
   dinal Wolsey, not close-fisted like Cardinal Mazarin,
I would raise and refit the Andrea Doria just for a cruise around
   Manhattan Island and set before my guests a feast Lucullan,
   yea, even Belshazzaran.
Upon arising next noon I would taper on to prodigality again by
   making the kind of humble propitiatory offering that Midas
   might have made to Zeus or Hera,
I would spend $1700 on an appropriate gift for President de
   Gaulle, an item advertised by a Park Avenue shop consisting of
   a limestone fossil fish plaque 60 million years old, a relic of the
   Eocene Era.
I would also, may my tribute increase,
Present every taxi-driver in New York with a lifetime supply of ci-
   gars costing not less than a dollar apiece.
Whether glory or infamy would be my lot I know not which,
But I would surely carve for myself a special niche among the rich.

IF HE WERE ALIVE TODAY, MAYHAP,
MR. MORGAN WOULD SIT
ON THE MIDGET'S LAP

"Beep-beep.
BANKERS TRUST AUTOMOBILE LOAN
You'll find a banker at Bankers Trust"
            —Advertisement in N.Y. Times

When comes my second childhood,
As to all men it must,
I want to be a banker
Like the banker at Bankers Trust.
I wouldn't ask to be president,
Or even assistant veep,

I'd only ask for a kiddie car
And permission to go beep-beep.

The banker at Chase Manhattan,
He bids a polite Good-day;
The banker at Immigrant Savings
Cries Scusi! and Olé!
But I'd be a sleek Ferrari
Or perhaps a joggly jeep,
And scooting around at Bankers Trust,
Beep-beep, I'd go, beep-beep.

The trolley car used to say clang-clang
And the choo-choo said toot-toot,
But the beep of the banker at Bankers Trust
Is every bit as cute.
Miaow, says the cuddly kitten,
Baa, says the woolly sheep,
Oink, says the piggy-wiggy,
And the banker says beep-beep.

So I want to play at Bankers Trust
Like a hippety-hoppy bunny,
And best of all, oh best of all,
With really truly money.
Now grown-ups dear, it's nightie-night
Until my dream comes true,
And I bid you a happy boop-a-doop
And a big beep-beep adieu.

WHAT'S HECUBA TO HIM?
A ONE-MINUTE CLOSE-UP
OR
SOME NOSES FOR NEWS ARE FOR TWEAKING

Once there was a TV Roving Reporter named Goucher Bumpus.
His nose for news was his compass.
His approach to his victims was sometimes hotly belligerent,
Sometimes cool as a refrigerant.

He had the manners of a hyena
And the persistence of a subpoena.
His questions were notable for their callosity
Because conscience never made a coward of him because he had no
conscience, only curiosity.
His hand never trembled as he thrust the mike at the widow of a
policeman or fireman killed on duty,
And his audio-video of the mother whose child had been run over
was a thing of beauty.
At probing the emotions of relatives waiting for the casualty list at
the airport he couldn't be bested,
And he had caused three murder convictions to be reversed be-
cause he had badgered confessions out of the accused right af-
ter they were arrested.
He was indeed a worthy Roving Reporter,
And only on his arrival at Heaven's gate did he meet a worthy re-
torter.
No hagiolater he, he didn't bother to wheedle,
He bluntly demanded of the guardian if he honestly believed that
a million angels can dance on the point of a needle.
The result was ideal;
Many previous interviewees had told him where to go, but this
time it was for real.

UNTITLED LIMERICK

Cried a teen-age protestor named Jill,
"Those C.I.A. squares make me ill!
First they bugged our martinis,
Our bras and bikinis,
And now they are bugging The Pill!"

UNTITLED

Happy Birthday, dear Eugene,
The first to give us a choice between.
Today in you we place our trust,
Not an alternative, but a must.

The kids are for you, glory be,
And so are wise old men like me.
How many statesmen of good intent
Would rather be right than president,
But I will gladly take my oath
That you're the man who can be both.
As your 52nd candle burns,
Many happy election returns!

Author's Note: Birthday verse for Senator Mc-
Carthy written at request of McCarthy for
President Committee. Written between 12 noon
and 1:30 P.M. on March 27, 1968. O.N.

THE FILIBUSTER

Once more the filibuster runs amok,
A kissin' cousin of the jabberwock.
And what might be this fabulous filibuster?
A beast composed of blathering and bluster.
Yet when it whiffles to the Senate floor
Brave statesmen quiver at its windy roar.
Reason and decency cry out in vain,
And human rights go swirling down the drain.
Though some set forth to slay the filibuster,
It stages more and better last stands than Custer.

YES-AND-NO MAN

Poor Manfred, always in bad odor,
Muddled middle-of-the-roader.
Veering Left toward visions bright,
Leftist jargon drives him Right
Until the Rightist hatchet men
Turn him to the Left again,
Searching for a category,
Spo-Radical or desul-Tory.

POLITICAL REFLECTION

Discretion is the better part of virtue;
Commitments the voters don't know about can't hurt you.

ROADBLOCK

Justice has been rerouted
From present to future tense;
The law is so in love with the law
It's forgotten common sense.

MINI-JABBERWOCKY

Most people would find rising unemployment
A source of unenjoyment.
Not so the anonymous presidential advisor
Whose comment might have been wiser.
He has informed the nation
That rising unemployment is merely a statistical aberration.
I don't want to argue or squabble,
But that gook I won't gobble.

THE COLLECTOR

I met a traveler from an antique show,
His pockets empty, but his eyes aglow.
Upon his back, and now his very own,
He bore two vast and trunkless legs of stone.
Amid the torrent of collector's jargon
I gathered he had found himself a bargain,
A permanent conversation piece post-prandial,
Certified genuine early Ozymandial,
And when I asked him how he could be sure,
He showed me P. B. Shelley's signature.

Eat, Drink, and Be Merry

REFLECTIONS ON ICE-BREAKING

Candy
Is dandy
But liquor
Is quicker.

PARSLEY FOR VICE-PRESIDENT!

I'd like to be able to say a good word for parsley, but I can't,
And after all what can you find to say for something that even the
dictionary dismisses as a biennial umbelliferous plant?
Speaking of which, I don't know how the dictionary figures it as
biennial, it is biennial my eye, it is like the poor and the iniq-
uitous,
Because it is always with us, because it is permanent and ubiquitous.
I will not venture to deny that it is umbelliferous,
I will only add that it is of a nasty green color, and faintly odorif-
erous,
And I hold by my complaint, though every cook and hostess in the
land indict me for treason for it,

That parsley is something that as a rhymer I can find no rhyme for
it and as an eater I can find no reason for it.
Well, there is one sin for which a lot of cooks and hostesses are
some day going to have to atone,
Which is that they can't bear to cook anything and leave it alone.
No, they see food as something to base a lot of beautiful dreams
and romance on,
Which explains lamb chops with pink and blue pants on.
Everything has to be all decorated and garnished
So the guests will be amazed and astarnished,
And whatever you get to eat, it's sprinkled with a lot of good old
umbelliferous parsley looking as limp and wistful as Lillian
Gish,
And it is limpest, and wistfulest, and also thickest, on fish.
Indeed, I think maybe one reason for the disappearance of Enoch
Arden
Was that his wife had an idea that mackerel tasted better if instead
of looking like mackerel it looked like a garden.
Well, anyhow, there's the parsley cluttering up your food,
And the problem is to get it off without being rude,
And first of all you try to scrape it off with your fork,
And you might as well try to shave with a cork,
And then you surreptitiously try your fingers,
And you get covered with butter and gravy, but the parsley lingers,
And you turn red and smile at your hostess and compliment her on
the recipe and ask her where she found it,
And then you return to the parsley and as a last resort you try to
eat around it,
And the hostess says, Oh you are just picking at it, is there some-
thing wrong with it?
So all you can do is eat it all up, and the parsley along with it,
And now is the time for all good parsleyphobes to come to the aid
of the menu and exhibit their gumption,
And proclaim that any dish that has either a taste or an appear-
ance that can be improved by parsley is *ipso facto* a dish unfit
for human consumption.

FURTHER REFLECTION ON PARSLEY

Parsley
Is gharsley.

A DRINK WITH SOMETHING IN IT

There is something about a martini,
A tingle remarkably pleasant;
A yellow, a mellow martini;
I wish that I had one at present.
There is something about a martini,
Ere the dining and dancing begin,
And to tell you the truth,
It is not the vermouth—
I think that perhaps it's the gin.

There is something about an old-fashioned
That kindles a cardiac glow;
It is soothing and soft and impassioned
As a lyric by Swinburne or Poe.
There is something about an old-fashioned
When dusk has enveloped the sky,
And it may be the ice,
Or the pineapple slice,
But I strongly suspect it's the rye.

There is something about a mint julep,
It is nectar imbibed in a dream,
As fresh as the bud of the tulip,
As cool as the bed of the stream.
There is something about a mint julep,
A fragrance beloved by the lucky.
And perhaps it's the tint
Of the frost and the mint,
But I think it was born in Kentucky.

There is something they put in a highball
That awakens the torpidest brain,
That kindles a spark in the eyeball,

Gliding singing through vein after vein.
There is something they put in a highball
Which you'll notice one day, if you watch;
And it may be the soda,
But judged by the odor,
I rather believe it's the scotch.

Then here's to the heartening wassail,
Wherever good fellows are found;
Be its master instead of its vassal,
And order the glasses around.
For there's something they put in the wassail
That prevents it from tasting like wicker;
Since it's not tapioca,
Or mustard, or mocha,
I'm forced to conclude it's the liquor.

HOME, 99 AND 44/100% SWEET HOME

Most of the time, oh most of the time,
I like to sit at home,
With a good fire, and a good chair,
And a good detective tome.
What can a man, can a family man
Ask in the way of cheer
More than a pipe, and a reading lamp,
And a modest mug of beer?
Most of the time, the wealth of the Indies
Wouldn't tempt me to blowouts or shindies.

But once in a while,
Oh, once in a while,
It's pleasant to paint the town,
To frolic and revel,
A regular devil,
And do the evening brown.
To buy an orchid, or maybe two,
And woo the way that you used to woo,
To press the loot from the babies' banks

On waiters who fail to murmur thanks.
To dine and wine and dance and sup,
And ride in a cab till the sun comes up,
And to feel thereafter, in sundry ways,
Simply awful for days and days.
Home is heaven and orgies are vile,
But I *like* an orgy, once in a while.

Home is the place, oh home is the place
That no place else is like,
So who would freeze in the South, like Byrd,
Or discover peaks, like Pike?
Who so animal, who so low
As to pant for the Great White Way?
Who would give up a night at home
For one in a cabaret?
Most of the time I'd swim to Australia
As soon as engage in a Saturnalia.

But once in a while,
Oh, once in a while,
It's pleasant to loop the loop,
To daringly seize
The flying trapeze
With a cry of Allez-oop!
To jump the rails, kick over the traces,
To go on the town and visit places,
Sit ten at a table meant for two,
And choke on smoke as you used to do,
To tread the floor with the dancing bears,
They on your feet, and you on theirs,
To have flings at things that philosophers true shun,
And undermine your constitue-shun.
Home is heaven and orgies are vile,
But you *need* an orgy, once in a while.

THE PARTY NEXT DOOR

I trust I am not a spoilsport, but there is one thing I deplore,
And that is a party next door.
I am by nature very fond of everybody, even my neighbors,
And I think it only right that they should enjoy some kind of diversion after their labors,
But why don't they get their diversion by going to the movies or the Little Theater or the Comédie Française or the Commedia dell'arte?
Why do they always have to be giving a party?
You may think you have heard a noise because you have heard an artillery barrage or an avalanche or the subway's horrendous roar,
But you have never really heard anything until you have heard a party next door.
At a party next door the guests stampede like elephants in wooden shoes and gallop like desperate polo players,
And all the women are coloratura sopranos and all the men are train announcers and hogcallers and saxophone solo players.
They all have screamingly funny stories to tell to each other,
And half of them get at one end of the house and half of them get at the other end of the yard and then they yell to each other,
And even if the patrolman looks in from his beat they do not moderate or stop,
No, they just seduce the cop.
And at last you manage to doze off by the dawn's early light,
And they wake you up all over again shouting good night,
And whether it consists of two quiet old ladies dropping in for a game of bridge or a lot of revelers getting really sort of out-of-bounds-like,
That's what a party next door always sounds like,
So when you see somebody with a hoarse voice and a pallid face and eyes bleary and red-rimmed and sore,
It doesn't mean they've been on a party themselves, no, it probably means that they have experienced a party next door.

ASSORTED CHOCOLATES

If some confectioner were willing
To let the shape announce the filling,
We'd encounter fewer assorted chocs,
Bitten into and returned to the box.

CELERY

Celery, raw,
Develops the jaw,
But celery, stewed,
Is more quietly chewed.

THE PARSNIP

The parsnip, children, I repeat,
Is simply an anemic beet.
Some people call the parsnip edible;
Myself, I find this claim incredible.

THE PEOPLE UPSTAIRS

The people upstairs all practice ballet.
Their living room is a bowling alley.
Their bedroom is full of conducted tours.
Their radio is louder than yours.
They celebrate weekends all the week.
When they take a shower, your ceilings leak.
They try to get their parties to mix
By supplying their guests with pogo sticks,
And when their orgy at last abates,
They go to the bathroom on roller skates.
I might love the people upstairs wondrous
If instead of above us, they just lived under us.

NOT EVEN FOR BRUNCH

When branches bend in fruitful stupor
Before the woods break out in plaid,
The supermarket talks more super,
The roadside stands go slightly mad.
What garden grew this goblin harvest?
Who coined these words that strike me numb?
I will not purchase, though I starvest,
The cuke, the glad, the lope, the mum.

In happier days I sank to slumber
Murmuring names as sweet as hope:
Fair gladiolus, and cucumber,
Chrysanthemum and cantaloupe.
I greet the changelings that awoke me
With warmth a little less than luke,
As farmer and florist crowd to choke me
With glad and lope, with mum and cuke.

Go hence, far hence, you jargon-mongers,
Go soak your head in boiling ads,
Go feed to cuttlefish and congers
Your mums and lopes, your cukes and glads.
Stew in the whimsy that you dole us
I roam where magic casements ope
On cantemum spiced, and cuciolus,
Or chrysanthecumber, and gladaloupe.

THE STRANGE CASE OF MR. PALLISER'S PALATE

Once there was a man named Mr. Palliser and he asked his wife,
   May I be a *gourmet?*
And she said, You sure may,
But she also said, If my kitchen is going to produce a Cordon Blue,
It won't be me, it will be you,
And he said, You mean *Cordon Bleu?*
And she said to never mind the pronunciation so long as it was him
   and not *heu.*

But he wasn't discouraged; he bought a white hat and *The Cordon Bleu Cook Book* and said, How about some *Huîtres en Robe de Chambre?*

And she sniffed and said, Are you reading a cookbook or *Forever Ambre?*

And he said, Well, if you prefer something more Anglo-Saxon,

Why suppose I whip up some tasty *Filets de Sole Jackson,*

And she pretended not to hear, so he raised his voice and said, Could I please you with some *Paupiettes de Veau à la Grecque* or *Cornets de Jambon Lucullus* or perhaps some nice *Moules à la Bordelaise?*

And she said, Kindly lower your voice or the neighbors will think we are drunk and *disordelaise,*

And she said, Furthermore the whole idea of your cooking anything fit to eat is a farce. So what did Mr. Palliser do then?

Well he offered her *Oeufs Farcis Maison* and *Homard Farci St. Jacques,* and *Tomate Farcie à la Bayonne* and *Aubergines Farcies Provençales,* as well as *Aubergines Farcies Italiennes,*

And she said, Edward, kindly accompany me as usual to Hamburger Heaven and stop playing the fool,

And he looked in the book for one last suggestion and it suggested *Croques Madame,* so he did, and now he dines every evening on *Crème de Concombres Glacée, Côtelettes de Volaille Vicomtesse,* and *Artichauds à la Barigoule.*

HOW DO YOU SAY HA-HA IN FRENCH?

There are several people who I can claim I am glad I am not, without being accused of pride and effrontery,

And one of them is the bartender of a French restaurant in an English-speaking country.

The conversation of the customers isn't calculated to keep a bartender young,

Even when they converse in their mother tongue;

How much more dispiriting it must be when after the second Martini

They request a third because the first two are, not finished, but *finis*.
They select a *Maryland*, or cigarette,
And instead of Gotta light? it is *Avez-vous une allumette?*
When they cry *Garçon* after the school of Stratford atte Bowe or
    New Rochelle or Nineveh,
It is moot whether they want the waiter or Mrs. Miniver.
Somehow, in a *bistro*, or French eatery,
Everybody suddenly discovers they can talk like Sasha Guitry,
But they really can't,
And if I were the bartender I should poke them in the *œil* with the
    plume de ma tante.

POSTCARD TO MISS ISABEL NASH
FROM CHICAGO, ILLINOIS

On the shores of Lake Michigan
I cut into whitefichigan.
It's simply delichigan.

POSTCARD TO MISS LINELL NASH
FROM CORPUS CHRISTI, TEXAS

Last night I ate a Mexican meal
Which would have melted a throat of steel,
But being used to Carrie's soups,
I finished it without the hiccoups.

THE PRIVATE DINING ROOM

Miss Rafferty wore taffeta,
Miss Cavendish wore lavender.
We ate pickerel and mackerel
And other lavish provender.
Miss Cavendish was Lalage,
Miss Rafferty was Barbara.

We gobbled pickled mackerel
And broke the candelabara,
Miss Cavendish in lavender,
In taffeta, Miss Rafferty,
The girls in taffeta lavender,
And we, of course, in mufti.

Miss Rafferty wore taffeta,
The taffeta was lavender,
Was lavend, lavender, lavenderest,
As the wine improved the provender.
Miss Cavendish wore lavender,
The lavender was taffeta.
We boggled mackled pickerel,
And bumpers did we quaffeta.
And Lalage wore lavender,
And lavender wore Barbara,
Rafferta taffeta Cavender lavender
Barbara abracadabra.

Miss Rafferty in taffeta
Grew definitely raffisher.
Miss Cavendish in lavender
Grew less and less stand-offisher.
With Lalage and Barbara
We grew a little pickereled,
We ordered Mumm and Roederer
Because the bubbles tickereled.
But lavender and taffeta
Were gone when we were soberer.
I haven't thought for thirty years
Of Lalage and Barbara.

SNAP, CRACKLE, POP

Breakfast foods grow odder and odder:
It's a wise child that knows its fodder.

THE INVITATION SAYS FROM FIVE TO SEVEN

There's nothing like an endless party,
A collection of clammy little groups,
Where a couple of the guests are arty
And the rest of the guests are goops.
There's the confidential girlish chatter—
It soothes you like a drug—
And the gentle pitter-patter
As the anchovies hit the rug.
There's the drip, drip, drip of the mayonnaise
As the customers slither through the canapés,
There are feuds that are born,
There are friendships that pine away,
And the big cigar that smolders on the Steinaway.
The major trouble with a party
Is you need a guest to give it for,
And the best part of any guest
Is the last part out the door.

There's nothing like an endless party,
And there hasn't been since ancient Rome.
Here's Silenus making passes at Astarte
While Mrs. Silenus begs him to go home.
There is bigamy about the boudoirs,
There is bundling at the bar,
And the sideboard where the food was
Has the aspect of an abattoir.
You wonder why they pursue each other's wives,
Who by now resemble the cream cheese and the chives.
There's a corpse on the floor
From New Rochelle or Scarborough,
And its mate is swinging from the candelabara.
The best location for a party
Is in a room without a floor,
And the best way to give a party
Is leave town the night before.

HOW TO TELL A KITCHEN FROM A CUISINE:
TAKE A QUICK LOOK AT OURS

Every time the menu lists *bleu* cheese I want to order *fromage* blue,
Don't you?
Yet when they call it *bleu* cheese I suppose they are right,
Because *bleu* cheese differs from blue cheese because it is usually white.
I must read up on this matter in the cheese cook book,
Which clutters up our kitchen along with the fish cook book, the game cook book, the wine cook book, the Colonial cook book, the French cook book, the Eskimo cook book and the Siamese cook book.
Yes, in our kitchen there are everywhere you look books,
There may be a stove, but you can't see the cook box for the cookbooks.
You know the way some larders are full of potatoes and lentils and beans?
That's the way ours is full of recipes clipped from newspapers and magazines.
Having perused this mass of culinariana I have one hope that is definite;
I hope we will always have a kitchen, but I hope I will never be the chef in it,
Because my few attempts to emulate Clementine Paddleford or Brillat-Savarin,
They have resulted in results something less than mouthwaterin', or slaverin'.
If there is one element of cookery I deplore,
It is that when you go to cook, the recipe suddenly calls for a roux or a stock or something that should have been started the day before.
I attribute the brilliance of Gian-Carlo Menotti
To the fact that he has never tasted my manicotti,
Because my ignorance is so profound
That I don't know whether manicotti should be rectangular or round.
In this respect even my limited knowledge of money is preciser;
I know that the round kind is nice but the rectangular kind is much nicer.

THE PIZZA

Look at itsy-bitsy Mitzi!
See her figure slim and ritzy!
She eatsa
Pizza!
Greedy Mitzi!
She no longer itsy-bitsy!

YOU'LL DRINK YOUR ORANGE JUICE
AND LIKE IT, COMRADE

Soviet Union agrees to absorb quantities of citrus
fruits to relieve Cyprus surplus.
—Newspaper item

There's a Cyprus citrus surplus,
Citrus surplus Cypriotic.
No Sicilian citrus surplus
But a Cyprus citrus surplus,
Not a Cyprus citron surplus
But a Cyprus citrus surplus,
Not a Cyprus citrus circus
But a Cyprus citrus surplus.
It's a special citrus surplus,
Cyprus citrus super surplus.
"Just a surface citrus surfeit,"
Says a cryptic Coptic skeptic.
But the bishop in his surplice
Certifies the surfeit citrus—
In his surplus Sunday surplice,
Certifies the citrus surfeit,
Who'll assimilate the surplus,
Siphon off the Cyprus citrus?
Sipping at the citrus cistern
Who'll suppress the Cyprus surplus?
Says the Soviet to Cyprus,
"Send us all your surplus citrus;
This is just a simple sample

Of Socialist assistance.
Should you show a similar surplus
In the simmering summer solstice,
Send a summons to the Soviet
For surplus citrus solace."

Now on Cyprus they're all reading
Victory, by Joseph Comrade.

YOU'VE GOT TO BE MR. PICKWICK
IF YOU WANT TO ENJOY A PICNIC

Perhaps it's just that I'm lazy,
But I think anybody over six who says "Let's have a picnic" is
    crazy.
For some years now I have been grown up,
And I get no pleasure out of a warm martini served in a paper cup.
Picnics consist almost entirely of paper, not only paper cups, but
    paper spoons, paper plates, paper napkins, waxed paper, and
    the asbestos newspaper that you try to start the fire with,
Paper that you and I dispose of after our picnics, but everybody
    else litters up the county, state, or shire with.
There is the Odyssey picnic with no planned picnic site, and this
    one it is better to be caught dead than alive in,
Because after miles of not being able to choose between bosky dell
    and shady river bank you end up by eating your picnic in the
    car in the parking lot of an abandoned drive-in.
There is the inland picnic where you start to tickle and discover
    that every tickle is a tick,
And the beach picnic where the host didn't realize that the tide
    would come in so quick.
I always say there is only one kind of picnic where it doesn't mat-
    ter if you have forgotten the salt and the bottle-opener, and the
    kids want to go to the bathroom, and the thunder clouds swell
    and billow like funeral drapery,
And that is where the meal is cooked in the kitchen and served on
    the dining room table, which is covered with snowy un-papery
    napery.

MENU MACABRE

Let us now get away from praise of anti-smoke pollution measures
    and plans for noise abatements,
Let us now praise famous gourmets and their equally famous ante-
    mortem statements.
The preoccupation of the gourmet with good food is psychological,
Just as the preoccupation of the White Russian with Dark Eyes is
    balalaikalogical.
The gourmet eats for the moment, because what at his back does
    he always hear?
The Great Headwaiter with *l'addition* hurrying near.
How then do gourmets approach the bottom of life's bill of fare?
Some with foresight, some with false courage, and some with *sang-
    froid* of the most debonair.
In the first group, Isaiah, a connoisseur of pottage, especially in his
    dotage.
That his future messes of pottage were numbered he had a fore-
    boding,
And he said, Let us eat and drink; for tomorrow we shall die, a
    message that needs no decoding.
In the second, Sydney Smith; Fate cannot harm me, I have dined
    today, was his remark,
A perfect example of whistling in the dark.
Now the third group:
Consider Raoul, Comte de Gruelle, epicure, sybarite, *bon vivant*,
    and world authority on soup.
He went on an expedition in search of herbs for the ultimate in ex-
    otic seasoning,
And he was captured by cannibals in a country which the State De-
    partment requests me to call Ruritania through obvious politi-
    cal reasoning.
As he stood in the cauldron with water scalding his fundament
He sampled each new condiment.
When the broth reached his lips he smacked them heartily, and his
    last words, at 212° F.,
Were, My compliments to the chef.

THE DARKEST HALF-HOUR
OR
TOO EARLY IS THE TIME FOR ALL GOOD GUESTS TO COME TO THE AID OF THE PARTY

They are ready for their party.

He feels as elegant as the Sun King and she as divine as the Moon Goddess, Astarte.

They have asked the guests for 7:30 on this, they hope, effulgent eve,

And by 7:05 they are in the living room, poised, braced, anticipatory, and on the *qui vive*.

Eagerly they await the doorbell, or, in certain climes,

The ripple of those melodious Wistful Vista chimes.

He starts to light a cigarette, but she halts him with gestures frenzied—

The ashtrays have just been cleansèd.

She starts to sit on the sofa, and he, the most impartial umpire who never umped,

Evens the count by reminding her that the sofa has just been plumped.

Then she divides the olives by the number of guests and hopes she has not been too frugal,

And wishes that the caviar were not the sticky reddish kind but genuinely Belugal.

He nervously whistles a snatch from the *Peer Gynt Suite* by Grieg,

And wonders if his vodka—domestic, not Polish—is fit for compounding a White Russian, an Orange Julius, a Bog Fog, or a Palm Bay Intrigue.

By 7:25 she is pacing the floor and nibbling at her fingernails, destroying the opalescent symmetry acquired at the afternoon manicure,

And he inquires, "Are you sure it was *this* Saturday and not next that you asked them for?"—a question not recommended as the ideal panic cure.

At 7:30 they are tense as mummers awaiting the rise of the curtain, and at 7:31 they have abandoned their mumming—

They are convinced that nobody is coming.

So he says how about a quick one, and just as he has one hand in the ice bucket and the other on the gin,

Why, the first couple walks in.
You will be glad to learn that the party turned out to be absolutely
fabulous;
Indeed, some say the best since the one at which a horse was
named consul by the late Emperor Heliogabulus.

TASTE BUDS, EN GARDE!

Although I'll eat the strawberry when frozen
It's not the very berry I'd have chosen.
The naughty admen claim with gall divine
That it is better than the genu-ine,
New language they devise to sing its praise,
But only *le bon Dieu* can coin a *fraise*.

TABLE TALK—NO. 1,
THE HOG

Some scientist may at last disperse
The mysteries of the universe,
But me, I cannot even think
Why pork is white and ham is pink.

NO TROUBLE AT ALL, IT'S AS EASY
AS FALLING OFF A PORTABLE BAR

I often appeal to the Lord of hosts, because a host I often find my-
self.
And to the frustrations of hostmanship I cannot blind myself.
I invariably fail the ultimate test:
Outguessing the guest.
Would that I could anticipate
How my guests will elect to dissipate.
Now ice and glasses glisten within easy reach,
The guests old friends, the liquors lined up on the bar in accor-
dance with the well-known taste of each.
Comes Polyhymnia, the semi-teetotaller for whom you have
bought her favorite brand of sherry;

Tonight she would like just straight bourbon on the rocks with
perhaps a little sugar and bitters and, if it's not too much trou-
ble, a slice of orange and a maraschino cherry.
And Alistair, his cheek by years of aged scotch all motley mot-
tled—
Beefeater gin for him with just an ounce and a half of lime juice,
preferably British-bottled.
Here's Otho, a martini man as sure as da Gama's name was Vasco;
He'll take a Bloody Mary, only with a tequila base and maybe an
extra dash of Worcestershire sauce and lemon and just two
drops of Tabasco.
And Ethel, for whose sole benefit a stock of Dubonnet you carry—
This time she requests Campari.
Wilfred is smugly off the stuff, so you have provided every current
alternative or proxy;
He declines tomato juice, ginger ale, Coke, Sprite, Squirt, Fresca,
and Bitter Lemon, and wistfully supposes you haven't anything
in the way of Bevo or Moxie.
At long last Lily, surely fairest flower of the lot;
You ask her what she would like, and she replies, "Oh, anything
at all, dear, what have you got?"
Well, I'll tell you what I've got and what she's going to get this
time, by cracky:
My customary aperitif, pawpaw juice and *sake*.

The Ages of Man

À BAS BEN ADHEM

My fellow man I do not care for.
I often ask me, What's he there for?
The only answer I can find
Is, Reproduction of his kind.
If I'm supposed to swallow that,
Winnetka is my habitat.
Isn't it time to carve Hic Jacet
Above that Reproduction racket?

To make the matter more succinct:
Suppose my fellow man extinct.
Why, who would not approve the plan
Save possibly my fellow man?
Yet with a politician's voice
He names himself as Nature's choice.

The finest of the human race
Are bad in figure, worse in face.
Yet just because they have two legs
And come from storks instead of eggs

They count the spacious firmament
As something to be charged and sent.

Though man created cross-town traffic,
The *Daily Mirror*, *News*, and *Graphic*,
The pastoral fight and fighting pastor
And Queen Marie and Lady Astor,
He hails himself with drum and fife
And bullies lower forms of life.

Not that I think that much depends
On how we treat our feathered friends,
Or claim the wart hog in the zoo
Is nearer God than me or you;
Just that I wonder, as I scan,
The wherefore of my fellow man.

MORE ABOUT PEOPLE

When people aren't asking questions
They're making suggestions
And when they're not doing one of those
They're either looking over your shoulder or stepping on your toes
And then as if that weren't enough to annoy you
They employ you.
Anybody at leisure
Incurs everybody's displeasure.
It seems to be very irking
To people at work to see other people not working,
So they tell you that work is wonderful medicine,
Just look at Firestone and Ford and Edison,
And they lecture you till they're out of breath or something
And then if you don't succumb they starve you to death or some-
thing.
All of which results in a nasty quirk:
That if you don't want to work you have to work to earn enough
money so that you won't have to work.

OLD MEN

People expect old men to die,
They do not really mourn old men.
Old men are different. People look
At them with eyes that wonder when . . .
People watch with unshocked eyes;
But the old men know when an old man dies.

THE SEVEN SPIRITUAL AGES
OF MRS. MARMADUKE MOORE

Mrs. Marmaduke Moore, at the age of ten
(Her name was Jemima Jevons then),
Was the quaintest of little country maids.
Her pigtails slapped on her shoulderblades;
She fed the chickens and told the truth
And could spit like a boy through a broken tooth.
She could climb a tree to the topmost perch,
And she used to pray in the Methodist church.

At the age of twenty her heart was pure,
And she caught the fancy of Mr. Moore.
He broke his troth (to a girl named Alice),
And carried her off to his city palace,
Where she soon forgot her childhood piety
And joined in the orgies of high society.
Her voice grew English, or, say, Australian,
And she studied to be an Episcopalian.

At thirty our lives are still before us,
But Mr. Moore had a friend in the chorus.
Connubial bliss was overthrown
And Mrs. Moore now slumbered alone.
Hers was a nature that craved affection;
She gave herself up to introspection;
Then, finding theosophy rather dry,
Found peace in the sweet Bahai and Bahai.

Forty! and still an abandoned wife.
She felt old urges stirring to life.
She dipped her locks in a bowl of henna
And booked a passage through to Vienna.
She paid a professor a huge emolument
To demonstrate what his ponderous volume meant.
Returning, she preached to the unemployed
The gospel according to St. Freud.

Fifty! she haunted museums and galleries,
And pleased young men by augmenting their salaries.
Oh, it shouldn't occur, but it does occur,
That poets are made by fools like her.
Her salon was full of frangipani,
Romanian, Russian and Hindustani,
And she conquered par as well as bogey
By reading a book and going Yogi.

Sixty! and time was on her hands—
Maybe remorse and maybe glands.
She felt a need for a free confession,
To publish each youthful indiscretion,
And before she was gathered to her mothers,
To compare her sinlets with those of others,
Mrs. Moore gave a joyous whoop,
And immersed herself in the Oxford Group.

That is the story of Mrs. Moore,
As far as it goes. But of this I'm sure—
When seventy stares her in the face
She'll have found some other state of grace.
Mohammed may be her Lord and master,
Or Zeus, or Mithros or Zoroaster.
When a lady's erotic life is vexed
God knows what God is coming next.

THE RETURN

Early is the evening,
Reluctant the dawn;
Once there was summer;
Sudden it was gone.
It fell like a leaf,
Whirled downstream.
Was there ever summer,
Or only a dream?
Was ever a world
That was not November?
Once there was summer,
And this I remember.

Cornflowers and daisies,
Buttercups and clover,
Black-eyed Susans, and Queen Anne's lace,
A wide green meadow,
And the bees booming over,
And a little laughing girl with the wind in her face.

Strident are the voices
And hard lights shine;
Feral are the faces;
Is one of them mine?
Something is lost now;
Tarnished the gleam;
Was there ever nobleness,
Or only a dream?
Yes, and it lingers,
Lost not yet;
Something remains
Till this I forget,

Cornflowers and clover,
Buttercups and daisies,
Black-eyed Susans under blue and white skies,
And the grass waist-high
Where the red cow grazes,
And a little laughing girl with faith in her eyes.

There is a thought that I have tried not to but cannot help but
    think,
Which is, My goodness how much infants resemble people who
    have had too much to drink.
Tots and sots, so different and yet so identical!
What a humiliating coincidence for pride parentical!
Yet when you see your little dumpling set sail across the nursery
    floor,
Can you conscientiously deny the resemblance to somebody who
    is leaving a tavern after having tried to leave it a dozen times
    and each time turned back for just one more?
Each step achieved
Is simply too good to be believed;
Foot somehow follows foot
And somehow manages to stay put:
Arms wildly semaphore,
Wild eyes seem to ask, Whatever did we get in such a dilemma for?
And their gait is more that of a duckling than a Greek goddessling
    or godling,
And in inebriates it's called staggering but in infants it's called tod-
    dling.
Another kinship with topers is also by infants exhibited,
Which is that they are completely uninhibited,
And they can't talk straight
Any more than they can walk straight;
Their pronunciation is awful
And their grammar is flawful,
And in adults it's drunken and maudlin and deplorable,
But in infants it's tunnin' and adorable.
So I hope you will agree that it is very hard to tell an infant from
    somebody who has gazed too long into the cup,
And really the only way you can tell them apart is to wait till next
    day, and the infant is the one that feels all right when it wakes
    up.

WILL CONSIDER SITUATION

These here are words of radical advice for a young man looking
    for a job:

Young man, be a snob.

Yes, if you are in search of arguments against starting at the bottom,

Why I've gottom.

Let the personnel managers differ;

It's obvious that you will get on faster at the top than at the bot-
    tom because there are more people at the bottom than at the
    top so naturally the competition at the bottom is stiffer.

If you need any further proof that my theory works,

Well, nobody can deny that presidents get paid more than vice-
    presidents and vice-presidents get paid more than clerks.

Stop looking at me quizzically;

I want to add that you will never achieve fortune in a job that
    makes you uncomfortable physically.

When anybody tells you that hard jobs are better for you than soft
    jobs be sure to repeat this text to them,

Postmen tramp around all day through rain and snow just to de-
    liver people's in cozy air-conditioned offices checks to them.

You don't need to interpret tea leaves stuck in a cup

To understand that people who work sitting down get paid more
    than people who work standing up.

Another thing about having a comfortable job is you not only ac-
    cumulate more treasure;

You get more leisure.

So that when you find you have worked so comfortably that your
    waistline is a menace,

You correct it with golf or tennis.

Whereas if in an uncomfortable job like piano-moving or steve-
    doring you indulge,

You have no time for exercise, you just continue to bulge.

To sum it up, young man, there is every reason to refuse a job that
    will make heavy demands on you corporally or manually,

And the only intelligent way to start your career is to accept a sit-
    ting position paying at least twenty-five thousand dollars an-
    nually.

THE MIDDLE

When I remember bygone days
I think how evening follows morn;
So many I loved were not yet dead,
So many I love were not yet born.

LET'S NOT CLIMB THE
WASHINGTON MONUMENT TONIGHT

Listen, children, if you'll only stop throwing peanuts and bananas
   into my cage,
I'll tell you the facts of middle age.
Middle age is when you've met so many people that every new per-
   son you meet reminds you of someone else,
And when golfers' stomachs escape either over or under their belts.
It is when you find all halfbacks anthropoidal
And all vocalists adenoidal.
It is when nobody will speak loud enough for you to hear,
And you go to the ball game and notice that even the umpires are
   getting younger every year.
It's when you gulp oysters without bothering to look for pearls,
And your offspring cannot but snicker when you refer to your
   classmates as boys and your bridge partners as girls.
It is when you wouldn't visit Fred Allen or the Aga Khan if it
   meant sleeping on a sofa or a cot,
And your most exciting moment is when your shoelace gets tan-
   gled and you wonder whether if you yank it, it will come clean
   or harden into a concrete knot.
Also, it seems simpler just to go to bed than to replace a fuse,
Because actually you'd rather wait for the morning paper than lis-
   ten to the eleven o'clock news,
And Al Capone and Babe Ruth and Scott Fitzgerald are as remote
   as the Roman emperors,
And you spend your Saturday afternoons buying wedding presents
   for the daughters of your contemporers.
Well, who wants to be young anyhow, any idiot born in the last
   forty years can be young, and besides forty-five isn't really old,
   it's right on the border;
At least, unless the elevator's out of order.

GOOD RIDDANCE, BUT NOW WHAT?

Come children, gather round my knee;
Something is about to be.

Tonight's December thirty-first,
Something is about to burst.

The clock is crouching, dark and small,
Like a time bomb in the hall.

Hark, it's midnight, children dear.
Duck! Here comes another year!

EHEU! FUGACES
OR
WHAT A DIFFERENCE A LOT OF DAYS MAKE

When I was seventeen or so,
I scoffed at moneygrubbers.
I had a cold contempt for dough,
And I wouldn't wear my rubbers.
No aspirin I took for pains,
For pests no citronella,
And in the Aprilest of rains
I carried no umbrella.

When I was young I was Sidney Carton,
Proudly clad in a Spartan tartan.
Today I'd be, if I were able,
Just healthy, wealthy, and comfortable.

When I was young I would not yield
To comforters and bed socks,
In dreams I covered center field
For the Giants or the Red Sox.
I wished to wander hence and thence,
From diamond mine to goldfield,
Or piloting a Blitzen Benz,
Outdistance Barney Oldfield.

When I subscribed to the *Youth's Companion*
I longed to become a second D'Artagnan.
Today I desire a more modest label:
He's healthy, wealthy, and comfortable.

When I was pushing seventeen,
I hoped to bag a Saracen;
Today should one invade the scene,
I'd simply find it embaracen.
Ah, Postumus, no wild duck I,
But just a waddling puddle duck,
So here's farewell to the open sky
From a middle-aged fuddy-duddle duck.

When I was young I was Roland and Oliver,
Nathan Hale and Simón Bolívar.
Today I would rather sidestep trouble,
And be healthy, wealthy, and comfortable.

I DIDN'T SAY A WORD
OR
WHO CALLED THAT PICCOLO
PLAYER A FATHER?

A man could be granted to live a dozen lives,
And he still wouldn't understand daughters and wives.
It may be because sometimes their ears are pierced for earrings,
But they have the most eccentric hearings.
Their hearings are in fact so sensitive
That you frequently feel reprehensive.
At home, for instance, when near you,
Nobody can hear you.
After your most brilliant fireside or breakfast table chats you can
    count on two fingers the responses you will have got:
Either, Don't mumble, dear, or, more simply, What?
I suppose if you're male and parental
You get used to being treated mental,
But you'd feel less psychically distant
If they weren't so inconsistent,

Because if you open your mouth in a hotel or a restaurant their
    eardrums quiver at every decibel,
And their embarrassment is almost, if not quite, inexprecibel.
Their eyes signal What's cooking? at you,
And their lips hiss, Shush, Daddy, everybody's looking at you!
Now, I realize that old age is a thing of beauty,
Because I have read Cicero's *De Senectute,*
But I prefer to approach senility in my own way, so I'll thank no-
    body to rush me,
By which I mean specifically that my voice in a tearoom is no
    louder than anybody else's, so why does everybody have to
    shush me?

YOU CAN BE A REPUBLICAN,
I'M A GERONTOCRAT

Oh, "rorty" was a mid-Victorian word
Which meant "fine, splendid, jolly,"
And often to me it has reoccurred
In moments of melancholy.
For instance, children, I think it rorty
To be with people over forty.

I can't say which, come eventide,
More tedious I find;
Competing with the juvenile stride,
Or meeting the juvenile mind.
So I think it rorty, yes, and nifty,
To be with people over fifty.

The pidgin talk the youthful use
Bypasses conversation.
I can't believe the code they choose
Is a means of communication.
Oh, to be with people over sixty
Despite their tendency to prolixity!

The hours a working parent keeps
Mean less than Latin to them,
Wherefore they disappear in jeeps

Till three and four A.M.
Oh, to be with people you pour a cup for
Instead of people you have to wait up for!

I've tried to read young mumbling lips
Till I've developed a slant-eye,
And my hearing fails at the constant wails
Of, If I can't, why can't I?
Oh, to be beside a septuagenarian,
Silent upon a peak in Darien!

They don't know Hagen from Bobby Jones,
They never heard of Al Smith,
Even Red Grange is beyond their range,
And Dempsey is a myth.
Oh golly, to gabble upon the shoulder
Of someone my own age, or even older!

I'm tired of defining hadn't oughts
To opposition mulish,
The thoughts of youth are long long thoughts,
And Jingo! Aren't they foolish!
All which is why, in case you've wondered
I'd like a companion aged one hundred.

THE VOLUBLE WHEELCHAIR

When you roll along admiring the view,
And everyone drives too fast but you;
When people not only ignore your advice,
But complain that you've given it to them twice;
When you babble of putts you nearly holed,
By gad, sir,
You are getting old.

When for novels you lose your appetite
Because writers don't write what they used to write;
When by current art you are unbeguiled,
And pronounce it the work of an idiot child;
When cacophonous music leaves you cold,

By gad, sir,
You are getting old.

When you twist the sheets from night to morn
To recall when a cousin's daughter was born;
When youngsters mumble and won't speak up,
And your dog dodders, who was a pup;
When the modern girl seems a hussy bold,
By gad, sir,
You are getting old.

When you scoff at feminine fashion trends;
When strangers resemble absent friends;
When you start forgetting the neighbors' names
And remembering bygone football games;
When you only drop in at the club to scold,
By gad, sir,
You are getting old.

But when you roar at the income tax,
And the slippery bureaucratic hacks,
And the ancient political fishlike smell,
And assert that the world is going to hell,
Why you are not old at all, at all;
By gad, sir,
You are on the ball.

BIRTHDAY ON THE BEACH

At another year
I would not boggle,
Except that when I jog
I joggle.

CROSSING THE BORDER

Senescence begins
And middle age ends
The day your descendants
Outnumber your friends.

COME ON IN, THE SENILITY IS FINE

People live forever in Jacksonville and St. Petersburg and Tampa,
But you don't have to live forever to become a grampa.
The entrance requirements for grampahood are comparatively mild,
You only have to live until your child has a child.
From that point on you start looking both ways over your shoulder,
Because sometimes you feel thirty years younger and sometimes
     thirty years older.
Now you begin to realize who it was that reached the height of im-
     becility,
It was whoever said that grandparents have all the fun and none
     of the responsibility.
This is the most enticing spiderweb of a tarradiddle ever spun,
Because everybody would love to have a baby around who was no
     responsibility and lots of fun,
But I can think of no one but a mooncalf or a gaby
Who would trust their own child to raise a baby.
So you have to personally superintend your grandchild from dia-
     pers to pants and from bottle to spoon
Because you know that your own child hasn't sense enough to
     come in out of a typhoon.
You don't have to live forever to become a grampa, but if you do
     want to live forever,
Don't try to be clever;
If you wish to reach the end of the trail with an uncut throat,
Don't go around saying Quote I don't mind being a grampa but I
     hate being married to a gramma Unquote.

EH?

One advantage of advancing years:
They do something to your ears.
A touch of deafness lightens one of life's heaviest chores:
Listening to bores.
Of bores I have suffered more than my portion,
And I now find that their conversation is improved by a little dis-
     tortion,

Which alleviates my malaise
At cocktail parties and buffets.
Cornered by the unkempt young woman to whom reading Allen
    Ginsberg aloud to unkempt young men is fun,
My ears persuade me she said "Xenophon," not "Zen is fun."
Thus I can loll in a wonderland more fantastic than Alice's,
Half Anabasis, half analysis.
The female movie addict to whom the annual Oscars are graven
    tablets from Hollywood's holy mountain
No longer irks me when I seem to hear her complain that this
    year's award-winning song is not as good as one of its prede-
    cessors, "Pork Loins in the Fountain."
With the aid of my aural deficiency I encounter many happy sur-
    prises in what was once tedious social verbosity,
And go home refreshed to listen to the TV pitchman selling me a
    floor polish which seems to be called
Whipped Cream, and a cigarette, the unique virtue of which seems
    to be its high ferocity.

THE SUNSET YEARS OF SAMUEL SHY

Master I may be,
But not of my fate.
Now come the kisses, too many too late.
Tell me, O Parcae,
For fain would I know,
Where were these kisses three decades ago?
Girls there were plenty,
Mint julep girls, beer girls,
Gay younger married and headstrong career girls,
The girls of my friends
And the wives of my friends,
Some smugly settled and some at loose ends,
Sad girls, serene girls,
Girls breathless and turbulent,
Debs cosmopolitan, matrons suburbulent,
All of them amiable,
All of them cordial,

Innocent rousers of instincts primordial,
But even though health and wealth
Hadn't yet missed me,
None of them,
Not even Jenny,
Once kissed me.

These very same girls
Who with me have grown older
Now freely relax with a head on my shoulder,
And now come the kisses,
A flood in full spate,
The meaningless kisses, too many too late.
They kiss me hello,
They kiss me goodbye,
Should I offer a light, there's a kiss for reply.
They kiss me at weddings,
They kiss me at wakes,
The drop of a hat is less than it takes.
They kiss me at cocktails,
They kiss me at bridge,
It's all automatic, like slapping a midge.
The sound of their kisses
Is loud in my ears
Like the locusts that swarm every seventeen years.

I'm arthritic, dyspeptic,
Potentially ulcery,
And weary of kisses by custom compulsory.
Should my dear ones commit me
As senile demential,
It's from kisses perfunctory, inconsequential.
Answer, O Parcae,
For fain would I know,
Where were these kisses three decades ago?

THE WRONGS OF SPRING
OR
NO ALL FOOLS' DAY
LIKE AN ALL OLD FOOLS' DAY

Just because I'm sixty-three,
Shall April folly forbidden be?
Though the locks above my scalp
Be thin as snow on August Alp,
Must I then leave April foibles
To sprouts of louts and hobbledehoibles?
I still remain the out-to-win type,
And I reply, "Not on your tintype!"
I will find a zany zebra,
I will teach the beast algebra;
Buy a Peugeot or a Simca
Present it to a worthy YMCA;
Seek me out a sporting bishop,
Fit him with slaloms from a ski shop;
Roam through Perth and other Amboys,
Gathering luscious fraises and framboise,
To feast on with meringues and Nesselrodes
The while I drink a toast to Cecil Rhodes.
I'll write to some forlorn Penelope,
"S(ealed) W(ith) A K(iss)" on the envelope;
I'll memorize the works of Euripides
And match the footwork of centipedes.
I'll turn my mind to projects grandiose—
Regal, imperial, Ozymandiose—
Be Orientally lethargical,
Sybaritic, Maharajical,
And write, while lolling in my tub,
A syllabus on syllabub.
So I'll pace out my seven ages
By various frolicsome ambages—
A word that means, in Webster's phrase,
By roundabout or winding ways.
Thus, when April hoots her girlish laughter
My senile cackle shall echo after.

A MAN CAN COMPLAIN, CAN'T HE?
(A LAMENT FOR THOSE WHO THINK OLD)

Pallid and moonlike in the smog,
Now feeble Phoebus 'gins arise;
The upper floors of Empire State
Have vanished into sooty skies.
Half missing, like the shrouded tower,
Lackluster, like the paten solar,
I draw reluctant waking breath;
Another day, another dolor.

That breath I draw was first exhaled
By diesel and incinerator;
I should have wakened not at all,
Or, were it feasible, even later.
Walls of the world close in on me,
Threats equatorial and polar;
Twixt pit and pendulum I lie;
Another day, another dolor.

Here's news about the current strike,
The latest, greatest test of fission.
A fatal mugging in the park,
An obit of the Geneva mission.
One envelope yields a baffling form
Submitted by the tax comptroller;
A jury summons completes my mail;
Another day, another dolor.

Once eager for, I've come to dread,
The nimble fingers of my barber;
He's training strands across my scalp
Like skimpy vines across an arbor.
The conversation at the club
Is all intestinal or molar;
What dogs the Class of '24?
Another day, another dolor.

Between the dotard and the brat
My disaffection veers and varies;

Sometimes I'm sick of clamoring youth,
Sometimes of my contemporaries.
I'm old too soon, yet young too long;
Could Swift himself have planned it droller?
Timor vitae conturbat me;
Another day, another dolor.

PREFACE TO THE PAST

Time all of a sudden tightens the tether,
And the outspread years are drawn together.
How confusing the beams from memory's lamp are;
One day a bachelor, the next a grampa.
What is the secret of the trick?
How did I get so old so quick?
Perhaps I can find by consulting the files
How step after step added up to miles.
I was sauntering along, my business minding,
When suddenly struck by affection blinding,
Which led to my being a parent nervous
Before they invented the diaper service.
I found myself in a novel pose,
Counting infant fingers and toes.
I tried to be as wise as Diogenes
In the rearing of my two little progenies,
But just as I hit upon wisdom's essence
They changed from infants to adolescents.
I stood my ground, being fairly sure
That one of these days they must mature,
So when I was properly humbled and harried,
They did mature, and immediately married.
Now I'm counting, the cycle being complete,
The toes on my children's children's feet.
Here lies my past, good-by I have kissed it;
Thank you, kids, I wouldn't have missed it.

The Curtain Rises—
Nashional Performances

UNTITLED

A pretty girl is like a melody and a pretty moustache cup is like Mr.
    Dewey,
And a pretty musical comedy is like an ugly race at Aqueduct or
    Bowie.
Please do not gather from this most tentative of discourses
That I mean to imply that a musical comedy is filled with unreli-
    able horses,
Because anyone with half an eye can distinguish a horse race from
    a musical comedy because horses take the saliva test,
While girls take the Godiva test,
No, I merely mean to aver through gritted dentures
That betting on horses and writing musical comedies are both
    highly speculative ventures,
Only if you are wrong about a horse race it takes just two minutes
    to find out, plus a little money, with which naturally you are
    rife,
While even to find out if you are right about a musical comedy re-
    quires fifteen of the best months of your life.

On the other hand if you win a bet, your satisfaction is private,
   you don't get any public plaudits or applauses.
Whereas if you conquer Broadway you get your name in the pa-
   pers, which leads to visits from the Bureau of Internal Revenue,
   and appeals to contribute to many worthy causes.
On the same hand, both gambles are fraught with hopes and doubts,
And well-wishers and ill-wishers who masquerade as friends but
   boil down to touts,
Who after your money is irrevocably down inform you after with
   the maximum of confidence and the minimum of tact
That what you need is a different horse or a different lovesong or
   a different jockey or a different first act.
And they are right because now I can hardly tell the paddock at
   Saratoga from the lobby of the Shubert in New Haven.
They are both filled with the voice of the raven.

FOUR PROMINENT SO-AND-SO'S

(ALSO PUBLISHED AS *QUARTET OF PROSPEROUS LOVE-CHILDREN*)

(Editor's Note: This is the first of Nash's published lyrics. This song was written for the March 1933 Dutch Treat Club performance in New York City. Robert Armbruster composed the music. The verses were published later in *Happy Days*—slightly Bowdlerized—but several private printings reverted to the original verses, initially known as "Pedigree," of which this is the most requested.)

I'm an autocratic figure in these democratic states,
I'm a dandy demonstration of hereditary traits.
As the children of the baker bake the most delicious breads,
As the sons of Casanova fill the most exclusive beds,
As the Barrymores, the Roosevelts, and others I could name
Inherited the talents that perpetuate their fame,
My position in the structure of society I owe
To the qualities my parents bequeathed me long ago.
My pappy was a gentleman, and musical, to boot,
He used to play piano in a house of ill repute.
The madam was a lady, and a credit to her cult,
She enjoyed my pappy's playing, and I was the result!
So my mammy and my pappy are the ones I have to thank
That I'm Chairman of the Board of the National Country Bank!

Chorus:
Oh, our parents forgot to get married,
Oh, our parents forgot to get wed,
Did a wedding bell chime? It was always a time
When our parents were somewhere in bed,
Tra la la la, parents were somewhere in bed.
Oh, thanks to our kind loving parents,
We are kings in the land of the free—
Your banker, your broker, your Washington joker—
Four prominent bastards are we, tra la la la
Four prominent bastards are we.

In a cozy little farmhouse in a cozy little dell
A dear old-fashioned farmer and his daughter used to dwell.
She was pretty, she was charming, she was tender, she was mild,
And her sympathy was such that she was frequently with child.
The year her hospitality attained a record high
She became the happy mammy of an infant, which was I.
Whenever she was gloomy I could always make her grin
By childishly inquiring who my pappy could have been.
The hired man was favored by the girls in Mammy's set
And a trav'ling man from Scranton was an even money bet.
But such were Mammy's motives, and such was her allure,
That even Roger Babson wasn't altogether sure.
Well, I took my mammy's morals and I took my pappy's crust
And I grew to be the founder of a big Investment Trust.

Chorus:

On a cozy little chain gang on a dusty southern road
My late lamented daddy had his permanent abode.
Now some were there for stealing, but Daddy's only fault
Was an overwhelming weakness for criminal assault.
His philosophy was simple, and free of moral tape:
Seduction is for sissies, but a he-man wants his rape.
Daddy's total list of victims was embarrassingly rich,
And though one of them was Mammy, he couldn't tell me which,
Well, I didn't go to college, but I got me a degree;
I reckon I'm the model of a perfect S.O.B.;
I'm a debit to my country but a credit to my dad,

The most expensive senator the nation ever had;
I remember Daddy's warning that raping is a crime
Unless you rape the voters a million at a time.

Chorus:

I'm an ordinary figure in these democratic states,
A pathetic demonstration of hereditary traits.
As the children of policemen possess the flattest feet,
As the daughter of the floozie has a waggle to her seat,
My position at the bottom of society I owe
To the qualities my parents bequeathed me long ago.
My father was a married man, and what is even more,
He was married to my mother, a fact which I deplore,
I was born in holy wedlock, consequently, by and by,
I was rooked by every bastard with plunder in his eye.
I invested, I deposited, I voted every fall,
And if I saved a penny, the bastards took it all.
At last I've learned my lesson and I'm on the proper track:
I'm a self-appointed bastard and I'm goin' to get it back.

Chorus

ONE TOUCH OF VENUS

Some girls have a touch of Venus,
It can help a girl a lot,
Why describe a touch of Venus?
You either have it or not.
If you have a touch of Venus,
Men will all react the same,
With a little touch of Venus,
A lady can beat the game.

The world belongs to men and women,
But the banks belong to men,
The world is just a green persimmon
If you're an average hen.
Venus found she was a goddess
In a world controlled by gods,
So she opened up her bodice,
And equalized the odds.

If you have a touch of Venus,
Men of Iron turn to clay.
Confidentially, between us,
They are suckers in the hay.
Look what Beatrice did to Dante,
What DuBarry did to France,
Venus showed them that the pantie
Is mightier than the pants.

Some girls have a touch of Venus,
They get diamonds every night.
If she has a touch of Venus,
When a girl does wrong she does it right.
I could use a touch of Venus,
It comes in handy in a pinch,
Mix a little touch of goddess,
A little touch of damsel,
And life is just a goddess damsel cinch.

HOW MUCH I LOVE YOU

More than a catbird hates a cat,
Or a criminal hates a clue,
Or the Axis hates the United States,
That's how much I love you.
As a sailor's sweetheart hates the sea,
Or a juggler hates a shove,
As a wife detests unexpected guests,
That's how much you I love.

I love you more than a wasp can sting,
And more than a hangnail hurts;
I love you more than commercials are a bore,
And more than a grapefruit squirts.
I swear to you by the stars above,
And below, if such there be,
As a bride would resent a blessed event,
That's how you are loved by me.

More than a waiter hates to wait,
Or a lioness hates the zoo,
Or a batter dislikes those called third strikes,
That's how much I love you.
As much as a lifeguard hates to swim
Or a writer hates to read,
Or the Hays office frowns on low-cut gowns,
That's how much you I need.

I love you more than a hive can itch
And more than a chilblain chills,
I yearn for you in an ivy-clad igloo
As a liver yearns for pills.
I swear to you by the earth below,
And above, if such there be,
As a dachshund abhors revolving doors,
That's how you are loved by me.

Tell me, is love still a popular suggestion,
Or merely an obsolete art?
Forgive me for asking this simple question,
I'm unfamiliar with his heart,
I'm a stranger here myself.

Why is it wrong to murmur I adore him
When it's shamefully obvious I do?
Does love embarrass him or does it bore him?
I'm only waiting for my cue,
I'm a stranger here myself.

I dream of a day, a gay warm day,
With my face between his hands;
Have I missed the path, have I gone astray?
I ask, and no one understands.

Love me or leave me, that seems to be the question,
I don't know the tactics to use,
But if he should offer a personal suggestion,
How could I possibly refuse,
When I'm a stranger here myself?

Please tell me, tell a stranger,
By curiosity goaded,
Is there really any danger
That love is now outmoded?
I'm interested especially
In knowing why you waste it,
True romance is so fleshly—
With what have you replaced it?
What is your latest foible?
Is gin rummy more exquisite?
Is skiing more enjoy'ble?
For heaven's sake, what is it?

I can't believe that love has lost its glamour,
That passion is really passé;
If gender is just a term in grammar

How can I ever find my way,
When I'm a stranger here myself?

How can he ignore my available condition?
Why these Victorian views?
You perceive before you a woman with a mission,
This is a case for a woman's intuition,
I must discover the key to his ignition,
Then if he should make a diplomatic proposition,
How can I possible refuse,
When I am a stranger here myself?

WEST WIND

I had a love, and my love was fair,
Fair as a summer's dawn.
I lost my love, I never knew where,
Suddenly she was gone.
The West Wind stirred the meadow
The night she slipped away,
And I seem to glimpse her shadow
When the West Wind brushes the day.

West Wind, can you waken my true love?
West Wind, can your whisper renew love?
Speak to her softly of the dream we lost,
The theme we lost,
The gleam we lost.

West Wind, can you call back an old love?
West Wind, can you kindle a cold love?
West Wind, can the magic of then
Become ours once again?
Breathe on the embers,
If by chance she remembers,
Then some day at last
We can recapture the past.

FOOLISH HEART

Will you tell me how these things happen?
Have I trusted in love too much?
When did the magic vanish?
Have I somehow lost my touch?
How gay the world could be
Could I love you, could he love me.

Love shouldn't be serious, should it?
You meet, perhaps you kiss, you start.
I fancied that I understood it;
I forgot my foolish heart.
Love can't be illogical, can it?
You kiss, perhaps you smile, you part.
It happens the way that you plan it,
If you hush your foolish heart.
Poor foolish heart,
Crying for one who ignores you!
Poor foolish heart,
Flying from one who adores you!
Ah, love used to touch me so lightly,
Why will my heart betray me so?
I could dance with a new lover nightly,
But my foolish heart says No.

THE TROUBLE WITH WOMEN

I once loved a girl out in Flatbush,
A picture of beauty and grace;
But she thought kittens came from a catbush,
And she never had heard of first base.
I travel no longer to Flatbush,
Though the girl is both wealthy and pure,
For whenever I tried my desires to confide
Her mind was upon her coiffure.

Oh, the trouble, the trouble with women,
They soften your heart till it melts,

And then at the critical moment
They are thinking about something else.

As a student my life was Parisian,
I languished, a captive of sex.
When specks interfered with my vision
They were lovely, voluptuous specks.
I toiled on a farm tilling soybeans,
In a struggle to chasten my brain,
But the girl beans got in with the boy beans,
And I never struggled again.

Oh, the trouble, the trouble with women,
You think you have left them behind,
You frolic in physical freedom,
And then they turn up in your mind.

The reason each day I grow frailer,
Is that I'm trapped in a one-way romance
With a lady who lives in a trailer,
With some devil-may-care debutantes.
Her love for her kin is exquisite,
She entertains uncles galore;
But whenever I pay her a visit
Them uncles won't open the door.

Oh, the trouble, the trouble with women,
I fear that their life is a lie,
While they stall you with maidenly murmurs
They are romping with some other guy.

When I drove in my glamorous Chevy
I would park in a suitable spot,
Then I'd turn to the girls like a heavy,
And inquire if they would, or would not.
I always implied that they had to,
But, oh Jimminies, was I perplexed,
On the night that one said she'd be glad to—
I didn't know what to do next.

Oh, the trouble, the trouble with women
They are either too cold or too warm.

Yes, they're either in flight or insatiable.
Oh, God give me strength to ignor'm.

One week end I rented a Packard
For a maiden of whom I was fond.
Her lips and her toenails were lacquered
And I think she was technically blond.
Her defenses had started to crumble,
I was bursting with masculine pride,
When up spoke a voice from the rumble—
Her mother had stolen a ride.

Oh, the trouble, the trouble with women,
They are constantly one jump ahead.
You touch what you think is a bosom,
And you find it's an eight-ball instead.

The reason I moan in my slumber
Is that I'm subject to female rebuffs,
Or if I make note of a number,
The laundry erases my cuffs.
If I droop like a lily in sadness,
The diagnosis is easy to see,
Every woman has moments of madness,
But never, no never with me.

Oh, the trouble, the trouble with women,
I repeat it again and again,
From Kalamazoo to Kamchatka
The trouble with women is men.

SPEAK LOW

Speak low when you speak love,
Our summer day
Withers away
Too soon, too soon.
Speak low when you speak love;
Our moment is swift,
Like ships adrift

We're swept apart too soon.
Speak low, darling, speak low,
Love is a spark,
Lost in the dark,
Too soon, too soon.
I feel, wherever I go,
That tomorrow is near,
Tomorrow is here,
And always too soon.
Time is so old, and love so brief,
Love is pure gold, and time a thief.
We're late, darling, we're late,
The curtain descends,
Everything ends,
Too soon, too soon.
I wait, darling, I wait—
Will you speak low to me,
Speak love to me,
And soon?

THAT'S HIM

You know the way you feel when there is autumn in the air?
That's him. . . . That's him. . . .
The way you feel when Antoine has finished with your hair?
That's him. . . . That's him. . . .
You know the way you feel when you smell bread baking,
The way you feel when suddenly a tooth stops aching?
Wonderful world, wonderful you,
That's him. . . . That's him. . . .

He's simple as a swim in summer,
Not arty, not actory,
He's like a plumber when you need a plumber,
He's satisfactory.
You know the way you feel when you want to knock on wood,
The way you feel when your heart is gone for good?
Wonderful world, wonderful you,
That's him.

You could shuffle him with millions,
Soldiers and civilians,
I'd pick him out.
In the darkest caves and hallways
I would know him always
Beyond a doubt.
Identification comes easily to me
Because—that's he.

You know the way you feel about the *Rhapsody in Blue*?
That's him. . . . That's him. . . .
The way you feel about a hat created just for you?
That's him. . . . That's him. . . .
You know the way you feel when the fireflies glimmer,
The way you feel when overnight your hips grow slimmer?
Wonderful world, wonderful you,
That's him. . . . That's him. . . .

He's like a book directly from the printer:
You look at him—he's so commenceable,
He's comforting as woolens in the winter,
He's indispensable.
You know the way you feel that you know you should conceal,
The way you feel that you really shouldn't feel?
Wonderful world, wonderful you,
That's him.

LOW AND LAZY

I used to be a girl with a vinegar tongue
And a tombstone for a heart,
So I feel a little funny when I find myself
So obviously falling apart.
What can a hard girl do when she goes soft
But throw the rules away,
What can she say, but

Low and lazy,
Can this be me so low and lazy,
Could it maybe
Be love?
Warm and wistful,
What makes you look so warm and wistful,
Could it maybe
Be love?
There was I who thought that holding hands was senseless,
Now I'm defenseless,
I'm walking wide-eyed.
Low and lazy,
I thank my heart my head is hazy.
Can I ever come to?
When I'm so low and lazy and with you.

Mother washed my mouth with soap the time I flirted,
Now I'm converted,
I'm sailing sky high.
Low and lazy,
I know why bees and flowers go crazy—
Let's find out what they do
When I'm so low and lazy and with you.

When you look life in the face
There's too much time, there's too much space,
There's too much future, too much past,
Man is so little, and the world so vast;
You may fancy yourself as an immortal creature
But you're just a cartoon between a double feature.

You go round about
And round about
And round about you go,
For an olden spell is wound about the game.
Then it's ring around
And swing around
Your partners as you go,
But the more they change, the more they are the same.
When the dancing is done,
You are back where you started,
When the music begins, it plays the same old tune.
Then it's round about
And round about
And round about again
As you pray again
Each day again to soar;
On your way again,
It's round about once more.

You wake each morning alive and gay,
You think today is another day,
Your future seems a primrose path,
You hum to your pillow and you sing in your bath.
Your stockings hug you along the seam,
Your girdle fits like a sophomore's dream,
You roam the world like a romantic rover,
You find today is just yesterday warmed over.
You meet a man and you're on the crest.
You think he's diff'rent from all the rest.
You start to dream of a cozy flat
With milk for the kids and cream for the cat,

And that's the moment not to be astounded
To find that you've been merry-go-rounded.

You go round about
And round about
And round about you go,
For an olden spell is wound about the game,
Then it's ring around
And swing around
Your partners as you go,
But the more they change, the more they stay the same.
When the dancing is done,
You are back where you started,
Each tomorrow the sun shines through your vacant heart.
Then it's round about
And round about
And round about again
As you pray again each day again to soar;
On your way again,
It's round about once more.

(Editor's Note: This song reappeared in the 1952 musical *Two's Company*)

A LITTLE LOVE, A LITTLE MONEY

A little love, a little money,
That's all that I'm praying for,
A little love, a little money,
Lord, I'm a beggar at your door.

A little love, a little money,
What more can a poor man use?
I'll spend the money on my baby
And take a chance on shoes.

I'm not praying for limousines
Or green turtle soup in golden tureens.
Lord, if it ain't too much to give
All I want is a chance to live.

A little love, a little money,
That's the reason the rich ain't poor
You know I'm broke, you know I'm lonely
Lord, there's no trouble I'd endure
That money and love can't cure.

A little love, a little money,
Will do what no preacher can.
A little love, a little money,
Might turn a bum into a man.

A little love, a little money,
Won't you send me before I die?
Just a little spending money
And someone standing by.

I'm not greedy, I do not dream
Of platinum sauce on diamond ice cream.
I've lived too long in shanty-town,
Someday I've got to settle down.

A little love, a little money,
A silver dollar, a pretty dove—
If that should be too much to ask for
I humbly tell the Lord above
I'll do without the love.

JUST LIKE A MAN

A girl can get along without a song,
A girl can get ahead without a sled,
She can find her Shangri-La without a bra,
But I don't think she can without a man. . . .

Just like a man,
He was like sugar when our thing began.
Just like a man,
When the going got rough he ran.
Just like a dame,
I found he was easy to blame,
But now that he's gone
It's beginning to dawn
Life is worse than it was before he came.

It's queer how a man can irritate you
When he's round you every day.
Yet even his cigar butts fascinate you
The moment he's gone away.

He was a man,
The charter member of the no-good clan,
And now life is empty
Because I never dreamt he
Would pick up his hat just like a man.

Just like a man,
He involved me in a nudist plan;
I'm not a man,
I got blisters when he got tan.
Just like a lynx,

I watched every one of his drinks
But should he come in
From wherever he's been,
I will smile while he drinks until he stinks.

He used to flood the bathtub with his splashes
While he bellowed like a cow.
When he lit my cigarettes, he lit my lashes.
Oh I wish they were burning now.

He drove me frantic humming Dardanella,
I can hear that flat note yet
On rainy nights he lost our umbrella
Now I'd welcome him wringing wet.

He was a man,
The only thing Del Monte cannot can.
But now that I've known him
I guess I want to own him,
Because he behaves just like a man.

He was a man,
A thing no other thing is lower than;
Though he was all headaches,
My heart aches and my bed aches
Because he has gone, just like a man.

(Editor's Note: This song later became Bette Davis's sig-
nature song in the 1952 musical revue *Two's Company*.)

OUT OF THE CLEAR BLUE SKY

Where was I just a-strolling, humming
Pavements were hot but rain was coming;
Swiftly the sky grew strange and dark
Fate strode beside me in the park.
I brooded on the sky above
When my heart felt a bump and a shove—

She came out of the clear blue sky,
Struck my heart and I don't know why,
Lost in lightning and thunder—
Now I wonder Where am I?

I was doing all right alone,
Am I ready to be her own?
Must I fall for a stranger
Who came out of the clear blue sky?

He came out of the clear blue sky,
Like the rain when your heart is dry,
Lost in lightning and thunder—
Now I wonder Where am I?

I feel young as an April breeze
And as old as the Seven Seas.
I'm in love with a stranger
Who came out of the clear blue sky.

I'm in love with a stranger
Who came out of the clear blue sky.

HAUNTED HOTSPOT

Used to know a sizzling hotspot
Crazy with jam and jive
The piano was so carefree
And the striptease so alive.

Sauntered by the club last Friday
And felt my blood run cold.
The entrance was boarded up
And the marquee was covered with mold.

That old haunted hotspot
It's stranger than most;
Got no cover charges
And features a genuine ghost.

There's mice in the bandstand
And cartons on the bar;
There's rust on the spotlight
That used to pick out the star.

Her price was high, the drummer man—he was her guy
Until that hot-dog pianist caught her eye.

Dust covers on the piano
A hole in the drum
In that haunted hotspot
A lady got slayed by a bum.

It's haunted until Kingdom come.

FLY NOW AND PAY LATER

I'm afraid our producers didn't trust you,
They made you pay for your tickets in advance.
That's the proper routine on the box office scene,
But it's not the right routine for romance.
You cannot pay in advance for romance.
No matter how much you have hoarded,
Paying in advance is kind of sordid.

I want to fly now and pay later;
Sample every thrill before the bill comes due
I want to buy now and pay later,
For the hidden love, forbidden love of you.
I want to burn our bridges behind us,
Gather rosebuds while we may,
The bill collector's sure to find us,
But not today, no, not today!
I want to fly now and pay later,
Want to soar with you to a sky of blue and gold
Want to fly now, riding high now,
I want to fly now before my wings grow old.

BORN TOO LATE

Once in a while I dream
Of a river that runs upstream,
Of a river flowing back to time gone by.
To a day when hearts beat high,
But the old earth keeps growing older,
While I'm glancing over my shoulder.

Born too late,
No more worlds to conquer,
Born too late,
All the deeds are done.
Long ago somewhere around the corner
Slumbered a princess waiting to be won.
The sky was bright with fiery dragons,
Mermaids filled the softly singing sea,
Now the sea and the sky are humdrum
And the princess, where is she?

Faint and far,
I can hear the music
Fade and die,
Leave me with my fate.
Faint and far,
I can hear the princess sighing,
"You were born too late."

THIS LOVELY WORLD

This lovely world
In which we slumbered
Outlives its time,
Its days are numbered.
Our world must pass
Like breath on glass—
The joys we share depart.

This lovely world
Fades into fable,
Like Roland's Horn
And Arthur's Table,
So clouds our sky
But you and I
Will face it heart to heart.

(Sung by Ashley to Melanie in
the *Twelve Oaks* theme.)

I'M TOO YOUNG TO BE A WIDOW

I'm too young to be a widow,
Widow's weeds are not for me,
Why should I be broken-hearted?
I was caged, and now I'm free.

Black material,
So funereal,
Makes me want to scream, I declare.
I won't falsify,
I would waltz if I—
If I met the man who would dare.

I don't want to be a widow,
I was never Charles's wife,
Brooding over Charles's memory
I don't want to spend my life.

I'll tiptoe warily
Temporarily,
Mourning like a true turtle-dove
(But) I'm too young to be a widow
And I'm old enough for love.

(Sung by Scarlett O'Hara after Charles's
death before she goes to Atlanta.)

EXCERPTS FROM RAVEL'S
"THE MOTHER GOOSE SUITE"
OR
FAIRY TALES FOR PROMENADES

PROLOGUE

Come one, come all, from village and town,
And turn the hourglass upside down.
See how the years, like grains of sand,
Sift backwards to a sweeter land,
A land that disappeared long since,
Where every frog might be a prince,
And every kitchen drudge, likewise,
A spellbound princess in disguise.
Just for a while forget the date,
Forget that you were born too late,
Too late to hear the mermaids singing
And dragons through the heavens winging,
Too late for simple tears and laughter
And living happily ever after.

Come join our game of make-believe,
Wear a child's heart upon your sleeve,
Pretend, with music soft, and rhyme,
That Now is Once Upon a Time.

HOP-O'-MY-THUMB

Hop-O'-My-Thumb, Hop-O'-My-Thumb,
Only three inches high, but bright as they come.
His father and mother were poverty-stricken,
Though they did have a pot, they did not have a chicken.
One night as he huddled in bed with his brothers
He overheard voices, his father's and mother's.
Said Papa, "We have nothing to cook or to carve,
And we can't bear to watch our little ones starve.
To the forest we'll take them at dawning of day;
While they're gathering firewood, we'll both slip away."

Said Mama, "But consider what fate will be theirs,
They will all be devoured by the wolves and the bears!"
He replied, "If they're eaten, they're eaten. So be it.
But remember, at least you won't be there to see it."
"Ah, what fortunate children," murmured Mama,
"To have such a kind-hearted thoughtful papa!"

Tiny Hop-O'-My-Thumb was the slyest of rebels,
He filled all his pockets with little white pebbles
Which he dropped on the ground wherever he could
As he and his family walked through the wood.
Thus the children at dusk, though abandoned, weren't lost,
For with bright shiny stones the path was embossed.
Said Hop-O'-My-Thumb, "I can see in the dark.
Don't cry, you're as safe as—well, in Central Park."
He led them all home, or its shabby equivalent,
Where their welcome may best be described as ambivalent.
"Now wasn't that fun?" said Papa, counting ten,
"I propose that tomorrow we do it again."

Now Hop-O'-My-Thumb searched around and around,
But search as he might, not a pebble was found.
When they entered the forest he scattered instead
A life-line of crumbs from his last bit of bread.
Night fell, and alas for poor Hop-O'-My-Thumb,
The birds of the forest had gulped every crumb.

But he didn't despair, he sniffed the air,
And followed his nose to an ogre's lair.
Cried the ogre, "You and your six plump siblings
Shall provide me juicy munchings and nibblings!"
But Hop-O'-My-Thumb didn't wish to be fed off,
He bamboozled that ogre and cut his head off,
And he seized the ogre's treasure hoard
And in seven-league boots he homeward soared,
Where he gave it all to his loving parents,
Which showed commendable forbearance.

EXCERPTS FROM TCHAIKOVSKY'S CHILDREN'S ALBUM—BETWEEN BIRTHDAYS AND OTHER INNOCENT VERSES

BETWEEN BIRTHDAYS

My birthdays take so long to start,
They come along a year apart.
It's worse than waiting for a bus;
I fear I used to fret and fuss,
But now, when by impatience vexed
Between one birthday and the next,
I think of all that I have seen
That keeps on happening in between.
The songs I've heard, the things I've done,
Make my un-birthdays not so un-.

WINTER MORNING

Winter is the king of showmen,
Turning tree stumps into snowmen
And houses into birthday cakes
And spreading sugar over lakes.
Smooth and clean and frosty white,
The world looks good enough to bite.
That's the season to be young,
Catching snowflakes on your tongue.

Snow is so snowy when it's snowing,
I'm sorry it's slushy when it's going.

THE HOBBY HORSE

I'll tell you the kind of horse I've got,
He'd rather gallop than trot trot trot,
He can jump like a wallaby, run like a wapiti,
He's my very own clippety-cloppety property.
He's herbivorous, so I call him Herbie,
And if he were alive, he'd win the Derby.

THE SWALLOW

Swallow, swallow, swooping free,
Do you not remember me?
I think last spring that it was you
Who tumbled down the sooty flue
With wobbly wings and gaping face,
A fledgling in the fireplace.
Remember how I nursed and fed you,
And then into the air I sped you?
How I wish that you would try
To take me with you as you fly.

THE NEW DOLL

My new doll is so squushy soft
She dimples where I touch her;
I loved my old doll very much,
But I love my new doll mucher.

MORNING PRAYER

Now another day is breaking,
Sleep was sweet and so is waking.
Dear Lord, I promised you last night
Never again to sulk or fight.
Such vows are easier to keep
When a child is sound asleep.
Today, O Lord, for your dear sake,
I'll try to keep them when awake.

SWEET DREAMS

I wonder as into bed I creep
What it feels like to fall asleep.
I've told myself stories, I've counted sheep,
But I'm always asleep when I fall asleep.
Tonight my eyes I will open keep,

And I'll stay awake till I fall asleep,
Then I'll know what it feels like to fall asleep,
Asleep,
Asleeep,
Asleeeep. . . .

THE CARNIVAL OF THE ANIMALS
(MUSIC BY CAMILLE ST. SAËNS)

INTRODUCTION

Camille St. Saëns was racked with pains
When people addressed him as "Saint Sains."
He held the human race to blame
Because it could not pronounce his name.
So he turned to metronome and fife
To glorify other forms of life.
Be quiet, please, for here begins
His salute to feathers, furs, and fins.

ROYAL MARCH OF THE LIONS

The lion is the king of beasts
And husband of the lioness.
Gazelles and things on which he feasts
Address him as your hioness.
There are those who admire that roar of his
In the African jungles and veldts
But I think wherever a lion is
I'd rather be somewhere else.

COCKS AND HENS

The rooster is a roistering hoodlum,
His battle-cry is a cock-a-doodlum.
Hands in pockets, cap over eye,
He whistles at pullets passing by.

WILD JACKASS

Have you ever harked to the jackass wild
Which scientists call the onager?
It sounds like the laugh of a backward child,
Or a hepcat on a harmoniger.

But do not sneer at the jackass wild,
There is method in his hee-haw,
For with maidenly blush and accent mild
The jenny-ass answers, shee-haw.

TURTLES

Come crown my brow with leaves of myrtle
I know the tortoise is a turtle.
Come carve my name in stone immortal,
I know the turtoise is a tortle.
I know to my profound despair;
I bet on one to beat a hare,
I also know I'm now a pauper
Because of its tortley turtley torpor.

ELEPHANTS

Elephants are useful friends
Equipped with handles at both ends.
They have a wrinkled, moth-proof hide:
Their teeth are upside down, outside.
If you think the elephant preposterous
You've probably never seen a rhinosterous.

KANGAROOS

The kangaroo can jump incredible,
He has to jump, because he's edible.
I could not eat a kangaroo
But many fine Australians do.
Those with cookbooks as well as boomerangs,
Prefer him in tasty kangaroo meringues.

THE AQUARIUM

Some fish are minnows, some are whales.
People have dimples. Fish have scales.

Some fish are slim, and some are round.
They don't catch cold, they don't get drowned.
But every fish wife fears for her fish
What we call mermaids and they call merfish.

THE MULES
In the world of mules
There are no rules.

THE CUCKOO IN THE WOODS
Cuckoos lead bohemian lives,
They fail as husbands and as wives;
Therefore they cynically disparage
Everybody else's marriage.

THE BIRDS
Puccini was Latin, and Wagner Teutonic,
And birds are incurably philharmonic.
Suburban yards and rural vistas
Are filled with avian Andrews sisters.
The skylark sings a roundelay,
The crow sings "The Road to Mandalay,"
The nightingale sings a lullaby
And the seagull sings a gullaby.
That's what shepherds listened to in Arcadia
Before they invented TV and radia.

THE PIANISTS
Some claim that pianists might be human,
And quote the case of Mr. Truman.
St. Saëns, upon the other hand,
Considered them a scurvy band.
Ape-like they are, he said, and simian,
Instead of normal men and wimian.

THE FOSSILS

At midnight in the museum hall
The fossils gathered for a ball.
There were no drums or saxophones
But just the clatter of their bones;
A rolling, rattling, carefree circus
Of mammoth polkas and mazurkas.
Pterodactyls and brontosauruses
Sang ghostly prehistoric choruses.
Amid the mastodonic wassail
I caught the eye of one small fossil.
Cheer up, old man, he said, and winked—
It's kind of fun to be extinct.

THE SWAN

The swan can swim while sitting down.
For pure conceit he takes the crown.
He looks in the mirror over and over,
And claims to have never heard of Pavlova.

GRAND FINALE

Now we reach the grand finale,
Animale, carnivale.
Noises new to sea and land
Issue from the skillful band.
All the strings contort their features
Imitating crawly creatures,
All the basses look like mumps
From blowing umpah umpah umps.
In out-doing Barnum and Bailey and Ringling
St. Saëns had done a miraculous thingling.

For Your Consideration

COMMON SENSE

Why did the Lord give us agility
If not to evade responsibility?

LOOK FOR THE SILVER LINING

I can't say that I feel particularly one way or the other towards
bellboys,
But I do admit that I haven't much use for the it's-just-as-well-
boys.
The cheery souls who drop around after every catastrophe and
think they are taking the curse off
By telling you about somebody who is even worse off.
No matter how deep and dark your pit, how dank your shroud,
Their heads are heroically unbloody and unbowed.
If you have just lost the one love of your life, there is no possible
doubt of it,
They tell you there are as good fish in the sea as ever came out of it.
If you are fined ten dollars for running past a light when you didn't
but the cop says you did,

They say Cheer up think of the thousand times you ran past them
   and didn't get caught so you're really ten thousand bucks
   ahead, Hey old kid?
If you lose your job they tell you how lucky you are that you've
   saved up a little wealth
And then when the bank folds with the savings they tell you you
   sure are lucky to still have your health.
Life to them is just one long happy game,
At the conclusion of which the One Great Scorer writes not
   whether you won it or lost it, but how you played it, against
   your name.
Kismet, they say, it's Fate. What is to be, will be. Buck up! Take
   heart!
Kismet indeed! Nobody can make me grateful for Paris Green in
   the soup just by assuring me that it comes that way Allah carte.

LINES TO A WORLD-FAMOUS POET WHO
FAILED TO COMPLETE A WORLD-FAMOUS POEM
OR
COME CLEAN, MR. GUEST!

Oft when I'm sitting without anything to read waiting for a train
   in a depot,
I torment myself with the poet's dictum that to make a house a
   home, livin' is what it takes a heap o'.
Now, I myself should very much enjoy makin' my house a home,
   but my brain keeps on a-goin' clickety-click, clickety-click,
   clickety-click,
If Peter Piper picked a peck o' heap o' livin', what kind of a peck
   o' heap o' livin' would Peter Piper pick?
Certainly a person doesn't need the brains of a Lincoln
To know that there are many kinds o' livin', just as there are many
   kinds o' dancin' or huntin' or fishin' or eatin' or drinkin'.
A philosophical poet should be specific
As well as prolific,
And I trust I am not being offensive
If I suggest that he should also be comprehensive.

You may if you like verify my next statement by sending a stamped, self-addressed envelope to either Dean Inge or Dean Gauss,
But meanwhile I ask you to believe that it takes a heap of other things besides a heap o' livin' to make a home out of a house.
To begin with, it takes a heap o' payin',
And you don't pay just the oncet, but agayin and agayin and agayin.
Buyin' a stock is called speculatin' and buyin' a house is called investin',
But the value of the stock or of the house fluctuates up and down, generally down, just as an irresponsible Destiny may destine,
Something else that your house takes a heap o', whether the builder came from Sicily or Erin,
Is repairin',
In addition to which, gentle reader, I am sorry to say you are little more than an imbecile or a cretin
If you think it doesn't take a heap o' heatin',
And unless you're spiritually allied to the little Dutch boy who went around inspectin' dikes lookin' for leaks to put his thumb in,
It takes a heap o' plumbin',
And if it's a house that you're hopin' to spend not just today but tomorrow in,
It takes a heap o' borrowin'.
In a word, Macushla,
There's a scad o' things that to make a house a home it takes not only a heap, or a peck, but at least a bushela.

HEARTS OF GOLD

OR

A GOOD EXCUSE IS WORSE THAN NONE

There are some people who are very resourceful
At being remorseful,
And who apparently feel that the best way to make friends
Is to do something terrible and then make amends.
They come to your party and make a great hit with your Victorian aunt and with her freely mingle,

And suddenly after another drink they start a lot of *double entendre* the *entendre* of which is unfortunately not *double* but single,

And if you say anything to them they take umbrage,

And later when you are emptying the ashtrays before going to bed you find them under the sofa where they have crept for a good night's slumbrage.

Then next day they are around intoning apologies

With all the grace and conviction of a high-paid choir intoning doxologies.

There are people in every group

Who will jog your elbow at table just when you are lifting a spoonful of very hot soup,

Or a musicale or something while you're listening to a ravishing obbligato

Will forget their cigarettes and burn a hole in your clothes the size of a medium-size tomato.

And then you are presented with a lot of form-fitting apologies

Quite good enough, I am sure, for inclusion in one of the higher-class anthologies.

Everybody says these people have hearts of gold,

But nevertheless they are always talking when you're putting, or splashing mud on you from their car, or giving you a cold,

And they are always sure that today you don't mind their inflicting on you any sorrow,

Because they'll give you so much pleasure when they smilingly apologize tomorrow.

But I myself would rather have a rude word from someone who has done me no harm

Than a graceful letter from the King of England saying he's sorry he broke my arm.

THE CASE OF IDENTITY

Some people achieve temporary fame

Because they never forget the face but never remember the name,

And others set a dizzy pace

By never missing a name but never recognizing a face,

And still others are sharpshooters for both names and faces and
   can at a glance fasten them to their proprietors in their proper
   positions,
And you want to look out for people with this charming social gift
   because they are either salesmen or politicians,
And finally there is a fourth unfortunate class of people who are
   constantly so embarrassed that they wish they could be swal-
   lowed up by a dozen Atlantics or Pacifics,
Because to their astigmatic eyes and wandering minds, faces are
   but a bouillabaisse of features, and names but an omelet of hi-
   eroglyphics,
And, if you too, dear reader, belong to this unhappy group,
I fear your life contains more woe is me than boop-boop-a-doop.
People come up to you and say You don't remember me, do you,
   and of course you say you do, and of course, you don't,
And the first two or three times it happens you think maybe they
   will eventually identify themselves but finally you get to know
   that they consistently won't,
And then when you walk along the street you are never off the
   horns of a dilemma,
Because you are always seeing somebody that you think you know
   but you can't quite rememma,
And if you don't speak to them they invariably turn out to have
   been somebody you like or somebody you like's wife,
And they get very angry and tell everybody you aren't speaking to
   your old friends anymore and they are off you for life,
And if you do speak to them, of the nearest policeman you are in
   danger
Because they invariably turn out to be a suspicious feminine
   stranger.
Then if you ever do happen to get a name by heart
It generally belongs to some single lady who immediately gets mar-
   ried or some married lady who immediately resumes her single
   name and you have to go back and make a fresh start.
And another thing you have to get used to
Is introducing people to people when you can't remember either
   the name of the people who are to be introduced or the people
   they are supposed to be introduced to,

And I wish all the people who are good at names or faces or both
  would retire to St. Helena or Elba or Taos,
And leave the rest of us to live quietly in cozy anonymous chaos.

ARE YOU A SNODGRASS?

It is possible that most individual and international social and eco-
  nomic collisions
Result from humanity's being divided into two main divisions.
Their lives are spent in mutual interference,
And yet you cannot tell them apart by their outward appearance.
Indeed the only way in which to tell one group from the other you
  are able
Is to observe them at the table,
Because the only visible way in which one group from the other
  varies
Is in its treatment of the cream and sugar on cereal and berries.
Group A, which we will call the Swozzlers because it is a very suit-
  able name, I deem,
First applies the sugar then swozzles it all over the place pouring
  on the cream,
And as fast as they put the sugar on they swozzle it away,
But such thriftlessness means nothing to ruthless egotists like they,
They just continue to scoop and swozzle and swozzle and scoop,
Until there is nothing left for the Snodgrasses, or second group.
A Snodgrass is a kind, handsome intelligent person who pours the
  cream on first,
And then deftly sprinkles the sugar over the cereal or berries after
  they have been properly immersed,
Thus assuring himself that the sugar will remain on the cereal and
  berries where it can do some good, which is his wish,
Instead of being swozzled away to the bottom of the dish.
The facts of the case for the Snodgrasses are so self-evident that it
  is ridiculous to debate them,
But this is unfortunate for the Snodgrasses as it only causes the sin-
  ister and vengeful Swozzlers all the more to hate them.
Swozzlers are irked by the superior Snodgrass intelligence and no-
  bility

And they lose no opportunity of inflicting on them every kind of
    incivility.
If you read that somebody has been run over by an automobile
You may be sure that the victim was a Snodgrass, and a Swozzler
    was at the wheel.
Swozzlers start wars and Snodgrasses get killed in them,
Swozzlers sell waterfront lots and Snodgrasses get malaria when
    they try to build in them.
Swozzlers invent fashionable diets and drive Snodgrasses crazy
    with tables of vitamins and calories,
Swozzlers go to Congress and think up new taxes and Snodgrasses
    pay their salaries,
Swozzlers bring tigers back alive and Snodgrasses get eaten by ana-
    condas,
Snodgrasses are depositors and Swozzlers are absconders,
Swozzlers hold straight flushes when Snodgrasses hold four of a
    kind,
Swozzlers step heavily on the toes of Snodgrasses' shoes as soon as
    they are shined.
Whatever achievements Snodgrasses achieve, Swozzlers always top
    them;
Snodgrasses say Stop me if you've heard this one, and Swozzlers
    stop them.
Swozzlers are teeming with useful tricks of the trade that are not
    included in standard university curricula;
The world in general is their oyster, and Snodgrasses in particular.
So I hope for your sake, dear reader, that you are a Swozzler, but
    I hope for everybody else's sake that you are not,
And I also wish that everybody else was a nice amiable Snodgrass
    too, because then life would be just one long sweet harmonious
    mazurka or gavotte.

GRASSHOPPERS ARE VERY INTELLIGENT

Ah woe, woe, woe, man was created to live by the sweat of his brow,
And it doesn't make any difference if your brow was moist yester-
    day and the day before, you've still got to get it moist again
    right now.

And you know deep in your heart that you will have to continue
  keeping it dewy
Right up to the time that somebody at the club says, I suppose we
  ought to go to what's-his-name's funeral, who won the fifth at
  Bowie?
That's a nasty outlook to face,
But it's what you get for belonging to the human race.
So far as I know, mankind is the only section of creation
That is doomed to either pers- or ex-piration.
Look at the birds flying around, and listen to them as their voices
  in song they hoist;
No wonder they sing so much, they haven't got any brows, and if
  they had they couldn't be bothered keeping them moist.
And bees don't do anything either, bees just have a reputation for
  industry because they are sharp enough to buzz,
And people hear a bee buzzing and don't realize that buzzing isn't
  any trouble for a bee so they think that it is doing more than it
  actually does,
So next time you are about to expend some enthusiasm on the
  bee's wonderful industrial powers,
Just remember that that wonderful bee would die laughing if you
  asked it to change places with you and get its brow moist while
  you went around spending the day smelling flowers.
But if you are humanity, it is far from so,
And that is why I exclaim Woe woe woe,
Because I don't see much good in being the highest form of life
If all you get out of it is a brow moist from perpetual struggle and
  strife.
Indeed sometimes when my brow is particularly moist I think I
  would rather be a humble amoeba
Than Solomon in all his glory entertaining the Queen of Sheba.

KINDLY UNHITCH THAT STAR, BUDDY

I hardly suppose I know anybody who wouldn't rather be a suc-
  cess than a failure,
Just as I suppose every piece of crabgrass in the garden would
  much rather be an azalea,

And in celestial circles all the run-of-the-mill angels would rather
    be archangels or at least cherubim and seraphim,
And in the legal world all the little process-servers hope to grow
    up into great big bailiffim and sheriffim.
Indeed, everybody wants to be a wow,
But not everybody knows exactly how.
Some people think they will eventually wear diamonds instead of
    rhinestones
Only by everlastingly keeping their noses to their ghrinestones,
And other people think they will be able to put in more time at
    Palm Beach and the Ritz
By not paying too much attention to attendance at the office but
    rather in being brilliant by starts and fits.
Some people after a full day's work sit up all night getting a col-
    lege education by correspondence,
While others seem to think they'll get just as far by devoting their
    evenings to the study of the difference in temperament between
    brunettance and blondance.
In short, the world is filled with people trying to achieve success,
And half of them think they'll get it by saying No and half of them
    by saying Yes,
And if all the ones who say No said Yes, and vice versa, such is the
    fate of humanity that ninety-nine percent of them still wouldn't
    be any better off than they were before,
Which perhaps is just as well because if everybody was a success
    nobody could be contemptuous of anybody else and everybody
    would start in all over again trying to be a bigger success than
    everybody else so they would have somebody to be contemp-
    tuous of and so on forevermore,
Because when people start hitching their wagons to a star,
That's the way they are.

SUPPOSE I DARKEN YOUR DOOR

It seems to me that if you must be sociable it is better to go and see
    people than to have people come and see you,
Because then you can leave when you are through.
Yes, the moment you begin to nod

You can look at your watch and exclaim Goodness gracious, is it ten o'clock already, I had no idea it was so late, how very odd!

And you politely explain that you have to get up early in the morning to keep an important engagement with a man from Alaska or Siam,

And you politely thank your host and hostess for the lovely time and politely say good night and politely scram,

But when you yourself are the home team and the gathering is under your own roof,

You haven't got a Manchurian's chance of being aloof.

If you glance at your watch it is a grievous breach of hospitality and a disgrace,

And if you are caught in the midst of a yawn you have to pretend you were making a face and say Come on everybody, let's see who can make the funniest face.

Then as the evening wears on you feel more and more like an unsuccessful gladiator,

Because all the comfortable places to sit in are being sat in by guests and you have to repose on the windowsill or the chandelier or the radiator,

And somebody has always brought along a girl who looks like a loaf of raisin bread and doesn't know anybody else in the room,

And you have to go over to the corner where she is moping and try to disperse her gloom,

And finally at last somebody gets up and says they have to get back to the country or back to town again,

And you feebly say Oh it's early, don't go yet, so what do they do but sit down again,

And people that haven't said a word all evening begin to get lively and people that have been lively all evening get their second wind and somebody says Let's all go out in the kitchen and scramble some eggs,

And you have to look at him or her twice before you can convince yourself that anybody who would make a suggestion like that hasn't two heads or three legs,

And by this time the birds are twittering in the trees or looking in the window and saying Boo,

But nobody does anything about it and as far as I know they're all
still here, and that's the reason I say that it is better to go and
see people than to have people come and see you.

MAY I DRIVE YOU HOME, MRS. MURGATROYD?

Here's a statement that anybody who feels so inclined is welcome
to make a hearty mental meal of:
People who possess operator's licenses ought never to ride in a car
that anybody else is at the wheel of.
It seems to be their point of view
That you are some kind of fanatic bent on murdering or mutilat-
ing them even in the face of the certainty that in so doing you
must murder or mutilate yourself too.
They are always jumping and wincing and jamming their feet
down on an imaginary brake,
Or making noises as if they had just discovered that their bed was
inhabited by a snake,
Or else they start a casual conversation that begins with remarks
about the weather and other banalities,
And leads up to a pointed comment on the horrifying number of
annual automobile fatalities.
They tell you not only about cars that actually are coming but also
cars that might be coming, and they do it so kindly and gently
That it's obvious they consider you deaf and blind as well as rather
deficient mently.
And when at last you somehow manage to get to where you've
been going to they say thank you in a voice full of plaster of
Paris and bitter aloes,
And get down out of the car as if they were getting down off the
gallows,
And they walk away with the Is-it-really-over expression of a lot
of rescued survivors
And you go off and make a lot of remarks to yourself about back-
seat drivers,
And you vow that come what may you yourself will never join
their ranks, no indeed,

And then the next day somebody gives you a lift and you find
   yourself bathed with cold moisture the moment they shift the
   gears into third speed.
The truth of the matter, mesdames and sirs,
Is that we are all born chauffeurs;
Or, to put it another way before retiring to curl up with a bad
   book on the sofa,
Everybody in the car can drive better than the chauffeur.

A PLEA FOR A LEAGUE OF SLEEP

Some people lead a feverish life,
For they with restlessness are rife.
They revel in labors energetic,
Their fare is healthful and ascetic,
Their minds are keen, their hands are earthy,
Each day they work on something worthy.
Something accomplished, something done,
Comprises their idea of fun.

My life with joy is sometimes fraught,
But mostly when I'm doing naught.
Yea, I could spend my whole career
A pillow underneath my ear.
How wise was he who wittily said
That there is nothing like a bed.
A mattress is what I like to creep on;
The right side is the one I sleep on.

Heroes who moil and toil and fight
Exist on eight hours' sleep a night.
I call this but a miserly budget,
Yet I assure you that they grudge it.
I've heard them groan, times without number,
At wasting a third of their lives in slumber.
All right, you Spartans who build and delve,
You waste eight hours, and I'll waste twelve.

No honester man is to be found
Than he who sleeps the clock around.
Of malice and ambition free,
The more he sleeps, the sleepier he.
No plots and schemes infest his head,
But dreams of getting back to bed.
His spirit bears no worldly taint;
Scratch a sluggard, and find a saint.

Stalin and Hitler while they sleep
Are harmless as a baby sheep;
Tyrants who cause the earth to quake
Are only dangerous when awake.
This world would be a happier place,
And happier the human race,
And all our pilots be less Pontius,
If people spent more time unconscious.

PORTRAIT OF THE ARTIST AS
A PREMATURELY OLD MAN

It is common knowledge to every schoolboy and even every Bach-
elor of Arts,
That all sin is divided into two parts.
One kind of sin is called a sin of commission, and that is very im-
portant,
And it is what you are doing when you are doing something you
ortant,
And the other kind of sin is just the opposite and is called a sin of
omission and is equally bad in the eyes of all right-thinking
people, from Billy Sunday to Buddha,
And it consists of not doing something you shuddha.
I might as well give you my opinion of these two kinds of sin as
long as, in a way, against each other we are pitting them,
And that is, don't bother your head about sins of commission be-
cause however sinful, they must at least be fun or else you
wouldn't be committing them.
It is the sin of omission, the second kind of sin,

That lays eggs under your skin.

The way you get really painfully bitten

Is by the insurance you haven't taken out and the checks you haven't
added up the stubs of and the appointments you haven't kept
and the bills you haven't paid and the letters you haven't written.

Also, about sins of omission there is one particularly painful lack
of beauty,

Namely, it isn't as though it had been a riotous red-letter day or
night every time you neglected to do your duty;

You didn't get a wicked forbidden thrill

Every time you let a policy lapse or forgot to pay a bill;

You didn't slap the lads in the tavern on the back and loudly cry
Whee,

Let's all fail to write just one more letter before we go home, and
this round of unwritten letters is on me.

No, you never get any fun

Out of the things you haven't done,

But they are the things that I do not like to be amid,

Because the suitable things you didn't do give you a lot more trou-
ble than the unsuitable things you did.

The moral is that it is probably better not to sin at all, but if some
kind of sin you must be pursuing,

Well, remember to do it by doing rather than by not doing.

GOOD-BY, OLD YEAR, YOU OAF
OR
WHY DON'T THEY PAY THE BONUS?

Many of the three hundred and sixty-five days of the year are fol-
lowed by dreadful nights but one night is by far, oh yes, by far
the worst,

And that, my friends, is the night of December the thirty-first.

Man can never get it through his head that he is born to be not a
creditor but a debtor;

Man always thinks the annual thought that just because last year
was terrible next year is bound to be better.

Man is a victim of dope

In the incurable form of hope;
Man is a blemishless Pollyanna,
And is convinced that the advent of every New Year will place him
   in possession of a bumper crop of manna.
Therefore Man fills himself up with a lot of joie de vivre
And goes out to celebrate New Year's Ivre;
Therefore millions of respectable citizens who just a week before
   have been perfectly happy to sit at home and be cozily Christ-
   mas carolized
Consider it a point of honor to go out on the town and get them-
   selves paralyzed;
Therefore the whistles blow toot toot and the bells ring ding ding
   and the confetti goes confetti confetti at midnight on the thirty-
   first of December,
And on January first the world is full of people who either can't
   and wish they could, or can and wish they couldn't remember.
They never seem to learn from experience;
They keep on doing it year after year from the time they are pul-
   ing infants till they are doddering octogenerience.
My goodness, if there's anything in heredity and environment
How can people expect the newborn year to manifest any culture
   or refironment?
Every New Year is the direct descendent, isn't it, of a long line of
   proven criminals?
And you can't turn it into a philanthropist by welcoming it with
   cocktails and champagne any more successfully than with
   prayer books and hyminals.
Every new year is a country as barren as the old one, and it's no
   use in trying to forage it;
Every new year is incorrigible; then all I can say is for Heaven's
   sakes, why go out of your way to incorrage it?

A CLEAN CONSCIENCE NEVER RELAXES

There is an emotion to which we are most of us adduced,
But it is one which I refuse to boost.
It is harrowing, browbeating, and brutal,
Besides which it is futile.

I am referring, of course,
To remorse.
Remorse is a violent dyspepsia of the mind,
But it is very difficult to treat because it cannot even be defined,
Because everything is not gold that glisters and everything is not a tear that glistens,
And one man's remorse is another man's reminiscence,
So the truth is that as far as improving the world is concerned, remorse is a duffer,
Because the wrong people suffer,
Because the very fact that they suffer from remorse proves they are innocuous,
Yes indeed, it is the man remorse passes over completely who is the virulent streptococcuous,
Do you think that when Nero threw a martyr to the lions remorse enveloped him like an affinity?
Why the only remorse in the whole Colosseum was felt by the martyr who was reproaching himself for having dozed through the sermon on the second Sunday after Trinity.
So I think remorse ought to stop biting the consciences that feed it,
And I think the Kremlin ought to work out some plan for taking it away from those who have it and giving it to those who need it.

JUST KEEP QUIET AND NOBODY WILL NOTICE

There is one thing that ought to be taught in all the colleges,
Which is that people ought to be taught not to go around always making apologies.
I don't mean the kind of apologies people make when they run over you or borrow five dollars or step on your feet,
Because I think that kind is sort of sweet;
No, I object to one kind of apology alone,
Which is when people spend their time and yours apologizing for everything they own.
You go to their house for a meal,
And they apologize because the anchovies aren't caviar or the partridge is veal;
They apologize privately for the crudeness of the other guests,

And they apologize publicly for their wife's housekeeping or their husband's jests;

If they give you a book by Dickens they apologize because it isn't by Scott,

And if they take you to the theater, they apologize for the acting and the dialogue and plot;

They contain more milk of human kindness than the most capacious dairy can,

But if you are from out of town they apologize for everything local and if you are a foreigner they apologize for everything American.

I dread these apologizers even as I am depicting them,

I shudder as I think of the hours that must be spent in contradicting them,

Because you are very rude if you let them emerge from an argument victorious,

And when they say something of theirs is awful, it is your duty to convince them politely that it is magnificent and glorious,

And what particularly bores *me* with them,

Is that half the time you have to politely contradict them when you rudely agree with them,

So I think there is one rule every host and hostess ought to keep with the comb and nail file and bicarbonate and aromatic spirits on a handy shelf,

Which is don't spoil the dénouement by telling the guests everything is terrible, but let them have the thrill of finding it out for themself.

A STITCH TOO LATE IS MY FATE

There are some people of whom I would certainly like to be one,
Who are the people who get things done.
They balance their checkbooks every month and their figures always agree with the bank's,
And they are prompt in writing letters of condolence or thanks.
They never leave anything to chance,
But always make reservations in advance.

When they get out of bed they never neglect to don slippers so they
never pick up athlete's foot or a cold or a splinter,
And they hang their clothes up on hangers every night and put their
winter clothes away every summer and their summer clothes
away every winter.
Before spending any money they insist on getting an estimate or a
sample,
And if they lose anything from a shoelace to a diamond ring it is
covered by insurance more than ample.
They have budgets and what is more they live inside of them,
Even though it means eating things made by recipes clipped from
the Sunday paper that you'd think they would have died of
them.
They serve on committees
And improve their cities.
They are modern knight errants
Who remember their godchildren's birthdays and the anniversaries
of their godchildren's parents.
And in cold weather they remember the birds and supply them
with sunflower seed and suet,
And whatever they decide to do, whether it's to save twenty-five
percent of their salary or learn Italian or write a musical com-
edy or touch their toes a hundred times every morning before
breakfast, why they go ahead and do it.
People who get things done lead contented lives, or at least I guess
so,
And I certainly wish that either I were more like them or they were
less so.

DON'T GRIN, OR YOU'LL HAVE TO BEAR IT

It is better in the long run to possess an abscess or a tumor
Than to possess a sense of humor.
People who have senses of humor have a very good time,
But they never accomplish anything of note, either despicable or
sublime,
Because how can anybody accomplish anything immortal

When they realize they look pretty funny doing it and have to stop
   to chortle?
Everybody admits that Michelangelo's little things in the Sistine
   Chapel are so immortal they have everybody reeling,
But I'll bet he could never have dashed them off if he had realized
   how undignified he looked lying up there with his stomach on
   the ceiling.
Yes, fatal handicaps in life are fortunately few,
But the most fatal of all is the faculty of seeing the other person's
   point of view,
And if your devoted mother suggests that you will someday be rich
   and famous, why perish the suggestion;
That is, perish it if you are afflicted with the suspicion that there
   are two sides to every question.
Good gracious, how could anybody corner wheat
If they were sissy enough to reflect that they were causing a lot of
   other people to be unable to afford to eat?
Look at mayors and congressmen and presidents, always except-
   ing college presidents, such as Harvard's Conant;
Do you think they could get elected if they admitted even to them-
   selves that there was anything to be said for their opponent?
No, no, genius won't get you as far as common everyday facility
Unless it is accompanied by a conviction of infallibility,
And people who have a sense of humor are extremely gullible,
But not enough so, alas, to believe that they are infullible.

EXPERIENCE TO LET

Experience is a futile teacher,
Experience is a prosy preacher,
Experience is a fruit tree fruitless,
Experience is a shoe-tree bootless.
For sterile wearience and drearience,
Depend, my boy, upon experience.
The burnt child, urged by rankling ire,
Can hardly wait to get back at the fire,
And, mulcted in the gambling den,
Men stand in line to gamble again.

Who says that he can drink or not?
The sober man? Nay, nay, the sot.
He who has never tasted jail
Lives well within the legal pale,
While he who's served a heavy sentence
Renews the racket, not repentance.
The nation bankrupt by a war
Thinks to recoup with just one more;
The wretched golfer, divot-bound,
Persists in dreams of the perfect round;
Life's little suckers chirp like crickets
While spending their all on losing tickets.
People whose instinct instructs them naught,
But must by experience be taught,
Will never learn by suffering once,
But ever and ever play the dunce.
Experience! Wise men do not need it!
Experience! Idiots do not heed it!
I'd trade my lake of experience
For just one drop of common sense.

INTEROFFICE MEMORANDUM

The only people who should really sin
Are the people who can sin with a grin,
Because if sinning upsets you,
Why, nothing at all is what it gets you.
Everybody certainly ought to eschew all offences however venial
As long as they are conscience's menial.
Some people suffer weeks of remorse after having committed the
    slightes peccadillo,
And other people feel perfectly all right after feeding their husband
    arsenic or smothering their grandmother with a pillow.
Some people are perfectly self-possessed about spending their lives
    on the verge of delirium tremens,
And other people feel like hanging themselves on a coathook just
    because they took that extra cocktail and amused their fellow
    guests with recitations from the poems of Mrs. Hemans.

Some people calmly live a barnyard life because they find monogamy dull and arid,

And other people have sinking spells if they dance twice in an evening with a lady to whom they aren't married.

Some people feel forever lost if they are riding on a bus and the conductor doesn't collect their fare,

And other people ruin a lot of widows and orphans and all they think is, Why there's something in this business of ruining widows and orphans, and they go out and ruin some more and get to be a millionaire.

Now it is not the purpose of this memorandum, or song,

To attempt to define the difference between right and wrong;

All I am trying to say is that if you are one of the unfortunates who recognize that such a difference exists,

Well, you had better oppose even the teensiest temptation with clenched fists,

Because if you desire peace of mind it is all right to do wrong if it never occurs to you that it is wrong to do it,

Because you can sleep perfectly well and look the world in the eye after doing anything at all so long as you don't rue it,

While on the other hand nothing at all is any fun

So long as you yourself know it is something you shouldn't have done.

There is only one way to achieve happiness on this terrestrial ball,

And that is to have either a clear conscience, or none at all.

IT'S SNUG TO BE SMUG

Oh, sometimes I wish I had the wings of an angel because then I could fly through the air with the greatest of ease,

And if I wanted to be somewhere else I could get there without spending any money on taxis or railroad tickets or tips or fees,

Yes, I could fly to Paris and do as a Parisian, or fly to Rome and do as a Roman.

But on the other hand wings would necessitate my sleeping on my abdomen,

So I don't really wish I had the wings of an angel, but sometimes I wish I had the sweet voice of a thrush,

And then if I sang an Indian Love Lyric why thousands of beauti-
ful beauties would harken and quiver and blush,
And it would be a treat to hear my rendition of Sweet Alice Ben
Bolt,
But on the other hand who would go to harken to anybody who
was known to eat insects and moult?
So I don't really wish I had the sweet voice of a thrush, but some-
times I wish I had the courage of a lion,
And then I could look life in the eye with a will of iron,
And to a goose, or a burglar, or even a butler, I wouldn't hesitate
to say Boo!
But on the other hand I might encounter a goose or a burglar or a
butler who had the courage of a lion too,
So I don't really wish I had the courage of a lion but sometimes I
wish I had the innocence of a lamb,
And then I would never wake up crying Fie on me! and Damn!
But on the other hand innocence is a security on which it is hard
to borrow,
Because all it means is that either you get eaten by a wolf today or
else the shepherd saves you from the wolf so he can sell you to
the butcher tomorrow,
So I do not really wish I had the innocence of a lamb,
I guess I'll stay just as I am.

MR. BARCALOW'S BREAKDOWN

Once there was a man, and he was named Mr. Barcalow, to be ex-
act,
And he prided himself on his tact,
And he said, One thing about an apple, it may have a worm in it,
and one thing about a chimney, it may have soot in it,
But one thing about my mouth, I never put my foot in it.
Whenever he entered a community
He inquired of his host and hostess what topics he could discuss
with impunity,
So no matter beside whom he was deposited,
Why, he could talk to them without disturbing any skeletons that
should have been kept closeted,

But one dire day he went to visit some friends,
And he started asking tactful questions about untactful conversa-
tional trends,
And his host said that here was one place that Mr. Barcalow
wouldn't need his tact,
Because taboos and skeletons were what everybody there lacked,
And his hostess said, That's right, but you'd better not mention
bathrooms to Emily, who you will sit by at lunch,
Because her grandmother was scalded to death in a shower shortly
after complaining that there was no kick in the punch,
And his host said, Oh yes, and steer away from education when
you talk to the Senator,
Because somebody said his seventeen-year-old nephew would have
to burn down the schoolhouse to get out of the third grade and
his nephew overheard them and did burn down the school-
house, including the music teacher and the janitor,
And his hostess said, Oh yes, and if you talk about love and marriage
to Mrs. Musker don't be surprised if her eye sort of wanders,
Because her daughter is the one who had the divorce suit with
thirty-seven co-responders.
And Mr. Barcalow said, Well, can I talk about sports,
And his hostess said, Well, maybe you'd better not because
Louise's sister, the queer one, was asked to resign from the club
because she went out to play moonlight tennis in shorts, and
Mr. Barcalow said That's not so terrible is it, everybody wears
shorts, and his hostess said, Yes, but she forgot the shorts.
So Mr. Barcalow said The hell with you all, and went upstairs and
packed.
And that was the last that was ever heard of Mr. Barcalow and his
tact.

PIPE DREAMS

Many people have asked me what was the most beautiful sight I
saw during the recent summer,
And I think the most beautiful sight was the day the water
wouldn't stop running and in came the plumber,
Because your cottage may be very cunning,

But you don't appreciate it when the water won't stop running,
And you would almost rather submit to burgling
Than to consistent gurgling.
And then the other most beautiful sight I saw during the summer
Was the day the water wouldn't run at all and in came the plumber,
Because one thing even less enticing than a mess of pottage
Is a waterless cottage,
So apparently all my beautiful memories of the summer
Are beautiful memories of the plumber,
And I am sorry they aren't more romantic,
I am sorry they are not memories of the moonlight rippling on the
 Atlantic,
Oh my yes, what wouldn't I give for some beautiful memories of
 the fields and the sky and the sea,
But they are not for the likes of me,
Nay, if you want to have beautiful memories of the summer,
Why the thing to do is to be a plumber,
Because then you can have some really beautiful beauties to re-
 member,
Because naturally plumbers wouldn't think plumbers were the
 most beautiful thing they saw between June and September,
And that's the great advantage plumbers have over me and you,
They don't have to think about plumbers, so they can concentrate
 on the view.

HOW NOW, SIRRAH? OH, ANYHOW

Oh, sometimes I sit around and think, What would you do if you
 were up a dark alley and there was Caesar Borgia,
And he was coming torgia,
And brandished a poisoned poniard,
And looked at you like an angry fox looking at the plumpest roos-
 ter in a boniard?
Why that certainly would be an adventure,
It would be much more exciting than writing a poem or selling a
 debenture,
But would you be fascinated,
Or just afraid of being assassinated?

Or suppose you went out dancing some place where you generally
dance a lot,
And you jostled somebody accidentally and it turned out to be Sir
Lancelot,
And he drew his sword,
Would you say Have at you! or would you say Oh Lord?
Or what if you were held up by a bandit,
And he told you to hand over your money, would you try to dis-
arm him and turn him over to the police, or would you over
just meekly hand it?
What would you do if you were in a luxurious cosmopolitan hotel
surrounded by Europeans and Frenchmen,
And a beautiful woman came up to you and asked you to rescue
her from some mysterious mastermind and his sinister hench-
men?
Would you chivalrously make her rescue your personal objective,
Or would you refer her to the house detective?
Yes, and what if you were on trial for murdering somebody whom
for the sake of argument we might call Kelly or O'Connor,
And you were innocent but were bound to be convicted unless you
told the truth and the truth would tarnish a lady's honor,
Would you elect to die like a gentleman or live like a poltroon,
Or put the whole thing in the hands of an arbitration committee
headed by Heywood Broun?
Yes, often as through life I wander
This is the kind of question I ponder,
And what puzzles me most is why I even bother to ponder when I
already know the answer,
Because anybody who won't cross the street till the lights are green
would never get far as a Musketeer or a Bengal Lancer.

NO WONDER OUR FATHERS DIED

Does anybody mind if I don't live in a house that is quaint?
Because, for one thing, quaint houses are generally houses where
plumbing ain't,
And while I don't hold with fanatical steel-and-glass modernistic
bigots,

Still, I do think that it simplifies life if you live it surrounded by efficient pipes and faucets and spigots.

I admit that wells and pumps and old oaken buckets are very nice in a poem or ode,

But I feel that in literature is where they should have their permanent abode,

Because suppose you want a bath,

It is pleasanter to be able to take it without leaving a comfortable stuffy room and going out into the bracing fresh air and bringing back some water from the end of a path.

Another thing about which I am very earnest,

Is that I do like a house to be properly furnaced,

Because if I am out in the bracing fresh air I expect to be frozen,

But to be frigid in a stuffy room isn't what I would have chosen.

And when you go to bed in a quaint house the whole house grumbles and mutters,

And you are sure the walls will be shattered by clattering shutters.

At least you hope it's the shutters but you fear it's a gang of quaint ghosts warming up for twelve o'clock,

And you would lock yourself snugly in but the quaint old key won't turn in the quaint old lock,

So you would pull the bedclothes snugly up over your head and lie there till a year from next autumn,

Were it not a peculiarity of bedclothes in quaint houses that if you pull them up on top, why your feet stick out at the bautum,

But anyhow you find a valley among the hilltops of your mattress and after a while slumber comes softly stealing,

And that is when you feel a kiss on your cheek and you think maybe it is a goodnight kiss from your guardian angel, but it isn't, it's a leak in the ceiling.

Oh, I yield to none in my admiration of the hardy colonists and their hardy spouses,

But I still feel that their decadent descendants build more comfortable houses.

NATURE KNOWS BEST

I don't know exactly how long ago Hector was a pup,
But it was quite long ago, and even then people used to have to start their day by getting up.
Yes, people have been getting up for centuries,
They have been getting up in palaces and Pullmans and penitentiaries.
The caveman had to get up before he could go out and track the brontosaurus,
Verdi had to get up before he could sit down and compose the Anvil Chorus,
Alexander had to get up before he could go around being dominant,
Even Rip Van Winkle had to get up from one sleep before he could climb the mountain and encounter the sleep which has made him prominent.
Well, birds are descended from birds and flowers are descended from flowers,
And human beings are descended from generation after generation of ancestors who got up at least once every twenty-four hours,
And because birds are descended from birds they don't have to be forced to sing like birds, instead of squeaking like rats,
And because flowers are descended from flowers they don't have to be forced to smell like flowers, instead of like burning rubber or the Jersey flats,
But you take human beings, why their countless generations of ancestors who were always arising might just as well have spent all their lives on their mattresses or pallets,
Because their descendants haven't inherited any talent for getting up at all, no, every morning they have to be forced to get up either by their own conscience or somebody else's, or alarm clocks or valets.
Well, there is one obvious conclusion that I have always held to,
Which is that if Nature had really intended human beings to get up, why they would get up naturally and wouldn't have to be compelled to.

UNTITLED

You resent me.
I resent you.
That's what we call
The point of view.

DON'T GUESS, LET ME TELL YOU

Personally I don't care whether a detective story writer was edu-
 cated in night school or day school
So long as they don't belong to the H.I.B.K. school.
The H.I.B.K. being a device to which too many detective story
 writers are prone,
Namely the Had I But Known.
Sometimes it is the Had I But Known what grim secret lurked be-
 hind that smiling exterior I would never have set foot within
 the door,
Sometimes the Had I But Known then what I know now I could
 have saved at least three lives by revealing to the Inspector the
 conversation I heard through that fortuitous hole in the floor.
Had-I-But-Known narrators are the ones who hear a stealthy creak
 at midnight in the tower where the body lies, and, instead of
 locking their door or arousing the drowsy policeman posted
 outside their room, sneak off by themselves to the tower and
 suddenly they hear a breath exhaled behind them,
And they have no time to scream, they know nothing else till the
 men from the D.A.'s office come in next morning and find them.
Had I But Known-ers are quick to assume the prerogatives of the
 Deity,
For they will suppress evidence that doesn't suit their theories with
 appalling spontaneity,
And when the killer is finally trapped into a confession by some
 elaborate device of the Had I But Known-er some hundred
 pages later than if they hadn't held their knowledge aloof,
Why they say Why Inspector I knew all along it was he but I
 couldn't tell you, you would have laughed at me unless I had
 absolute proof.

Would you like a nice detective story for your library which I am
sorry to say I didn't rent but owns?
I wouldn't have bought it had I but known it was impregnated
with Had I But Knowns.

HUSH, HERE THEY COME

Some people get savage and bitter when to backbiters they refer,
But I just purr.
Yes, some people consider backbiters to be the rankest of the rank,
But frankly, I prefer them to people who go around being frank,
Because usually when you are backbitten behind your back you
don't know about it and it doesn't leave a trace,
But frankness consists of having your back bitten right to your
face,
And as if that weren't enough to scar you,
Why you are right there in person to scotch the defamation, and
if you don't happen to be able to scotch it, why where are
you?
Frank people are grim, but genuine backbiters are delightful to
have around,
Because they are so anxious that if what they have been saying
about you has reached your ears you shouldn't believe it, that
they are the most amiable companions to be found;
They will entertain you from sunset to dawn,
And cater encouragingly to all your weaknesses so that they can
broadcast them later on,
So what if they do gnaw on your spine after enjoying your beer
and skittles?
I don't blame them the least of jots or tittles,
Because certainly no pastime such diversion lends
As talking friends over analytically with friends,
So what if as they leave your house or you leave theirs backbiters
strip your flesh and your clothes off,
At least it is your back that they bite, and not your nose off.
I believe in a place for everything and everything in its place,
And I don't care how unkind the things people say about me so
long as they don't say them to my face.

EVERYBODY TELLS ME EVERYTHING

I find it very difficult to enthuse
Over the current news.
Just when you think that at least the outlook is so black that it can
    grow no blacker, it worsens,
And that is why I do not like the news, because there has never
    been an era when so many things were going so right for so
    many of the wrong persons.

DON'T LOOK FOR THE SILVER LINING,
JUST WAIT FOR IT

The rabbit loves his hoppity and the wallaby loves his hippity.
I love my serendipity.
Let none look askance;
Serendipity is merely the knack of making happy and unexpected
    discoveries by chance.
Only yesterday I was bored by a bore—there is no topic that he
    isn't inept on it—
And when I pointed out a piece of chewing gum on the sidewalk,
    he was too busy talking to listen, so I soon made the happy and
    unexpected discovery that he had stepped on it.
It was serendipity when a recent hostess of mine in Philadelphia
    apologized for serving ham and eggs because she had forgotten
    to order scrapple,
Just as it was when I found a bow tie I could wear that didn't rise
    and fall with my Adam's apple.
Also when I found a hole in my pocket which I had tickets for a
    harp recital in, or in which I had tickets for a harp recital, to
    put it properer,
So instead of the harp recital we had to see the Marx Brothers in
    A Night at the Opera.
If your coat catches on a branch just as you are about to slip over
    a precipice precipitous,
That's serendipitous,
But when you happily and unexpectedly discover that you don't
    have to go to the dentist or the chiropodist,
That's serendopitist.

I'LL WRITE THEIR NUMBER DOWN
WHEN WE GET HOME

Words, idle words, are what people's social life contains a goodly
store of,

And the idlest words are contained in the wishful phrase begin-
ning, Why don't we see more of?

By the time your age is medium,

Well, your most exotic evenings are placid to the point of tedium,

Because whenever you step out you find yourself stepping out
amid faces and ideas that are, to say the least, familiar,

Which is a situation which moves only from the willy-nilly to the
willy-nillier,

But once in every eleven blue moons you encounter a newcomer in
your little coterie,

And it doesn't matter whether he is a veteran or a veterinary or a
vestryman or a vegetarian or a notable or a Notogæn or a no-
tary,

Because his fresh point of view is as beneficial to anemic conver-
sation as a transfusion or a tonic,

And his wife is equally attractive and stimulating, and the future
would be cute as a button if it weren't so inevitably ironic,

Because on the way home you say "My I like those people, why
don't we see more of them?" and it is agreed that Yes we cer-
tainly must, and from then on they might as well be living in
the ancient Anglian kingdom of Mercia,

Because you never see them again because you never do anything
about it except to murmur "Why don't we see more of them?"
and that is why the best definition I can think of for at least one
man's social life is simply inertia.

SUPPOSE HE THREW IT IN YOUR FACE

Please don't anybody ask me to decide anything, I do not know a
nut from a meg,
Or which came first, the lady or the tiger, or which came next, the
chicken or the egg.
I am, alas, to be reckoned
With the shortstop who can't decide whether to throw to first or
second,
Nor can I decide whether to put, except after c,
E before i, or i before e.
But where this twilight mind really goes into eclipse
Is in the matter of tips.
I stand stricken before the triple doom,
Whether, and How Much, and Whom.
Tell me, which is more unpleasant,
The look from him who is superior to a tip and gets it, or from him
who isn't and doesn't?
I had rather be discovered playing with my toes in the Aquarium
Than decide wrongly about an honorarium.
Oh, to dwell forever amid Utopian scenery
Where hotels and restaurants and service stations are operated by
untippable unoffendable machinery.

ALLOW ME, MADAM, BUT IT WON'T HELP

Adorable is an adjective and womankind is a noun,
And I often wonder why, although adorable womankind elects to
talk standing up, it elects to put on its coat sitting down.
What is the outstanding characteristic of matinees, tearooms and
table d'hôtes?
Women, sitting firmly and uncomfortably on their coats;
Woman at whose talents a contortionist would hesitate to scoff,
Because they also sat down on their coats to take them off.
What is *savoir faire*?
It is the ability to pick up eighty-five cents in nickels and a lipstick
with the right hand while the left hand is groping wildly over
the back of a chair.

· 385 ·

Yes, and if you desire savoir faire that you could balance a cup on,
Consider the calmness of a woman trying to get her arm into the
    sleeve of a coat that she has sat down on too far up on.
Women are indeed the salt of the earth,
But I fail to see why they daily submit themselves voluntarily to an
    operation that a man only undergoes when he is trying to put
    on his trousers in an upper berth.

SEEING EYE TO EYE IS BELIEVING

When speaking of people and their beliefs I wear my belief on my
    sleeve;
I believe that people believe what they believe they believe.
When people reject a truth or an untruth it is not because it is a
    truth or an untruth that they reject it,
No, if it isn't in accord with their beliefs in the first place they sim-
    ply say, "Nothing doing," and refuse to inspect it.
Likewise when they embrace a truth or an untruth it is not for ei-
    ther its truth or its mendacity,
But simply because they have believed it all along and therefore re-
    gard the embrace as a tribute to their own fair-mindedness and
    sagacity.
These are enlightened days in which you can get hot water and
    cold water out of the same spigot,
And everybody has something about which they are proud to be
    broad-minded but they also have other things about which you
    would be wasting your breath if you tried to convince them
    that they were a bigot,
And I have no desire to get ugly,
But I cannot help mentioning that the door of a bigoted mind
    opens outwards so that the only result of the pressure of facts
    upon it is to close it more snugly.
Naturally I am not pointing a finger at me,
But I must admit that I find any speaker far more convincing when
    I agree with him than when I disagree.

YOU AND ME AND P. B. SHELLEY

What is life? Life is stepping down a step or sitting in a chair,
And it isn't there.
Life is not having been told that the man has just waxed the floor,
It is pulling doors marked PUSH and pushing doors marked PULL
     and not noticing notices which say PLEASE USE OTHER DOOR.
It is when you diagnose a sore throat as an unprepared geography
     lesson and send your child weeping to school only to be re-
     turned an hour later covered with spots that are indubitably
     genuine,
It is a concert with a trombone soloist filling in for Yehudi Menuhin.
Were it not for frustration and humiliation
I suppose the human race would get ideas above its station.
Somebody once described Shelley as a beautiful and ineffective an-
     gel beating his luminous wings against the void in vain,
Which is certainly describing with might and main,
But probably means that we are all brothers under our pelts,
And Shelley went around pulling doors marked PUSH and pushing
     doors marked PULL just like everybody else.

WILL YOU HAVE YOUR TEDIUM
RARE OR MEDIUM?

Two things I have never understood: first, the difference between
     a Czar and a Tsar,
And second, why some people who should be bores aren't and oth-
     ers, who shouldn't be, are.
I know a man who isn't sure whether bridge is played with a puck
     or a ball,
And he hasn't read a book since he bogged down on a polysylla-
     ble in the second chapter of *The Rover Boys at Putnam Hall.*
His most thrilling exploit was when he recovered a souvenir of the
     World's Fair that had been sent out with the trash,
And the only opinion he has ever formed by himself is that he
     looks better without a mustache.
Intellectually speaking, he has neither ears to hear with nor eyes to
     see with,

Yet he is pleasing to be with.
I know another man who is an expert on everything from witch-
craft and demonology to the Elizabethan drama,
And he has spent a weekend with the Dalai Lama,
And substituted for a mongoose in a fight with a cobra, and per-
formed a successful underwater appendectomy,
And I cannot tell you how tediously his reminiscences affect me.
I myself am fortunate in that I have many interesting thoughts
which I express in terms that make them alive,
And I certainly would entertain my friends if they always didn't
have to leave just when I arrive.

I WILL ARISE AND GO NOW

In far Tibet
There live a lama,
He got no poppa,
Got no momma,

He got no wife,
He got no chillun,
Got no use
For penicillun,

He got no soap,
He got no opera,
He don't know Geritol
From copra,

Got no opinions
Controversial,
He never hear
TV commercial.

He got no teeth,
He got no gums,
Don't eat no Spam,
Don't need no Tums.

He love to nick him
When he shave;

He also got
No hair to save.

Got no distinction,
No clear head,
Don't call for Calvert;
Drink milk instead.

He use no lotions
For allurance,
He got no car
And no insurance.

No Alsop warnings,
No Reston rumor
For this self-centered
Nonconsumer.

Indeed, the
Ignorant Have-Not
Don't even know
What he ain't got.

If you will mind
The box-tops, comma,
I think I'll go
And join that lama.

TWO GOES INTO TWO ONCE,
IF YOU CAN GET IT THERE

All my life I have been a witness of things,
Among which I keep witnessing the eternal unfitness of things.
Daily it is my wont
To notice how things that were designed to fit each other, don't.
Getting a cigarette into a cigarette holder is like the round hole and
the square peg,
And getting the cork back into the vermouth bottle is like rein-
serting the cuckoo in the egg.
Why is the card-case always just a smidgin smaller than the deck?

Why does it take a 15¾ collar to encircle a 15½ neck?

Experience is indeed a teacher, and I have learned this fact from it,

That no suitcase is large enough to recontain the clothes you just unpacked from it.

No wonder the grapes set on edge the teeth of the little foxes;

The minute you buy a dozen silver or brocade or leather matchbox holders the matchbox makers change the size of the boxes.

I am baffled, I weave between Scylla and Charybdis, between a writ of replevin and a tort;

I shall console myself with the reflection that even in this world, ever perverse and ever shifting, two pints still make one cavort.

WHAT'S IN A NAME?
SOME LETTER I ALWAYS FORGET

Not only can I not remember anecdotes that are racy,

But I also can't remember whether the names of my Scottish friends begin with M-c or M-a-c,

And I can't speak for you, but for myself there is one dilemma with me in the middle of it,

Which is, is it Katharine with a K or Catherine with a C, and furthermore is it an A or is it an E in the middle of it?

I can remember the races between Man o' War and Sir Barton, and Epinard and Zev,

But I can't remember whether it's Johnson or Johnston any more than whether you address a minister as Mr. or Dr. or simply Rev.

I know a cygnet from a gosling and a coney from a leveret,

But how to distinguish an I-double-T from an E-double-T Everett?

I am familiar with the nature of an oath,

But I get confused between the Eliot with one L and one T, and the Elliot with two L's and one T, and the Eliott with one L and two T's, and the Elliott with two of both.

How many of my friendships have lapsed because of an extra T or a missing L;

Give me a simple name like Taliaferro or Wambsganss or Torporcer or Joralemon or Mankiewicz that any schoolboy can spell,

Because many former friends thought I was being impolite to them
When it was only because I couldn't remember whether they were
Stuarts with a U or Stewarts with an E-W that I didn't write to
them.

I'LL EAT MY SPLIT-LEVEL TURKEY
IN THE BREEZEWAY

A lady I know disapproves of the vulgarization of Christmas; she
believes that Christmas should be governed purely by spiritual
and romantic laws;
She says all she wants for Christmas is no more suggestive songs
about Santa Claus.
Myself, I am more greedy if less cuddle-y.
And being of '02 vintage I am perforce greedy fuddy duddily,
So my own Christmas could be made glad
Less by the donation of anything new than just by the return of a
few things I once had.
Some people strive for gracious living;
I have recurrent dreams of spacious living.
Not that I believe retrogression to be the be-all and the end-all,
Not that I wish to spend the holidays sitting in a Turkish corner
smoking Sweet Caps and reading *Le Rouge et le Noir* by
Stendhal,
Nor do I long for a castle with machicolations,
But I would like a house with a porte-cochere so the guests
wouldn't get wet if it rained the evening of my party for my
rich relations.
Also, instead of an alcove I'd like a dining room that there wasn't
any doubt of,
And a bathtub that you didn't have to send $7.98 to Wisconsin for
a device that enables you to hoist yourself out of,
And if there is one thought at which every cockle of my heart perks
up and warms,
It is that of an attic in which to pile old toys and magazines and
fancy dress costumes and suitcases with the handle off and
dressmaker's forms.

I'd like a house full of closets full of shelves,
And above all, a house with lots of rooms all with doors that shut
so that every member of the family could get off alone by them-
selves.
Please find me such a relic, dear Santa Claus, and when you've
done it,
Please find me an old-fashioned cook and four old-fashioned maids
at $8.oo a week and a genial wizard of a handyman to run it.

IT WOULD HAVE BEEN QUICKER TO WALK
OR
DON'T TELL ME WE'RE THERE ALREADY

Let us call her Mrs. Mipping, but her name is legion,
And she is to be found in any taxi helping to congest any congested
region.
Human experience largely consists of surprises superseding surmises,
And most surprises are unpredictable, which is why they come as
surprises,
There is one surprise, however, that is as predictable as a statement
by a Republican or Democratic national chairman or a picture
window in a pre-fab,
And that is the surprise of Mrs. Mipping when she gets to where
she was going in a cab.
In fact, she gets two surprises at a clip:
The first, that she has reached her destination, and the second, that
she is expected to pay for the trip.
If she is heading down to 5th Avenue and 52nd Street she doesn't
start to assemble her packages at 57th or 55th or even 53rd,
But when the cab pulls up at her corner she flutters like a bewil-
dered bird,
And she proceeds to gather up her impedimenta
While the faces of the several dozen drivers blocked behind her
turn magenta,
And only then does she realize that a figure has been registered on
the meter,
And she is thunderstruck as by an explosion of gunpowder, which
is largely composed of sulphur, charcoal and saltpeter.

Down go the packages on the seat again,
And she fumbles in her bag for her purse and fumbles in her purse
    for change and finally hands the driver a ten.
By the time the transaction is completed it is growing dark,
And traffic is backed up all the way to Central Park.
I believe that the Traffic Commissioner could soon iron out the sit-
    uation as smooth as silk
Simply by opening charge accounts with the taxi companies for
    Mrs. Mipping and her addlepated ilk.

SO I RESIGNED FROM THE CHU CHIN
CHOWDER AND MARCHING CLUB

The thing about which I know the least
Is the inscrutable East.
Neither is my ignorance immutable,
I find that every hour the East grows more inscrutable.
Day by day
I memorize pithy witticisms beginning "Confucius say."
I retire to leafy bowers
And immerse myself in *Kai-Lung's Golden Hours*,
In the evening I beat assiduously on a gong,
Picking out "Slow Boat to China" and "Why Did I Tell You I Was
    Going to Shanghai?" and "Chong He Come from Hong Kong."
In a valiant effort the inscrutable Oriental mind to explore
I have lost a fortune at mah-jongg to an inscrutable Pekinese
    puppy who lives next door,
All to no avail;
Scrutably speaking, I am beyond the pale.
I have only one accomplishment about which I would write home
    to Mother:
I can tell at least one Celestial from at least one other;
I can tell you, for a modest price,
The difference between a mandarin waving his hat over a prostrate
    palanquin bearer and a mandarin sitting on a cake of ice.
Do you want to know, really and truly?
Well, the first mandarin is fanning his coolie.

NEVER MIND THE OVERCOAT,
BUTTON UP THAT LIP

Persons who have something to say like to talk about the arts and
politics and economics,
And even the cultural aspects of the comics.
Among persons who have nothing to say the conversational con-
tent worsens;
They talk about other persons.
Sometimes they talk about persons they know personally, and re-
arrange their lives for them,
And sometimes they talk about persons they know through the
tabloids, and rearrange their husbands and wives for them.
I have better things to talk about than fortune hunters who harry
debs;
The causerie in my coterie is of how come Sir Arthur rewrote "The
Red-headed League" under the title of "The Adventure of the
Three Garridebs."
Gossip never darkens my doors
And I wouldn't trade one Gaboriau for a hatful of Gabors.
Do not praise me because to curious ears I will not pander,
I myself am not responsible for my abstention from libel and slan-
der.
For this laudable trait there is a coony little old lady whom I am
under obligation to;
She taught me that if you hear a juicy tidbit and don't repeat it
within twenty-four hours, why, after that it is juiceless and
there is no temptation to.
If you heed this precept you will never find yourself in a gossiper's
role;
I know, because in 1915 when I discovered that Marie Jeanne Bécu
Du Barry wasn't married to Louis XV I sat on the item for
twenty-four hours and from that day till this I haven't breathed
it to a living soul.

I SPY

OR

THE DEPRAVITY OF PRIVACY

My voice is a minor one, but I must raise it;
I come not only to bury privacy, but to praise it.
Yes, this is my long farewell to privacy;
Democracy seems to have turned into a sort of Lady Godivacy.
We are living in an era by publicity bewitched,
Where the Peeping Toms are not blinded, but enriched.
Keyhole-itis is contagious, and I fear that by our invasion of the
    privacy of the people who clamor for their privacy to be in-
    vaded,
Well, we are ourselves degraded;
And now that we can't leave the privacy of public personalities
    alone
We end up by invading our own.
What puts a neighbor's teeth on edge?
Your growing a hedge.
He is irked because he can't see what you're doing on your own
    lawn, raising tulips,
Or swigging juleps,
And curiosity is what he is in his knees up to,
And also exhibitionism, because he not only wants to know what
    you are doing, he wants you to know what *he's* up to,
So he has a picture window to look out through that he never low-
    ers the blinds on, so you can't help looking in through it,
And you are forced to observe the nocturnal habits of him and his
    kin through it.
Things have reached a pretty pass; even my two goldfish, Jael and
    Sisera,
Complain that they have no more privacy than a candidate's vis-
    cera.
Well, privacy is a wall,
And something there is that does not love it: namely, the Pry fam-
    ily, Pauline and Paul.

JACK DO-GOOD-FOR-NOTHING: A CURSORY
NURSERY TALE FOR TOT-BAITERS

Once there was a kindhearted lad named Jack Do-Good-for-
Nothing, the only son of a poor widow whom creditors did
importune,
So he set out in the world to make his fortune.
His mother's blessing and a crust of bread was his only stake,
And pretty soon he saw a frog that was about to be devoured by
a snake.
And he rescued the frog and drove the snake away,
And the frog vowed gratitude to its dying day,
And a little later on in his walk,
Why, he saw a little red hen about to be carried off by a hawk,
And he rescued the little red hen and drove the hawk away,
And the little red hen vowed that whenever he was in trouble his
kindness she would repay,
And he walked a few more country blocks,
And he saw a bunny rabbit about to be gobbled up by a fox,
And he rescued the bunny rabbit before the fox could fall on it,
And the bunny rabbit thanked Jack and told him any time he
needed help, just to call on it,
And after all this rescuing, Jack was huffing and puffing,
And a little farther on the snake and the hawk and the fox jumped
him, and out of him they beat the stuffing;
They even stole his crust of bread and each ate a third of it,
And the frog and the little red hen and the bunny rabbit said they
were very sorry when they heard of it.
You see, Jack against a cardinal rule of conduct had been a trans-
gressor:
Never befriend the oppressed unless you are prepared to take on
the oppressor.

UNFORTUNATELY,
IT'S THE ONLY GAME IN TOWN

Often I think that this shoddy world would be more nifty

If all the ostensibly fifty-fifty propositions in it were truly fifty-fifty.

How unfortunate that the odds

Are rigged by the gods.

I do not wish to be impious,

But I have observed that all human hazards that mathematics would declare to be fifty-fifty are actually at least fifty-one-forty-nine in favor of Mount Olympius.

In solitaire, you face the choice of which of two black queens to put on a red king; the chance of choosing right is an even one, not a long one,

Yet three times out of four you choose the wrong one.

You emerge from a side street onto an avenue, with the choice of turning either right or left to reach a given address.

Do you walk the wrong way? Yes.

My outraged sense of fair play it would salve

If just once I could pull the right curtain cord the first time, or guess which end of the radiator lid conceals the valve.

Why when choosing between two lanes leading to a highway toll-house do I take the one containing a lady who first hands the collector a twenty-dollar bill and next drops her change on the ground?

Why when quitting a taxi do I invariably down the door handle when it should be upped and up it when it should be downed?

By the cosmic shell game I am spellbound.

There is no escape; I am like an oyster, shellbound.

Yes, surely the gods operate according to the fiercest exhortation W. C. Fields ever spake:

Never give a sucker an even break.

A STRANGE CASEMENT OF
THE POETIC APOTHECARY

Poets are always in search of the right word, the adjective that is
inevitable,

Because an ill-chosen adjective induces levity in the reader, and no
poet wishes to be levitable.

A poem filled with the right words is more enjoyable, and there-
fore takes longer to read;

Hence the old Louisiana saying "The *mot juste*, the less speed."

When, for instance, Keats refers to "magic" casements he is no
poetaster who a mass of trite, meaningless phrases spawns;

He did not slap down the first adjective that came to mind because
he had left his thesaurus at Fanny Brawne's.

Whosoever thinks so, his ignorance of both Keats and casements
is absurd;

If Keats speaks of a casement as "opening," then "magic" is the
only possible word.

In the matter of casements Keats was no dreamy lotophagic;

He knew that if a casement was either openable or shuttable it was
manifestly magic.

Keats could have written a lot more odes and died with money in
the bank

But for the long hours he wasted trying to twist little widgets that
were rusted stuck and yanking handles that wouldn't yank.

If his casements were like mine, when open they would not admit
the breeze, and when shut they would not exclude the rain,

And when he looked through them he could not see Shelley or any-
thing else plain.

So anybody who thinks there is a *juster mot* than "magic," I sug-
gest they join the lowing herd and wind slowly o'er the lea,

And leave casements to Keats and me.

BOSTON ROBBERY

I'd expect to be robbed in Chicago,
But not in the home of the cod.
So I hope that the Cabots and Lowells
Will mention the matter to God.

O TEMPORA, OH-OH!

The sober journal that I read
Reports the news discreetly;
When faced with carnal goings-on
It treads the tightrope featly.

It chronicles in dispassionate terms
Divorce and defloration,
And circumspectly drops its voice
To mention deviation.

No juicy tidbits does it toss
To those for thrills esurient—
Naught lickerish or snickerish
To gratify the prurient.

But oh, the Sunday Book Review!
I realize my stodginess
As children leaf it through with cries
Of "Daddy, what's erogenous?"

I'm grateful to the critics who
Submit for our advisements
Their résumés of current books—
But, boy, the advertisements!

Read all about that cultured cad
De Sade and his diversions,
Or sexual practices (unrestrained)
Of ancient Medes and Persians.

For bashful couples in despair
Who fear themselves mismated,
The latest marriage manual,
Profusely illustrated.

And here's another picture book
To pique the jaded vision,
The pictures quite legitimate,
Pompeian, not Parisian.

So let us leave the Book Review,
That strangely blended torrent

Of all the news that's fit to print
And all the ads that orrent.

GOD BLESS THE GIDEONS
OR
THERE'S ALWAYS THE KING JAMES VERSION

High near the mountain or low near the ocean,
Hard by the spa, it's the same old hotel,
Born of a Middle Victorian notion,
Reaching full stature, with ell tacked on ell.

Septuagenarians crowd its verandas,
Leathery lady and fragile old man,
Sunning like lizards or dozing like pandas,
Dreaming of dinner, American plan.

Far past the TV room, far past the cardroom,
Deep in a cranny encompassed by nooks,
Dim as a dungeon and grim as a guardroom,
There is the library, these are the books—

Gone the gay jackets with blurbs parading,
Along the spine the titles are fading:
If Winter Comes, by A. S. M. Hutch.,
Castle Craneycrow, George Barr McCutch.,
The Amateur Gentleman, Jeffery Farnol,
Hilda Lessways, Bennett, Arnol',
Calvin Coolidge, C. Bascom Slemp,
Over the Top, Arthur Guy Emp.,
The Green Hat, Michael Arlen,
Blind Raftery, Donn Byrne's Irish darlin'.
Here lie Cosmo Hamilton, A. Hamilton Gibbs,
Joan Lowell, Trader Horn and their fabulous fibs,
The Art of Thinking, a tattered *Freckles*,
And an early, early Beverely Nichols.

Forty years on, when, afar and asunder,
Ashes are those who are reading today,
Strangers will gaze on our leavings with wonder,
Sum up an era and turn to croquet.

Behind glass doors not wholly hidden,
A literary kitchen midden,
The musty rubble of a race
Which fed on Kinsey and *Peyton Place.*
De Sade and *Valley of the Dolls* consort
With *Story of O* and *The Chapman Report,*
The *Tropics,* and other tins of sex;
Also, *The Agony and the Ecs.,*
Advise and Consent, by a Mr. Drury,
That life of Harlow, unhappy houri,
And yes, *How Probate to Avoid,*
And *Papa Hemingway,* not by Freud;
Memoirs of Getty, mystery Croesus,
And *Are You Running with Me, Jesus?*
In a corner, *This Is My Beloved,*
Penned by a twentieth-century Ovid,
And at one end, cleared by the courts,
A mildewed batch of Grove Press orts.

Golden pens and royalties must,
As chimney sweepers, come to dust.

JUST HOLMES AND ME,
AND MNEMOSYNE MAKES THREE

I am told that my character has as many layers as an onyx,
But one layer is missing, which is an aptitude for mnemonics.
Mnemosyne (daughter of Uranus and Gaea, date of birth destroyed
    in fire at Alexandria) was the goddess of memory,
So she never said "Hail, Amory!" to a minor deity whose name
    was Emory.
She became a mother by Zeus—as what nubile Grecian female
    didn't?—and the children turned out to be the Muses, who
    later on helped Homer with their reminiscences of Achilles and
    Hector,
And she needed her innate talent, because she had nine names to
    remember when she summoned them to their ambrosia and
    nectar.

Me, I can never be elected to any office, because I am nearsighted and frequently forget the face of an acquaintance, and, worse, I invariably forget the name,

So I am solaced by the discovery that my lifelong hero Mr. Sherlock Holmes was once the same.

In "The Adventure of the Speckled Band" (*The Complete Sherlock Holmes*, Doubleday, 1953), the proposed victim of a fiendish plot introduces herself on page 294 as Miss Helen Stoner, stepdaughter of Dr. Grimesby Roylott, of Stoke Moran,

An unpleasant man,

Yet on page 299 Holmes says to her, "Miss Roylott . . . you are screening your stepfather," a slip that Miss Stoner left uncorrected, either through tact or because her mind was upon her approaching wedding,

For she had recently become betrothed to Mr. Percy Armitage, second son of Mr. Armitage, of Crane Water, near Reading.

Well, whatever caused Holmes's error and Miss Stoner's overlooking it, I have this reflection to cheer me as I step from the mounting block to the saddle of my high-wheeled bike:

Great minds forget alike.

IF A BODER MEET A BODER, NEED A BODER CRY? YES

I haven't much faith in bodings; I think that all bodings are daft bodings.

Forebodings are bad enough, but deliver me from aftbodings.

Aftbodings are what too many of us suffer from subsequent to making decisions even of the most inconsequential and niggling.

Aftbodings prevent people in restaurants from enjoying their haunch of venison, because they keep wondering if they shouldn't have ordered the roast crackling suckling pigling.

Aftbodings are what women are constantly up to their midriffs amid,

Because they are always afraid that the hats or dresses they didn't buy are more becoming than the ones they did.

Aftbodings trouble the young executive who has opted for a martini instead of a Bloody Mary, and plague the rascally artist who too late feels that he should have forged that Gainsborough instead of this Romney.

Aftbodings are the major cause of insomny.

Consider the lines "Of all sad words . . . the saddest are these: 'It might have been!'" whittled by J. G. Whittier;

As an example of aftboding, what could be prettier?

Indeed, I deem this an example of aftboding *in excelsis,*

Because J. G. Whittier wasn't even boding after his own decision but somebody else's.

I myself am more and more inclined to agree with Omar and with Satchel Paige as I grow older:

Don't try to rewrite what the moving finger has writ, and don't ever look over your shoulder.

THE FERRY

The ferry is constantly to-ing and fro-ing,
I never can tell is it coming or going,
Thanks to him who designed this ambiguous scow
With two bows and no stern or two sterns and no bow.

BET YOU A NICKEL MY UNHAPPINESS
CAN LICK YOUR UNHAPPINESS

The world is full of bath towels and cocktail glasses and washrooms marked Hers and His,

And even fuller of darling little aphorisms and apothegms beginning Happiness is.

Perhaps my sense of whimsy has withered, has shriveled, is wizened,

But I think it's time to take a look at unhappiness, which is what happiness isn't.

Unhappiness is having aisle seats in the theatre and people stumble over your feet with or without an apologetic smile;

It is also having seats in the center of the row and you stumble over
the feet of people sitting on the aisle.

Unhappiness is being trapped on a rainy highway with a slow-
moving truck in front of you and a fast-moving truck coming
up behind you.

Unhappiness is forgetting what it was of which you had meant to
remind your wife to remind you.

It is a female teenager in the family whose very ideal is Raquel
Welch or Faye Dunaway;

It is the corner of the rug that keeps curling up and it is the three-
way lightbulb that works only one-way.

It is when you finally manage to fit both your check and that
computer-slotted slat into the envelope with the window slit pro-
vided by your utility cartel, and it is at best an awkward fit,

And you stamp it and seal it only to find that you have to rip it
open again because the wrong side of the slotted slat is facing
the slit.

Yes, the world is truly full of a number of things.

No wonder we are all usually as unhappy as kings.

WHICH THE CHICKEN, WHICH THE EGG?

He drinks because she scolds, he thinks;
She thinks she scolds because he drinks;
And neither will admit what's true,
That he's a sot and she's a shrew.

HE DIDN'T DARE LOOK
OR
THE PUZZLING UNIQUENESS
OF MR. SALTBODY'S MEEKNESS

I speak of Standish Saltbody, Harvard '24, a loyal Cantabridgin,

A timid man, a bashful man, whose makeup contained of arro-
gance not a modicum or a smidgin.

You would travel far to discover a character more retiring, more
innately diffident,

His overdeveloped sense of self-unimportance was pathetically ev-
ident,
Yet in him a kindred soul is what Galileo's persecutors might well
have found
Because his very timidity led him to fear that Standish Saltbody
was what the universe revolved around.
Small wonder that he was continually discomfited by a runaway
pulse;
He was convinced that his most trivial act could generate the most
appalling results.
He had not once attended the Yale game since undergoing gradu-
ation and valedictory
Because he was sure that his presence alone, although unsuspected
by his team, was sufficient to guarantee an Eli victory.
Although Willie Mays was his hero, his very ideal, he would never
watch him on TV
Because he was sure that although Willie couldn't know that Stan-
dish Saltbody was watching him from a distance of 2500 miles,
that one fact would hoodoo him into looking at strike three.
His sense of responsibility and guilt reached a point at which from
any positive move he was likely to refrain;
He was certain that any candidate he voted for would be defeated,
just as his washing the car would bring on a torrential rain.
Thus we see that this meekest and most self-depreciative of God's
creatures paradoxically felt himself to be omnipotent,
Since of any contretemps in his immediate world his words or
deeds were obviously the precipitant;
And indeed, if of the cosmos he was not the hub,
How is it that he could make the telephone ring merely by settling
down in the tub?

Nash's World

THE REWARD

In my mind's reception room
Which is what, and who is whom?
I notice when the candle's lighted
Half the guests are uninvited,
And oddest fancies, merriest jests,
Come from these unbidden guests.

SPRING COMES TO MURRAY HILL

I sit in an office at 244 Madison Avenue
And say to myself You have a responsible job, havenue?
Why then do you fritter away your time on this doggerel?
If you have a sore throat you can cure it by using a good goggerel,
If you have a sore foot you can get it fixed by a chiropodist,
And you can get your original sin removed by St. John the Bopodist,
Why then should this flocculent lassitude be incurable?
Kansas City, Kansas, proves that even Kansas City needn't always
   be Missourible.
Up up my soul! This inaction is abominable.

The pilgrims settled Massachusetts in 1620 when they landed on a
    stone hummock.
Maybe if they were here now they would settle my stomach.
Oh, if I only had the wings of a bird
Instead of being confined on Madison Avenue I could soar in a
    jiffy to Second or Third.

INTROSPECTIVE REFLECTION

I would live all my life in nonchalance and insouciance
Were it not for making a living, which is rather a nouciance.

HYMN TO THE SUN AND MYSELF

Well! Well!
The day's at the morn!
Dandy old day!
Dandy old morn!
Oh! Look!
The hillside's dew-pearled!
Nicely old hillside!
Nicely dew-pearled!
And oh! Look!
The snail's on the thorn!
Lucky old snail!
Lucky old thorn!
Well! Well!
All's right with the world!
Hurrah for the right!
Hurrah for the world!

For oh! what a day it is today, my lads!
Oh! my lads, what a day it is today!
At 11:07 A.M. I'll be 27¾ years old,
An age dear to me because it was once passed through by Edna St.
    Vincent Millay.
Oh what fun to be young and healthy and alive

And privileged to do some of the work of the world from nine to
     five!
Oh let me be truly thankful for every one of those 27¾ years;
For not having been run over by the Lexington Avenue Express or
     gored by runaway steers;
For not having been able to afford a passage on the *Titanic*,
For not having had any money to lose in the recent stock market
     panic;
For never having written a best-seller, only to be wounded by the
     critics;
And for never having gotten impeached for making millions in dirty
     politics;
For never having made any enemies by getting ahead too speedily;
For not finding the world at my feet while still as young as Lind-
     bergh or Gertrude Ederle;
For not having tried to impress my girl but being naturaler with
     her and naturaler;
So that now instead of having to marry and all that I can continue
     to be a careless baturaler;
Above all let me be thankful for something rarer than gold—
Viz: that at 11:07 A.M. I'll be 27¾ years old.
Oh let my future be as lucky as my past!
Oh let every day for a long time not be my last!

LINES TO BE MUTTERED THROUGH
CLENCHED TEETH AND QUITE
A LOT OF LATHER, IN THE COUNTRY

"Hark! Hark! The lark at Heaven's gate sings—"
Shut up, lark!
"And Phoebus 'gins arise—"
Sit down, Phoebus, before I knock you down!

Larks barking like beagles around a person's windows,
Sun-gods sneaking in at dawn and socking a person in the eye—
Why doesn't Nature go back to the Orient where it came from and
     bother the Mohammedans and Hindows
Instead of turning night into day every morning in Westchester
     County N.Y.?

I speak for a community of commuters who toil for a pittance per
  diem—
Who spend 12½ percent of their waking lives on the N.Y., N.H.,
  & H.—
Who would swap a billion shiny new A.M.'s for a secondhand P.M.—
I do not presume to speak for late risers such as Mr. Shubert and
  Mr. Winchell and Mr. Bache.

Why do we submit to a regime so tyrannical and despotic?
Why don't we do something about getting a lot less dawn and a lot
  more dusk?
I mean seriously, without any cracks about six months of night in
  the Arctic—
Because I think if it could be arranged life would be not nearly so
  grotusque.

Daybreak is one of the greatest disadvantages of living under the
  solar system:
It means having to get up almost the very minute you go to bed,
And bathe and shave and scrub industriously at your molar system
And catch a train and go to the office and try to earn some bread.

Come, let us leave the flowers and the birds and the beasts to their
  sun-worship,
All of us human beings ought to be more skeptical than a flower
  or a bird or a beast,
And a little serious thought should convince us that sunshine is
  something to unworship
And that if we want to salute the daybreak we should say not
  "Goodie goodie" but "Ah Cheest."

NO, YOU BE A LONE EAGLE

I find it very hard to be fair-minded
About people who go around being air-minded.
I just can't see any fun
In soaring up up up into the sun
When the chances are still a fresh cool orchid to a paper geranium
That you'll unsoar down down down onto your (to you) invalu-
  able cranium.

I know the constant refrain
About how it's safer up in God's trafficless heaven than in an automobile or a train
But—
My God, have you ever taken a good look at a strut?
Then that one about how you're in Boston before you can say antidisestablishmentarianism
So that preferring to take five hours by rail is a pernicious example of antiquarianism.
At least when I get on the Boston train I have a good chance of landing in the South Station
And not in that part of the daily press which is reserved for victims of aviation.
Then, despite the assurance that aeroplanes are terribly comfortable I notice that when you are railroading or automobiling
You don't have to take a paper bag along just in case of a funny feeling.
It seems to me that no kind of depravity
Brings such speedy retribution as ignoring the law of gravity.
Therefore nobody could possibly indict me for perjury
When I swear that I wish the Wright brothers had gone in for silver fox farming or tree surgery.

WHEN YOU SAY THAT, SMILE!
OR
ALL RIGHT, THEN, DON'T SMILE

When the odds are long,
And the game goes wrong,
Does your joie de vivre diminish?
Have you little delight
In an uphill fight?
Do you wince at a Garrison finish?
Then here's my hand, my trusty partner!
I've always wanted a good disheartener.

For Courage is preached by bellicose preachers,
Courage is taught by belligerent teachers,

To congregations, and eager students,
And nobody says a word for Prudence.
And people fly the Atlantic solo,
And other people play hockey and polo,
Say No! to shampoos in barber shops,
And voice their opinions to traffic cops,
And earn the coveted laurel wreath
With ebony optics and missing teeth.
But you and I, my trusty partner,
My indispensable disheartener,
Stand fast on critical occasions
Avoiding contusions and abrasions.
Let heroes carry on the torch;
It's pleasanter rocking on the porch.

Oh, things are frequently what they seem,
And this is wisdom's crown:
Only the game fish swims upstream,
But the sensible fish swims down.

Well, how is your pulse
When a cad insults
The lady you're cavaliering?
Are you willing to wait
To retaliate
Till the cad is out of hearing?
Then here's my hand, my trusty companion,
And may neither one of us fall in a canyon.

Oh, Courage is grand for muscular giants,
And midgets mighty with self-reliance.
Burglars use it, and aviators,
And people who wrestle with alligators.
Steeplejacks need it, and so do firemen,
And in soldiers it's maybe the chief requiremen',
But you and I, my trusty companion,
Who I hope will never fall in a canyon,
I see no reason for us to crave
The rotogravures and a hero's grave,
For he who fighteth and runneth away

Liveth to sip his pousse-café,
And the quickest route to the greatest distance,
Lies in the line of least resistance.
Leave derring-do to courageous strangers;
Who are we to be dog-in-the-mangers?

Things are frequently what they seem,
And this is wisdom's crown:
Only the game fish swims upstream,
But the sensible fish swims down.

CAT NAPS ARE TOO GOOD FOR CATS

Oh, early every afternoon
I like a temporary swoon.
I do not overeat at luncheon,
I do not broach the bowl or puncheon;
Yet the hour from two to three
Is always sleepy-time to me.

Bolt upright at my desk I sit,
My elbows digging into it,
My chin into my hands doth fit,
My careful fingers screen my eyes,
And all my work before me lies,
Which leads inquisitive passer-bys
Who glance my way and see me nod,
To think me wide awake, if odd.

I would not sell my daily swoon
For all the rubies in Rangoon.
What! Sell my swoon? My lovely swoon?
Oh, many and many's the afternoon
I've scoured the woods with Daniel Boone,
And sipped a julep with Lorna Doone
And former Governor Ruby Laffoon.
I'll sell my soul before my swoon,
It's not for sale, my swoon's immune.

From two to three each afternoon
Mine are the Mountains of the moon,
Mine a congenital silver spoon.
And I can lead a lost platoon
Or dive for pearls in a haunted lagoon,
Or guide a stratosphere balloon.
Oh, where the schooner schoons, I schoon,
I can talk lion, or baboon,
Or make a crooner cease to croon.
I like to swoon, for when I swoon
The universe is my macaroon.
Then blessings on thee, my afternoon torpor,
Thou makest a prince of a mental porpor.

THE WISHING WELL

Oh, what a really wonderful world this fairly wonderful world would be,
If only it had been designed by me!
Because if wishes were automobiles, beggars would not suffer with hitchhiker's thumb.
But I don't want my wishes to turn out to be automobiles, because I think there are enough automobiles now; I want them to turn out to be true, and then life would be the opposite of glum,
Because I wish that either felt hats were as cool as straw hats or straw hats were as comfortable as felts,
And I wish everybody liked everybody else,
And I wish nobody was poor and everybody was rich,
And I wish that when you scratch a mosquito bite, it would cease to itch,
And I wish your friends wouldn't get divorces,
And that nations didn't covet other nations' natural resources.
I also wish that all bottles had the kind of stopper that you could open them without pushing in the corks,
And that babies were brought by storks.
Another wish is that some literary explorer would discover about a thousand hitherto unpublished tomes,

And they turned out to be further adventures just as good as the
first adventures of the Three Musketeers and Mr. Pickwick and
Sherlock Holmes.

And I wish every play and every movie had a uniformly competent
cast instead of a lot of highly paid, untalented amateurs and
one box-office star in it,

And as an old oyster lover, I do wish every month had an R in it.

I wish pajama strings would stop disappearing into the waistband
of the pajamas, and that when you took the pins out of a new
shirt, you didn't have to put it on and sit down before locating
the final pin,

And I wish that politicians who are out of office wouldn't be so
shocked and horrified when politicians who are in office play
politics just the way they themselves look forward to doing
when they get back in,

And I am against accidents and disasters and hurricanes and floods,

And oh, yes, Mexican jumping collar buttons and studs,

And I wish that all war consisted of was flags flying and maybe a
general getting shot once in a while, and a campfire with sol-
diers sitting singing Annie Laurie about it,

And I wish that when you had done something you wish you hadn't
done, you could make it not done just by being sorry about it.

And I wish that Sweet Adeline and I've Been Working on the Rail-
road roared from a rumble seat returning from a party at the
country club sounded as sweet to the people who are trying to
get to sleep as they do to the people who roar them,

And I also wish that if the time ever arrives when wishes come
true, why, everybody will let me make their wishes for them.

SPLASH!

Some people are do-it-some-other-timers and other people are do-
it-nowers.

And that is why manufacturers keep on manufacturing both bath-
tubs and showers,

Because some bathers prefer to recline

On the cornerstone of their spine,

While others, who about their comfort are less particular,
Bathe perpendicular.
Thus from the way people lave themselves
You can tell how under other circumstances they will behave them-
selves.
Tubbers indulge in self-indulgence,
And they loll soaking until they are a moist mass of warm rosy ef-
fulgence,
And finally they regretfully hoist themselves up and shiver and say
Brrr! even though the atmosphere is like an orchid-house and
the mirror is coated with steam,
And they pat at their moistness with a towel as soft as whipped
cream,
So it is obvious that the tubber is a sybaritic softie,
And will never accomplish anything lofty.
How different is the showerer, whose chest is often festooned with
hair such as bedecked our ancestors arboreal!
He has no time to waste on luxuriousness, but skims through the
spray with the speed of a Democratic politician skimming
through a Republican editorial,
After which he grates himself on something which he calls a towel,
But which anybody covered with human skin instead of cowhide
would call a file or a spur or a rowel,
And thus at the same time he avoids procrastination
And improves his circulation,
So we see that the showerer is a Spartan,
And sternly guides his ambitious life along the lines laid down by
baccalaureate preachers and Bruce Barton,
And this is the reason that in the game of life although occasional
points are won by the tubber,
The showerer always gets game and rubber.
Sometimes tubbers and showerers get into arguments about tubs
and showers and become very warlike and martial,
But I myself have always been strictly impartial,
Yes, I am neutrally anchored halfway between Calais and Dover,
And all I will impartially and neutrally say is that there are three
things you can't do in a shower, and one is read, and the other
is smoke, and the other is get wet all over.

WAITING FOR THE BIRDIE

Some hate broccoli, some hate bacon,
I hate having my picture taken.
How can your family claim to love you
And then demand a picture of you?
The electric chair is a queasy chair,
But I know an equally comfortless pair;
One is the dentist's, my good sirs,
And the other is the photographer's.
Oh, the fly in all domestic ointments
Is affectionate people who make appointments
To have your teeth filled left and right,
Or your face reproduced in black and white.
You open the door and you enter the studio,
And you feel less cheerio than nudio.
The hard light shines like seventy suns,
And you know that your features are foolish ones.
The photographer says, Natural, please,
And you cross your knees and uncross your knees.
Like a duke in a high society chronicle
The camera glares at you through its monocle
And you feel ashamed of your best attire,
Your nose itches, your palms perspire,
Your muscles stiffen, and all the while
You smile and smile and smile and smile.
It's over; you weakly grope for the door;
It's not; the photographer wants one more.
And if this experience you survive,
Wait, just wait till the proofs arrive.
You look like a drawing by Thurber or Bab,
Or a gangster stretched on a marble slab.
And all your dear ones, including your wife,
Say There he is, that's him to the life!
Some hate broccoli, some hate bacon,
But I hate having my picture taken.

Seated one day at the dictionary I was pretty weary and also pretty
  ill at ease,
Because a word I had always like turned out not to be a word at
  all, and suddenly I found myself among the v's.
And suddenly among the v's I came across a new word which was
  a word called *velleity,*
So the new word I found was better than the old word I lost, for
  which I thank my tutelary deity,
Because velleity is a word which gives me great satisfaction,
Because do you know what it means, it means *low degree of voli-
  tion not prompting to action,*
And I always knew I had something holding me back but I didn't
  know what,
And it's quite a relief to know it isn't a conspiracy, it's only velle-
  ity that I've got,
Because to be wonderful at everything has always been my ambi-
  tion,
Yes indeed, I am simply teeming with volition,
So why I never was wonderful at anything was something I
  couldn't see
While all the time, of course, my volition was merely volition of a
  low degree,
Which is the kind of volition that you are better off without it,
Because it puts an idea in your head but doesn't prompt you to do
  anything about it.
So you think it would be nice to be a great pianist but why bother
  with practicing for hours at the keyboard,
Or you would like to be the romantic captain of a romantic ship
  but can't find time to study navigation or charts of the ocean
  or the seaboard;
You want a lot of money but you are not prepared to work for it,
Or a book to read in bed but you do not care to go into the noc-
  turnal cold and murk for it;
And now if you have any such symptoms you can identify your
  malady with accurate spontaneity;
It's velleity,

So don't forget to remember that you're velleitous, and if anybody
    says you're just lazy,
Why, they're crazy.

KIND OF AN ODE TO DUTY

Oh Duty,
Why hast thou not the visage of a sweetie or a cutie?
Why displayest thou the countenance of the kind of conscientious
    organizing spinster
That the minute you see her you are aginster?
Why glitter thy spectacles so ominously?
Why art thou clad so abominously?
Why art thou so different from Venus
And why do thou and I have so few interests mutually in common
    between us?
Why art thou fifty percent martyr
And fifty-one percent Tartar?
Why is it thy unfortunate wont
To try to attract people by calling on them either to leave undone
    the deeds they like, or to do the deeds they don't?
Why art thou so like an April post mortem
On something that died in the ortumn?
Above all, why dost thou continue to hound me?
Why art thou always albatrossly hanging around me?
Thou so ubiquitous,
And I so iniquitous.
I seem to be the one person in the world thou art perpetually
    preaching at who or to who;
Whatever looks like fun, there art thou standing between me and
    it, calling yoo-hoo.
O Duty, Duty!
How noble a man should I be hadst thou the visage of a sweetie or
    a cutie!
Wert thou but houri instead of hag
Then would my halo indeed be in the bag!
But as it is thou art so much forbiddinger than a Wodehouse hero's
    forbiddingest aunt

That in the words of the poet, When Duty whispers low, Thou
   must, this erstwhile youth replies, I just can't.

GOLLY, HOW TRUTH WILL OUT!

How does a person get to be a capable liar?
That is something that I respectfully inquiar,
Because I don't believe a person will ever set the world on fire
Unless they are a capable lire.
Some wise men said that words were given to us to conceal our
   thoughts,
But if a person has nothing but truthful words why their thoughts
   haven't even the protection of a pair of panties or shoughts,
And a naked thought is ineffectual as well as improper,
And hasn't a chance in the presence of a glib chinchilla-clad whop-
   per.
One of the greatest abilities a person can have, I guess,
Is the ability to say Yes when they mean No and No when they
   mean Yes.
Oh to be Machiavellian, oh to be unscrupulous, oh, to be glib!
Oh to be ever prepared with a plausible fib!
Because then a dinner engagement or a contract or a treaty is no
   longer a fetter,
Because liars can just logically lie their way out of it if they don't
   like it or if one comes along that they like better;
And do you think their conscience prickles?
No, it tickles.
And please believe that I mean every one of these lines as I am writ-
   ing them
Because once there was a small boy who was sent to the drugstore
   to buy some bitter stuff to put on his nails to keep him from
   biting them,
And in his humiliation he tried to lie to the clerk
And it didn't work,
Because he said My mother sent me to buy some bitter stuff for a
   friend of mine's nails that bites them, and the clerk smiled
   wisely and said I wonder who that friend could be,
And the small boy broke down and said Me,

And it was me, or at least I was him,
And all my subsequent attempts at subterfuge have been equally grim,
And that is why I admire a suave prevarication because I prevaricate so awkwardly and gauchely.
And that is why I can never amount to anything politically or socially.

SO THAT'S WHO I REMIND ME OF

When I consider men of golden talents,
I'm delighted, in my introverted way,
To discover, as I'm drawing up the balance,
How much we have in common, I and they.

Like Burns, I have a weakness for the bottle,
Like Shakespeare, little Latin and less Greek;
I bite my fingernails like Aristotle;
Like Thackeray, I have a snobbish streak.

I'm afflicted with the vanity of Byron,
I've inherited the spitefulness of Pope;
Like Petrarch, I'm a sucker for a siren,
Like Milton, I've a tendency to mope.

My spelling is suggestive of a Chaucer;
Like Johnson, well, I do not wish to die
(I also drink my coffee from the saucer);
And if Goldsmith was a parrot, so am I.

Like Villon, I have debits by the carload,
Like Swinburne, I'm afraid I need a nurse;
By my dicing is Christopher out-Marlowed,
And I dream as much as Coleridge, only worse.

In comparison with men of golden talents,
I am all a man of talent ought to be;
I resemble every genius in his vice, however heinous—
Yet I only write like me.

UNTITLED

Bow down, bow down to wood and stone,
To cleverly fashioned mud;
But if you want your soul your own
Kneel not to flesh and blood.

UNTITLED

Time walks on and people die;
Other people, never I.

NO DOCTORS TODAY, THANK YOU

They tell me that euphoria is the feeling of feeling wonderful, well,
    today I feel euphorian,
Today I have the agility of a Greek god and the appetite of a Vic-
    torian.
Yes, today I may even go forth without my galoshes,
Today I am a swashbuckler, would anybody like me to buckle any
    swashes?
This is my euphorian day,
I will ring welkins and before anybody answers I will run away.
I will tame me a caribou
And bedeck it with marabou.
I will pen me my memoirs.
Ah youth, youth! What euphorian days them was!
I wasn't much of a hand for the boudoirs,
I was generally to be found where the food was.
Does anybody want any flotsam?
I've gotsam.
Does anybody want any jetsam?
I can getsam.
I can play chopsticks on the Wurlitzer,
I can speak Portuguese like a Berlitzer.
I can don or doff my shoes without tying or untying the laces be-
    cause I am wearing moccasins,

And I practically know the difference between serums and anti-
toccasins.
Kind people, don't think me purse-proud, don't set me down as
vainglorious,
I'm just a little euphorious.

NOT GEORGE WASHINGTON'S,
NOT ABRAHAM LINCOLN'S, BUT MINE

Well, here I am thirty-eight,
Well, I certainly thought I'd have longer to wait.
You just stop in for a couple of beers,
And gosh, there go thirty-seven years.
Well, it has certainly been fun,
But I certainly thought I'd have got a lot more done.
Why if I had been really waked up and alive,
I could have been a Congressman since I was twenty-one or Presi-
dent since I was thirty-five.
I guess I know the reason my accomplishments are so measly:
I don't comprehend very easily.
It finally dawned on me that in life's race I was off to a delayed
start
When at the age of thirty-three I had to be told that I could swim
faster if I'd keep my fingers together instead of spreading them
apart.
And I was convinced that precociousness was not the chief of my
faults
When it was only last winter that I discovered that the name of
that waltz that skaters waltz to is "The Skater's Waltz."
After thirty-seven years I find myself the kind of a man that any-
body can sell anything to,
And nobody will ever tell anything to.
Whenever people get up a party of which I am to be a member to
see some picture which I don't want to see because I am unin-
terested in the situation that Scarlett and Mr. Chips are estranged
over,
Why my head is what it is arranged over.
Contrariwise, I myself not only can't sell anybody anything,

I can't even ever tell anybody anything.
I have never yet had a good gossip bomb all poised and ready to
    burst
That somebody hasn't already told everybody first.
Yes, my career to date has certainly been a fiasco;
It would not have made a thrilling dramatic production for the late
    Oliver Morosco or the late David Belasco.
But in spite of the fact that my career has been a fiasco to date,
Why I am very proud and happy to be thirty-eight.

SO DOES EVERYBODY ELSE,
ONLY NOT SO MUCH

O all ye exorcizers come and exorcize now, and ye clergymen draw
    nigh and clerge,
For I wish to be purged of an urge.
It is an irksome urge, compounded of nettles and glue,
And it is turning all my friends back into acquaintances, and all my
    acquaintances into people who look the other way when I heave
    into view.
It is an indication that my mental buttery is butterless and my men-
    tal larder lardless,
And it consists not of "Stop me if you've heard this one," but of
    "I know you've heard this one because I told it to you myself,
    but I'm going to tell it to you again regardless,"
Yes I fear I am living beyond my mental means
When I realize that it is not only anecdotes that I reiterate but what
    is far worse, summaries of radio programs and descriptions of
    cartoons in newspapers and magazines.
I want to resist but I cannot resist recounting the bright sayings of
    celebrities that everybody already is familiar with every word of;
I want to refrain but cannot refrain from telling the same audience
    on two successive evenings the same little snatches of domes-
    tic gossip about people I used to know that they have never
    heard of.
When I remember some titillating episode of my childhood I figure
    that if it's worth narrating once it's worth narrating twice, in
    spite of lackluster eyes and drooping jaws,

And indeed I have now worked my way backward from titillating
   episodes in my own childhood to titillating episodes in the
   childhood of my parents or even my parents-in-laws,
And what really turns my corpuscles to ice,
I carry around clippings and read them to people twice.
And I know what I am doing while I am doing it and I don't want
   to do it but I can't help doing it and I am just another Ancient
   Mariner,
And the prospects for my future social life couldn't possibly be
   barrener.
Did I tell you that the prospects for my future social life couldn't
   possibly be barrener?

COMPLIMENTS OF A FRIEND

How many gifted pens have penned
That Mother is a boy's best friend!
How many more with like afflatus
Award the dog that honored status!
I hope my tongue in prune juice smothers
If I belittle dogs or mothers,
But gracious, how can I agree?
I know my own best friend is Me.
We share our joys and our aversions,
We're thicker than the Medes and Persians,
We blend like voices in a chorus,
The same things please, the same things bore us.
If I am broke, then Me needs money;
I make a joke, Me finds it funny.
I know what I like, Me knows what art is;
We hate the people at cocktail parties,
When I can stand the crowd no more,
Why, Me is halfway to the door.
I am a dodo; Me, an auk;
We grieve that pictures learned to talk;
For every sin that I produce
Kind Me can find some soft excuse,
And when I blow a final gasket,

Who but Me will share my casket?
Beside us, Pythias and Damon
Were just two unacquainted laymen.
Sneer not, for if you answer true,
Don't you feel that way about You?

WHO DID WHICH?
OR
WHO INDEED?

Oft in the stilly night,
When the mind is fumbling fuzzily,
I brood about how little I know,
And know that little so muzzily.
Ere slumber's chains have bound me,
I think it would suit me nicely,
If I knew one tenth of the little I know,
But knew that tenth precisely.

O Delius, Sibelius,
And What's-his-name Aurelius,
O Manet, O Monet,
Mrs. Siddons and the Cid!
I know each name
Has an oriflamme of fame,
I'm sure they all did something,
But I can't think what they did.

Oft in the sleepless dawn
I feel my brain is hominy
When I try to identify famous men,
Their countries and Anno Domini.
Potemkin, Pushkin, Ruskin,
Velásquez, Pulaski, Laski;
They are locked together in one gray cell,
And I seem to have the passkey.

O Tasso, Picasso,
O Talleyrand and Sally Rand,
Elijah, Elisha,

Eugene Aram, Eugène Sue,
Don Quixote, Donn Byrne,
Rosencrantz and Guildenstern,
Humperdinck and Rumpelstiltskin,
They taunt me, two by two.

At last, in the stilly night,
When the mind is bubbling vaguely,
I grasp my history by the horns
And face it Haig and Haigly.
O, *Snow-Bound* was written by Robert Frost,
And Scott Fitzgerald wrote *Paradise Lost*,
Croesus was turned into gold by Minos,
And Thomas à Kempis was Thomas Aquinas.
Two Irish Saints were Patty and Micah,
The Light Brigade rode at Balalaika,
If you seek a roué to irk your aunt,
Kubla-Khan but Immanuel Kant,
And no one has ever been transmogrified
Until by me he has been biogrified.

Gently my eyelids close;
I'd rather be good than clever;
And I'd rather have my facts all wrong
Than have no facts whatever.

HOW TO GET ALONG WITH YOURSELF
OR
I RECOMMEND SOFTENING OF THE OUGHTERIES

When I was young I always knew
The meretricious from the true.
I was alert to call a halt
On other people's every fault.
My creed left no more chance for doubt
Than station doors marked IN and OUT.
A prophet with righteousness elated,
Dogmatic and opinionated,
Once self-convinced, I would not budge;

I was indeed a hanging judge.
I admitted, in either joy or sorrow,
No yesterday and no tomorrow.
My summary of life was reckoned
By what went on that very second.
I scoffed when kindly uncles and aunts
Said age would teach me tolerance,
For tolerance implies a doubt
That IN is IN and OUT is OUT.
But now that I am forty-nine.
I'm tolerant, and like it fine,
Since the faults of others I condone,
I can be tolerant of my own.
I realize the sky won't fall
If I don't pay my bills at all.
The King of Sweden it will not irk
To hear that I neglect my work,
And tombfuls of historic dead
Care not how late I lie abed.
Oh, tolerance is the state of grace
Where everything falls into place,
So now I tolerantly think
I could tolerate a little drink.

EACH JUNE I MAKE A PROMISE SOBER

Every summer I truly intend
My intellectual sloth to end,
Leave Dumas and Conan Doyle behind me,
And let the dog days, when they find me,
Find me beside the sea perusing
Volumes of Mr. Hutchins' choosing,
Congesting my uncultured head
With famous books I haven't read—
With Milton's *Areopagitica*,
The almanacs of Gotha and Whitaker,
With *Lysistrata* and *The Frogs*
And lots of Plato's dialogues,

With Darwin's *Voyage of the Beagle*,
Erasmus, and Tyl Eulenspiegel,
Corneille and Moliere and Racine
And *Rasselas* and *The Faerie Queen*,
Every summer with me I wager
That I'll read these masterpieces major.

Each June I make a promise sober,
That I'll be literate by October.
Lose d'Artagnan and Sherlock Holmes
In worthier and weightier tomes,
In Nietzsche and even preachier Germans,
And Donne's more esoteric sermons,
The lofty thoughts of Abelard,
And Rilke, Kafka, and Kierkegaard;
Loop in one comprehensive lasso
Turgeniev, Thomas Aquinas and Tasso,
The Conquest of Peru, by Prescott,
And *David Harum*, by Edward Westcott.
Of the classics, from *Beowulf* to Baedeker,
I know less than a first or second gradeker,
So every summer I truly intend
My intellectual sloth to end,
And every summer, for years and years
I've read *Sherlock Holmes* and *The Three Musketeers*.

I CAN HARDLY WAIT FOR THE SANDMAN

There are several differences between me and Samuel Taylor
   Coleridge, whose bust I stand admiringly beneath;
He found solace in opium, I found it in Codman's Bayberry Chew-
   ing Gum—at least until it started loosening my teeth.
Another difference between me and Samuel Taylor Coleridge is
   more massive in design:
People used to interrupt him while he was dreaming his dreams,
   but they interrupt me while I am recounting mine.
Now, if anybody buttonholes you to tell you about how they
   dreamt they were falling, or flying, or just about to die and they
   actually would have died if they hadn't woken up abruptly.

Well, they deserve to be treated interruptly,

But when somebody with a really interesting dream takes the floor,

I don't think people ought to break away and start listening to the neighborhood bore.

Therefore I feel I need offer no apology

For having gathered a few of my more representative dreams into a modest anthology.

Once I dreamt I was in this sort of, you know, desert with cactuses only they were more like caterpillars and there were skulls and all the rest,

And right in the middle of this desert was a lifeboat with the name *Mary Celeste*,

And if I hadn't woken up because the heat was so blistery,

Why, I bet I would have solved this mystery of nautical history.

Another time I dreamt I was climbing this mountain although actually it was more like a beach,

And all of a sudden this sort of a merry-go-round I forgot to tell you about turned into a shack with a sign saying, LEDA'S PLACE, SWAN-BURGERS 10¢ EACH.

I hope you will agree that of dreams I am a connoisseur,

And next time I will tell you about either how I dreamt I went down the rabbit hole or through the looking glass, whichever you prefer.

RING OUT THE OLD, RING IN THE NEW, BUT DON'T GET CAUGHT IN BETWEEN

1. FIRST CHIME

If there is anything of which American industry has a superfluity

It is green lights, know-how, initiative and ingenuity.

If there is one maxim to American industry unknown

It is, Let well enough alone.

Some people award American industry an encomium

Because it not only paints the lily, it turns it into a two-toned job with a forward look and backward fins and a calyx trimmed with chromium.

I don't propose to engage in a series of Lincoln-Douglas debates,

But take the matter of paper plates.

The future of many a marriage would have been in doubt
But for paper plates, which have imparted tolerability to picnics
    and the maid's day out,
But the last paper plates I handled had been improved into plastic
    and they are so artistic that I couldn't throw them away,
And I ended up by washing them against another day.
Look at the automotive industry, how it never relaxes;
It has improved the low-priced three so much that instead of a
    thousand dollars they now cost twenty-nine seventy-five, not
    including federal and local taxes.
Do you know what I think?
Ordinary mousetraps will soon be so improved that they will be
    too good for the mice, who will be elbowed out by mink.

2. SECOND CHIME

That low keening you hear is me bemoaning my fate;
I am out of joint, I was born either too early or too late.
As the boll said to the weevil,
Get yourself born before the beginning or after the end, but never
    in the middle of a technological upheaval.
I am adrift, but know not whether I am drifting seaward or shore-
    ward,
My neck is stiff from my head trying to turn simultaneously back-
    ward and forward.
One way I know I am adrift,
My left foot keeps reaching for the clutch when the car has an au-
    tomatic shift.
Another way that I am adrift I know,
I'm in a car that I've forgotten has a clutch and I stall it when the
    light says STOP and again when the light says GO.
I find that when dressing I behave as one being stung by gallinip-
    pers
Because half my trousers are old style and half new and I am for-
    ever zipping buttons and buttoning zippers.
I can no longer enjoy butter on my bread;
Radio and TV have taught me to think of butter as "You know
    what" or "The more expensive spread."
I am on the thin ice of the old order while it melts;

I guess that perhaps in this changing world money changes less
    than anything else.
That is one reason money is to me so dear;
I know I can't take it with me, I just want the use of some while I
    am here.

COME, COME, KEROUAC!
MY GENERATION IS BEATER THAN YOURS

My dictionary defines progress as an advance toward perfection.
There has been lots of progress during my lifetime, but I'm afraid
    it's been heading in the wrong direction.
What is the progress that I see?
The headwaiter has progressed to being a maitre d';
The airways have advanced backward like so many squids,
And the radio jokes about Bing's horses have become the TV jokes
    about Bing's kids.
We have progressed from a baseball czar to a football czar, and I
    suppose we'll eventually have a huntin' and a shootin' and a
    swimmin' czar,
And now the designers of automobile seats tell us that men's hip
    spreads have progressed to being broader than women's are.
Oriental menaces have not let progress pass them by,
And we have advanced from Fu-Manchu to Chou En-Lai.
Once, you just put "The Two Black Crows" on the talking ma-
    chine and wound the handle and it played, but now science has
    stacked the deck,
And if you want to hear one Little Golden Record you must be a
    graduate of Cal. Tech or M.I.T. (which is sometimes known as
    No-Cal. Tech).
Progress may have been all right once, but it went on too long;
I think progress began to retrogress when Wilbur and Orville
    started tinkering around in Dayton and at Kitty Hawk, because
    I believe that two Wrights made a wrong.

UNTITLED

I'd rather, if I dared or dast,
Conceal my academic past,
But the horrid truth is bound to pop out,
You behold in me a Harvard drop out.
With freshman year my studies ended,
But since I wasn't fired or suspended,
I could knock today on the Dean's front door
And be a full-fledged sophomore.
But why should I toil two years or three
To gain a simple B.A. degree?
I needn't be by Brahmins buffeted
To gain a distinction much more coveted.
For home in New Hampshire, here in Henniker
Are philosophers wise as Plato and Seneca
Whose sensitive nerves were so unstrung
By my losing fight with the mother tongue
That they raised me up beside my betters
And pronounced me to be a Doctor of letters.
How fitting, for letters gave me my start,
I know most of the alphabet by heart.
Spurred on by the honor you've done me this fall
I'm going to dig in and learn it all.
You've been kind to this synthetic Yankee;
Thankee.

Author's Note: Response to award of degree at tiny New
England College, Henniker, N.H., 9/28/67. I have now
two honorary degrees from New England College, Adel-
phi (Garden City, L.I., NY) and Franklin and Marshall.
Nothing as yet from Harvard, Oxford, Notre Dame, or
Wofford. O. N.

THE NONBIOGRAPHY OF A NOBODY

There is one major compensation for being a minor literary figure,
Said Mr. Curmudgel, a minor literary figure.
Particularly, said Mr. Curmudgel,
A minor literary figure who

Has led a life bespectacled and unspectacular,
The kind of life, said Mr. Curmudgel,
The kind of life that Solomon Grundy lived,
Leaving behind no meat, just a white skeleton of dates.
Born, married, sickened, died and that's the lot.
There's little there for ghouls to feed on.
At least I know, said Mr. Curmudgel,
That when the reticent New Hampshire soil
Reluctant yields me one small oblong of nonbreathing space
There will be none to grind my bones to make their bread,
To speculate both on my sex and what strange uses
I may have made of it,
To snivel over my death wish drowned in alcohol or blood sports,
My secret gnawing envy of my peers,
To cram the public maw with spiteful hearsay
Authenticate only by vociferous claim to intimacy,
To friendship, good fellowship, and unique piquant revelations
Garnered over the rum pot.
Let me say once for all, said Mr. Curmudgel,
I was never a Golden Boy by self destroyed,
And the hairs on my chest at last count numbered three.
No spate of As I Knew Hims
Will lie like empty beer cans around my modest stone,
No carrion crows regurgitate juiceless shreds of me,
No middle-aged actors searching for the comeback trail
Clamor to cast their versions of me on the screen.
Two inches or one in the *Times* and the printers are through with
    me, I'll rest in peace,
A Solomon Grundy of American letters.
Solomon Grundy, said Mr. Curmudgel thoughtfully,
Married on Wednesday, took sick on Thursday, died on Saturday.
By God, said Mr. Curmudgel,
Obviously an alcoholic with a death wish!
He slipped the cover from his dusty typewriter.

THE QUACK FROWN SOX LUMPS OVEN THE—
OR
FAREWELL PHI BETA KAFKA

If my mind is wandery,
Well, I'm in a quandary.
I am recovering from a temporary secretary, a girl from Bennington,
Who neither resembled nor had heard of such dream girls of my youth as Louise Groody or Ann Pennington.
She came to me under the misapprehension that she could thereby pick up experience in an easy school, not a hard school,
Which would lead her to producing and directing off-Broadway plays of the avant-, or prenez-garde school.
Her eyes and her conversation glistened,
But she never listened.
When she encountered such a Nordic name as Georg she carefully pronounced it Gay-org,
But when transcribing a reference to *The Raven* she typed it *Mr. Raven*, which led me into fruitless speculation as to what Thornton Burgess would have named the ape in *Murders in the Rue Morgue*.
I played Polonius to this pixie, plying her with admonitions both as a kindly pa and as a harsh pa,
But when I handed her a package for Parcel Post she sent it Marcel Proust, as I only realized when it eventually returned to me stamped *Marcel Proust ne marche pas*.
To sum up, let me say that I am at present capable of living, or viable,
But I am also easily crumbled or reduced to powder, which is friable.
Being both viable and friable I wish to prolong my existence, not to wreck it,
And I am now looking for a good listener who just squeaked through high school in Feeble Bluff, Nebraska, and never heard of Joyce or Samuel Beckett.

CHANT AT THE END OF
A BEGINNINGLESS SUMMER

The sky is overcast and I am undercast and the fog creeps in on
    little iceberg feet
And there is no retreat.
I would don my Job-like false whiskers and my straggly King Lear
    wig;
I shake them, and out drops an earwig.
Oh dank, dank, dank, there is no chill in the martini nor warmth
    in the toddy,
The aura of the house is that of a damp demd moist unpleasant
    body.
You will note that I cannot even quote Dickens correctly, as once
    I used,
In this weather, all my Dickens have gone back to Proust.
In this weather, in this weather
One hundred six-cent stamps and fifty air-mails have become per-
    manently glued together.
At night eaves drip and foghorn moans in tuneless timeless an-
    tiphony,
I have not seen the moon since the second Sunday after Epiphany.
Strangely, I find I miss the moon no whit,
Nor have I since the two U.S.'s have changed her from "she" to "it."
I want to return to the womb,
No matter of whom.
Respect my gloom, my gloom is lodged in my craw,
Do not mark, fold, tear or staple my gloom, it is recommended for
    mature audiences, it is void where prohibited by law.
Summer that never was, of seeing yoursel as other see ye I'll gie ye
    the giftie;
No maiden of bashful fifteen like other summers hae ye been, but
    unco like, as Richard Brinsley Sheridan almost said,
A weirdo of fifty.

NEVER WAS I BORN
TO SET THEM RIGHT

Since the non-book and the anti-hero are now accepted elements
of modern negative living
I feel justified in mentioning a few examples of the march of
progress for which I suggest a heartfelt non-thanksgiving.
I not only like Turkish towels or a reasonable facsimile on emerg-
ing from the tub,
I also like towels after washing my hands, even paper ones that
you rip untimely from a reluctant device that warns you, Blot,
do not rub.
I do not like the contraptions that have replaced towels in every
washroom from the humblest Howard Johnson to the haugh-
tiest Statler or Hilton,
These abominations which you stand cringingly in front of wait-
ing for them to scorch you with a blast of air from a hell hot-
ter than any imagined by Dante or Milton.
I like the common incandescent lamp whose light is produced in a
filament rendered luminous by the passage of current through
it,
I do not like the fluorescent lamp in which light is produced by
passage of electricity through a metallic vapor or gas enclosed
in a tube or bulb, I resent it, I rue it, I eschew it.
You stumble into a dark room and press a switch and then stand
in continuing darkness for half a minute wondering if you have
blown a fuse sky high,
And then the fluorescent fixture flickers and hesitates and finally
lights up and you see your face in the mirror and it is yellow
and green and purple like a recently blackened eye.
I do not like bottle openers shaped like a mermaid or a fish or even
an axolotl,
They may be all right for driving thumbtacks with but they're no
good for opening a bottle.
I do not like the substitution at toll-booths of the electronic coin-
basket for the human collector,
I accept it as grudgingly as Hecuba might have accepted the sub-
stitution of Polyphemus for Hector.

The collector would even lean into your car to accept the coin from your right hand, but you have to toss it at the basket with your left,

And I happen to be the least ambidextrous northpaw who ever chunked a pebble at a newt or an eft.

I do not like thrifty European airmail stationery combining envelope with letter, I have never faced one but I trembled;

You need a well-honed paper knife to open it, and even then end up with eight or sixteen fragments which must be painstakingly reassembled.

Speaking of envelopes, I particularly dislike in our non-civilization the return envelope with postage prepaid which the Internal Revenue Service does not enclose with its annual demands; of needlessly irritating the taxpayer this is the most picayune of their many ways;

When I drain my bank account to write them a check I think they might at least blow me to a nickel's worth of postage, especially as it wouldn't cost them anything anyways.

THE MAVERICK

I face each day as sweet as clover,
Sweet under-arm and sweet all over.
Don't smell of ocean spray or pine,
No thrilling he-man odor is mine;
For cleanliness I place my hope
On a daily bath and honest soap,
And since I'm quite deodorant-free,
If you don't smell anything, that's me.

I DIDN'T GO TO CHURCH TODAY

I didn't go to church today,
I trust the Lord to understand.
The surf was swirling blue and white,
The children swirling on the sand.
He knows, He knows how brief my stay,
How brief this spell of summer weather,
He knows when I am said and done
We'll have plenty of time together.

Index of Poems

Index of First Lines

A NOTE ON THE AUTHOR

Ogden Nash was born in 1902 in Rye, New York, and grew up there and in Savannah, Georgia. He dropped out of Harvard after his freshman year and went to work as an editor with Doubleday in New York. When he began publishing humorous poems in *The New Yorker*, and when he worked at the magazine, he became part of the fabled literary circle that included E. B. and Katharine White, Dorothy Parker, Harold Ross, and S. J. Perelman. He went on to publish more than two dozen books of verse as well as sceenplays, lyrics and scripts for the theater, children's stories, and essays. He later became a favorite on radio and at lecture platforms around the country, but the bedrock of his art always remained his poems with their uncanny wit. He died in 1971 in Baltimore.